AF479035

This book is published in
conjunction with the exhibition
**Painting and Sculpture –
From Classical Modernism
to the Present Day**

Exhibition
Uwe Wieczorek
Texts
Angela Schneider AS
Uwe Wieczorek UW

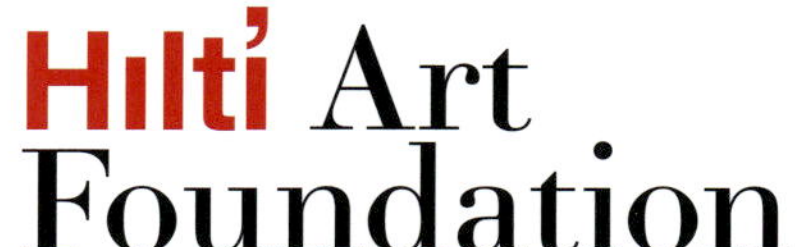

Painting and Sculpture

From Classical Modernism to the Present Day

HATJE
CANTZ

Preface

Michael Hilti

Hilti Art Foundation

We ventured into the public arena for the first time in 2005, when we showed some sixty works from the collection of the Hilti Art Foundation. The exhibition *From Paul Gauguin to Imi Knoebel* was on view at the Kunstmuseum Liechtenstein. Now, ten years later, we have the privilege once again of presenting our steadily developing and growing collection to the public. This time, however, it is not in the form of a temporary exhibition but in museum premises of our own, built with the intention of making the collection permanently accessible to the public in regularly changing exhibitions. Such a step is not possible without the long-term financial and personal commitment of the Hilti Art Foundation; it also entails substantial obligations and responsibilities. It might have been easier to hand over some of the collection to a museum on permanent loan. But that would not accord with the spirit of our collection: if we have to do without individual works for longer periods of time, then we want to contribute actively to their presentation.

The unique possibility of building and curating a museum in the centre of Vaduz in close cooperation with the Kunstmuseum Liechtenstein, the latter indebted to the initiative of my father Prof. Martin Hilti, is an exceptional opportunity to consolidate resources, to enhance the presence of the Kunstmuseum Liechtenstein and to offer viewers a much wider spectrum of art. And it is an opportunity to contribute to the vibrancy of cultural life in Liechtenstein.

The combination of a public and a private collection has great potential, for it is as fruitful in complementary dialogue as it is in mutual contradiction. It is our privilege as a private entity to be governed by different laws from those of a public collection. We do not have to commit exclusively to the guidance of art historical considerations; we are free. Our collection is an expression of this freedom; it testifies to our preferences, to quality, and to what we consider important. And, ultimately, it is the expression of our emotional involvement. But freedom in collecting does not mean randomly amassing works from all ages. Collections acquire coherence and cogency by focusing on specific areas and epochs and, further, by exercising discipline in building and enlarging their holdings. We have always aimed to collect art that radiates a certain harmony and sense of balance, art that is inspiring and stimulates new thoughts, and most especially art that is a source of pleasure. We collect works because we enjoy their company and want to live with them. That is why it is so hard for a private collector to part with works for extended periods of time. Collecting is inseparable from passion and enthusiasm. May you also experience this enthusiasm and share the love of art that underlies it.

The Collection and the Exhibition

Uwe Wieczorek

Curator

The collection of the Hilti Art Foundation has grown substantially, quantitatively, and qualitatively since first presented to the public at the Kunstmuseum Liechtenstein in 2005. The holdings currently comprise some 200 paintings, sculptures, objects, and photographs from classical Modernism to the present day. After more than twenty years of thoughtfully targeted collecting, increasingly important keynotes of the collection have come to include Cubism, Futurism, Expressionism, Concrete Art, and ZERO. Some of the artists, for instance Kirchner, Picasso, Beckmann, Giacometti, Fontana, Graubner, Knoebel, and Scully, are represented by several works.

It is a distinguishing feature of private collections that they reflect the specific interests and personal preferences of the collector. The collection of the Hilti Art Foundation is no exception. A deep appreciation of beauty and aesthetic values, which precludes ugliness without negating the dark side of life, has resulted in a collection of exceptionally gratifying works. At the same time, however, the collection has developed in response to the formal and conceptual changes that influenced art throughout the late nineteenth and twentieth centuries. The sheer unlimited expansion of knowledge in the sciences and the humanities in conjunction with the advances unleashed in technology and commerce have profoundly altered our view of the world and reality. This has motivated radical reactions in the fine arts by giving artists fruitful opportunities to experiment with new forms of composition and expression. Thus, in Cubism, conceived by Picasso and Braque, the mimetic representation of the empirical world yielded to autonomous compositions based on elementary stereometric shapes, as also demonstrated by Gris and Léger (cats. 20/21). Their work abandoned the laws of central perspective that had prevailed for centuries, and instead linked space and object as an aperspectival unit. Futurism enthusiastically embraced and, indeed, revered the accelerated movement, technology, and machines of modern life. In *Forme uniche,* Boccioni (cat. 4), whose work was hailed as the quintessence of Futurism, presents humankind as a product of speed divested of any individual features. Taking a more sceptical approach to civilization, artists like Gauguin (cat. 13), Schmidt-Rottluff, and Kirchner (cats. 15/16/17) cherished the unspoiled tranquillity of "primitive" and non-European cultures, adopting and adapting them in content and style to resonate with their own artistic needs. As an alternative to city life, the Expressionists associated with the Brücke and the Blaue Reiter (cats. 18/19) turned to nature as a pristine place of creaturely existence and physical and spiritual regeneration. Surrealists like Miró, Magritte, Ernst, and Tanguy (cats. 24/25/26/27) found inspiration for their art in poetry and magic, play and eros, and most especially in the unfathomable depths of the unconscious. For their universe of emblematic imagery, such artists as Klee and Dubuffet (cats. 29/31) sourced visual reality as much as their own imaginations and also found fruitful soil in the unusually creative, artistic output of children and the mentally ill.

War and suffering, crucial aspects of the twentieth century, inform the work of Beckmann (cats. 6/7/30) and Richier (cat. 8). Beckmann's self-portrait is one of art history's great testimonials not only to human self-reassurance between despair and hope, but also to the incontrovertible willingness to see and speak untarnished truths in the face of historical events. After the global catastrophes of the 1930s and 1940s, the existence of humankind was called into question, both physically and morally. Coming to terms with these experiences, Giacometti (cats. 9/10/33) focused his attention on the human figure, specifically on what constitutes the essence of being human. Wols (cat. 32), gazing both within and without, reacted to the turbulence of the times and the instability of his own life by renouncing figuration, using only line and colour to express his emotions in deliberately small format, with a physical immediacy as sensitive as it is forceful.

Contemporaneously with Giacometti and Wols, Fontana (cat. 37) was at work on an entirely different artistic approach, embracing technological innovation with an enthusiasm comparable to the Futurists. His *spazialismo* launched a new artistic and intellectual beginning in the wake of the Second World War. By slashing a monochrome white canvas, he drew abrupt and radical attention to the facts of material, plane, space, and light, thereby establishing the premises for an expanded understanding of the image, unconditionally liberated from tradition. Reacting directly or indirectly to Fontana, artists like Klein, Manzoni, Schoonhoven, Graubner, Uecker, and the ZERO artists (cats. 38/39/45/43/42) followed suit, coming to entirely distinctive conclusions of their own. The immanent concerns of art—material, plane, space, and light as well as form, colour, movement, and rhythm—came under scrutiny, as in the work of

Albers and Colombo (cats. 35/36), revealing the fundamentally relative nature of perception, or, as in the case of Fruhtrunk (cat. 46), aiming at life experience heightened through the intensification of seeing. In contrast, the concrete and constructive works of Honegger and Loewensberg (cats. 47/48) take a rational yet playful approach in their non-teleological treatment of composition and design.

Knoebel (cats. 44/50) revisits the questions Duchamp asked before the outbreak of the First World War: what is a work of art and what meaning does it have in view of ceaselessly changing notions of reality? His appreciation of classical modernism, in particular Malevich and Mondrian (cat. 22), applies not only to geometrical compositions, but also to forms of expression in the art of the Informel, as shown in works that cross the boundaries of genre to include reliefs, sculptures, and assemblage. Oscillating between cool concept and pure sensuality, between construction and deconstruction, between devotion and rejection, Knoebel demonstrates a both serious and wry delight in creating work that defies reduction to dogma.

Briefly summarized here, the collection seeks to represent the salient features of movements in art history since classical modernism as exemplified in the exhibition and accompanying publication. It is the first exhibition to be organized by the Hilti Art Foundation in its own building adjoining the Kunstmuseum Liechtenstein. Fifty selected paintings, sculptures, and objects will be presented on the three floors of the building, each focusing on a specific theme: "The Mystery of Humankind", "Experiment and Existence", "Immanence and Transcendence". The first theme, oriented toward seemingly familiar and yet enigmatic forms of human figuration, includes works ranging from about 1910 to 1970. Shown on the lower level of the building, these works draw attention to an increasingly important aspect of the collection. The second theme, on the first floor, foregrounds the experimental endeavours and existential concerns that motivated artists of classical modernism from about 1880 to 1950. The top floor comprises art after 1950 to the present day, addressing a theme that not only refers to the pure facticity of the work of art but also reveals the potential of exclusively non-figurative means to cross boundaries from the worldly to the otherworldly, from matter to spirit.

Since they still hold true, let me repeat, in slightly different form, the thoughts expressed in our first exhibition catalogue of 2005: May all the work to be displayed in the new building of the Hilti Art Foundation find inspiration from the insight that collecting art is not merely a question of personal pleasure or self-interest. Above all, the exhibitions are meant to draw attention, through art, to the best qualities of a society and its exceptional creative and human potential. Through a sense of responsibility and active citizenship, a *res privata* has now also acquired the character of a *res publica.*

My gratitude goes to the following people:

Michael and Caroline Hilti along with all the members of the Hilti family and the Martin Hilti Family Trust. In addition, I thank Marco Auderset, Roland Bauer, Claudia Büchel, Barbara Bühler, Kurt Dornig, Sebastian Frommelt, Eva Grünwald, Shandor Hayde, Sylvio Hoffmann, Robert Iten, Brigitte Lampert, Friedemann Malsch and the staff of the Kunstmuseum Liechtenstein, Meinrad Morger, Karin Osbahr, Heinz Preute, Martin Rogy-Hinse, Catherine Schelbert, Angela Schneider, Thomas Soraperra, Vajra Spook, Claudia Steinfels, Martin Wichert and Hatje Cantz Publishers, Cornelia Wieczorek, Arthur Willi and the production team, Hanna Züllig, and all the many other people who have been indispensable to this project.

I am grateful to them all for their consistently competent, cooperative, reliable, trustworthy, considerate, inspiring, critical, and active support. It is thanks to their contribution that the collection of the Hilti Art Foundation has acquired a distinctive individuality and a permanent home.

Uwe Wieczorek

The Mystery of Humankind

Wilhelm Lehmbruck
1881 Meiderich, Duisburg – 1919 Berlin

Stone cast
Signed on right thigh: LEHMBRUCK
118 × 50 × 37 cm

Inv. no.: S55T
Acquired 2013

01 Wilhelm Lehmbruck
Torso der Grossen Stehenden
1910

Wilhelm Lehmbruck went to Paris in 1910 after completing a conventional academic education in Düsseldorf. Having become a member of the Societé Nationale des Beaux-Arts in 1907, he was familiar with the French capital through his participation in the annual exhibitions. In 1910, he began contributing to the Salon d'Automne, where he made the acquaintance of important artists such as Archipenko, Brancusi, Derain, Léger, and Modigliani. In 1904, Lehmbruck had already seen a large retrospective of Rodin's work at the International Art Exhibition in Düsseldorf.

At the Salon d'Automne of 1910, he exhibited his larger-than-life *Grosse Stehende* (*Large Standing Nude*), cast in tinted plaster. It was the twenty-nine-year-old artist's first major work. The elongated limbs of this full-length figure were to become characteristic of sculptures made between 1911 and 1918. That same year Lehmbruck made his *Torso der Grossen Stehenden* (Torso of the Large Standing Nude). As Dietrich Schubert explains, the decision to depict only the torso enabled the artist to capture the quintessence of the figure by reducing it to essentials. The exquisitely balanced result clearly embodies Lehmbruck's artistic principle: "All art is scale, scale against scale, that is all." As in the work of Hans von Marées, to whom he was deeply indebted by his own account, Lehmbruck constructed the body as a piece of architecture seen from the front, with an axial skeleton around which the classically moulded thighs, hips, breasts, and shoulders are grouped. The contours of the figure reinforce the harmony of its self-contained presence. The inclined head and lowered eyes are not so much an expression of melancholy, as often observed, but rather a sign of inner peace and concentration. In comparison to Maillol's nudes—Lehmbruck studied them in Paris—the nude torso is neither erotically seductive nor overly modest. The artist has made a visual statement of existential and serene beauty.

This *Torso der Grossen Stehenden* is one of the two casts produced in Lehmbruck's lifetime. Parts of the grey "stone mass", as he called it, show a flesh-tinted pink, quickening the torso with a touch of animate life. AS

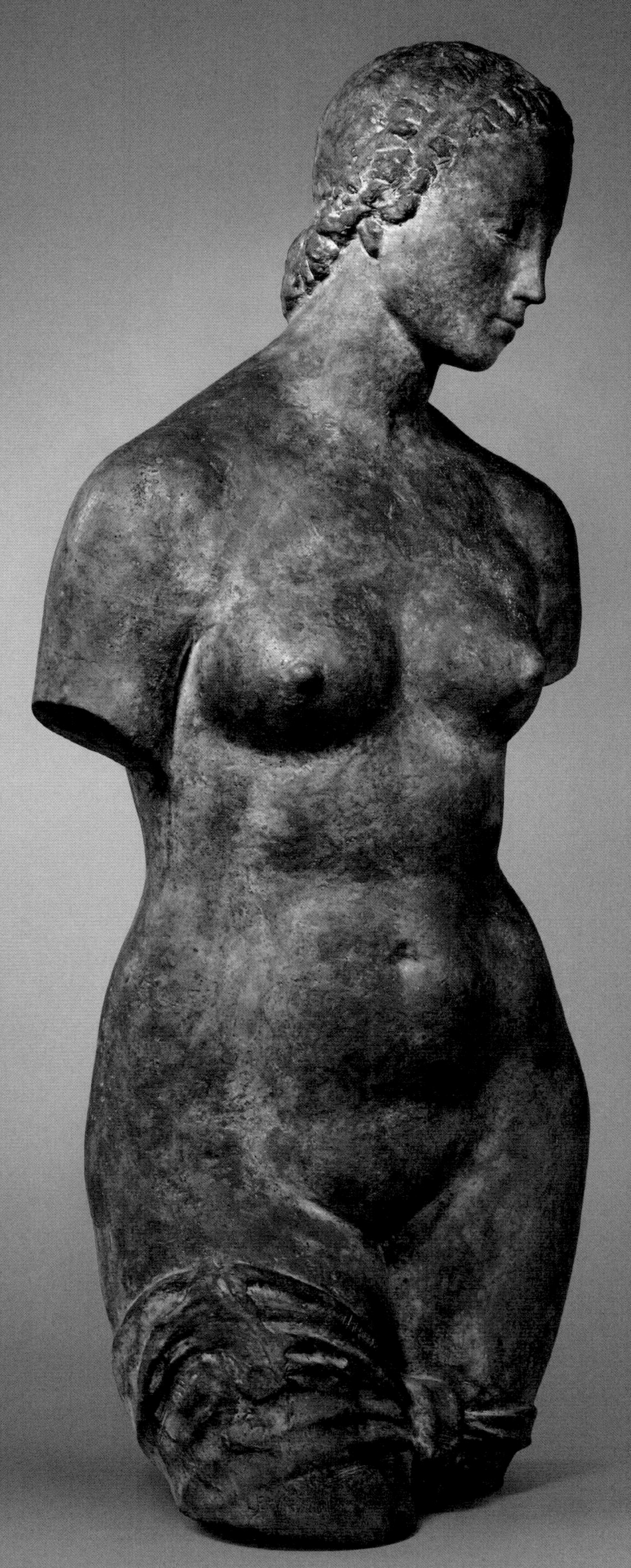

Ferdinand Hodler
1853 Bern – 1918 Geneva

Oil on canvas
Signed and dated lower right:
1909 F. Hodler
41.8 × 40.5 cm

Inv. no.: P52T
Acquired 2012

02 Ferdinand Hodler
Valentine Godé-Darel (La Parisienne I)
1909

Hodler presumably first met the actress and porcelain painter Valentine Godé-Darel in Geneva in 1908. Born in Paris in 1873, Godé-Darel was much younger than her lover for whom she was muse, model, and finally the mother of their daughter Paulette. Hodler's love affair was no doubt painful for his wife Berthe, but after Valentine's premature death, she raised Paulette with the help of a governess. Godé-Darel is known to the world primarily through the numerous paintings Hodler made of her agonizing death. His analytic gaze captures all the phases of an illness that broke out just a few weeks after the birth of their daughter and led to Valentine's death two years later in January 1915.

For Hodler, Valentine was the love of his life. In *La Parisienne,* as she was called, he pictures her as a beautiful woman in the prime of life, with sensitive features and yet subtly flirtatious, as she glances at the viewer over her bare left shoulder, her red lips slightly open and her luxurious hair exquisitely coiffed. The intimate portrait bust is preceded by nude studies made in connection with the painting *Linienherrlichkeit* (Linear Glory, 1908) and showing Valentine's body in eurythmic movement with her head similarly positioned. The almost square painting features the face and shoulders of the sitter, clearly outlined but executed with painterly and in part rather sketchy brushstrokes against a reddish grey ground. The richly nuanced colouring of her complexion seems to mirror a gently excited state of mind. Hodler painted a variation on this picture of the same size against a greenish grey ground followed by a third, smaller version that clearly emphasizes the sitter's refinement, for she is pictured wearing a fashionable high-collared garment and a lavish hat.

This first version of *La Parisienne,* combining aspects of neo-Impressionism, Art Nouveau, and Expressionism, probably gives the closest impression of the intimate relationship between painter and sitter. Knowing the tragic fate that awaited Valentine Godé-Darel, one cannot banish the sorrowful thought that a premonition of the imminent end of their love lies in the ephemerality of her gaze. UW

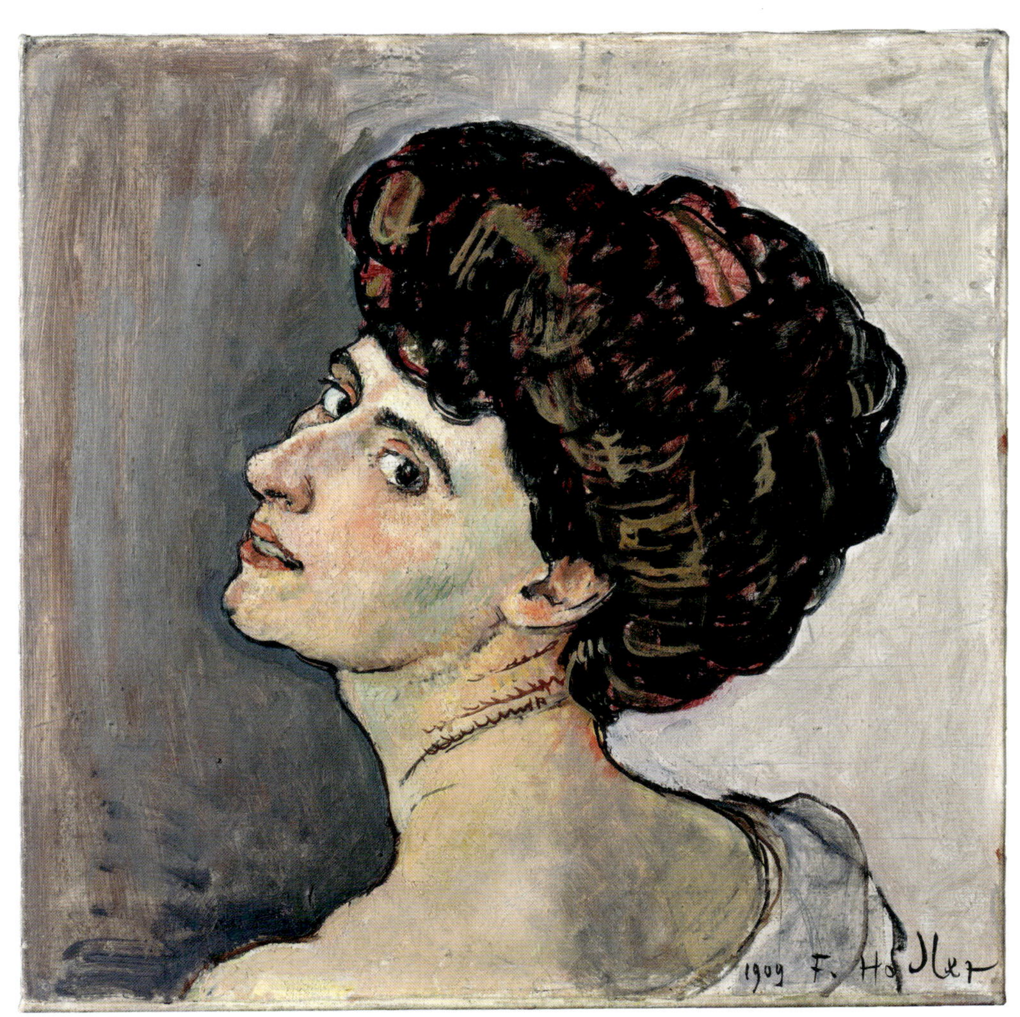

Raymond Duchamp-Villon
1876 Damville – 1918 Cannes

Cement with terra-cotta patina
Signed, dated, and numbered:
R. Duchamp Villon 1911 E/A
41 × 27 × 22 cm

Inv. no.: S32T
Acquired 2005

03 Raymond Duchamp-Villon
Baudelaire
1911

The French art critic, translator, essayist, and poet Charles Baudelaire (1821–1867) bestowed upon the world a poetic masterpiece with the publication of *Les Fleurs du Mal* in 1857. Painted in his lifetime by Deroy, Courbet, and Manet and photographed by Nadar, Carjat, and Neyt, he was honoured once again fourty-four years after his death for his trailblazing contribution to modern European literature, especially Symbolism—this time in the form of a sculpture. It was the literary journalist Jacques Crépet, editor and connoisseur of Baudelaire's oeuvre, who commissioned Duchamp-Villon in 1911 to create a monument in honour of the writer. A pencil drawing made by the sculptor gives a vague impression of this unexecuted sculpture, which was to have been crowned by the voluminous head of Baudelaire. Duchamp-Villon produced only this head in plaster, terracotta, bronze, and, as in the present work, in cement. The patina of surface and colour of these versions vary considerably. Raymond and Marcel Duchamp's older brother, Jacques Villon, reproduced the poet's portrait as an etching in 1920, titled *Baudelaire au socle*.

Initially, Duchamp-Villon worked in a style that shows an affinity with Rodin's oeuvre and Art Nouveau, but by 1911 he had taken up the formal idiom of Cubism, eschewing all accidental and anecdotal details. The portrait is pared down to the essential features of Baudelaire's physiognomy and the distinctive shape of the poet's head, drawing attention, perhaps, to the locus of the human intellect. The sculptor worked from a photograph. Nadar (1855), Carjat (1862), and Neyt (1864) equally capture the severity and melancholy of Baudelaire's features, indicative of the existential life crises from which he suffered: narrow, tightly closed lips and eyes focused on the viewer with great intensity. In contrast, the eyes in the sculpture have neither iris nor pupil. The countenance has the austerity of an ancient Egyptian bust, spiritual in appearance and stoically removed from the real world, which Baudelaire famously compared to an "oasis of horror in a desert of boredom". It was with a mixture of curiosity and profound scepticism that the poet perceived modern civilization's march of triumph and, attendant upon it, the global spread of "fuel, steam, and turntable", of industry, photography, and advertising. Baudelaire pitted the lifestyle of the dandy against the nauseating tedium and ugliness of bourgeois society, which had led to the loss of spiritual dignity *(honorabilité spirituelle)* and creativity *(imagination)*. The dandy as the actual hero of Modernism, embodied by himself, renounced utilitarian objectives in order to devote all thought and action exclusively to salvaging beauty through art and poetry as mnemonic devices. UW

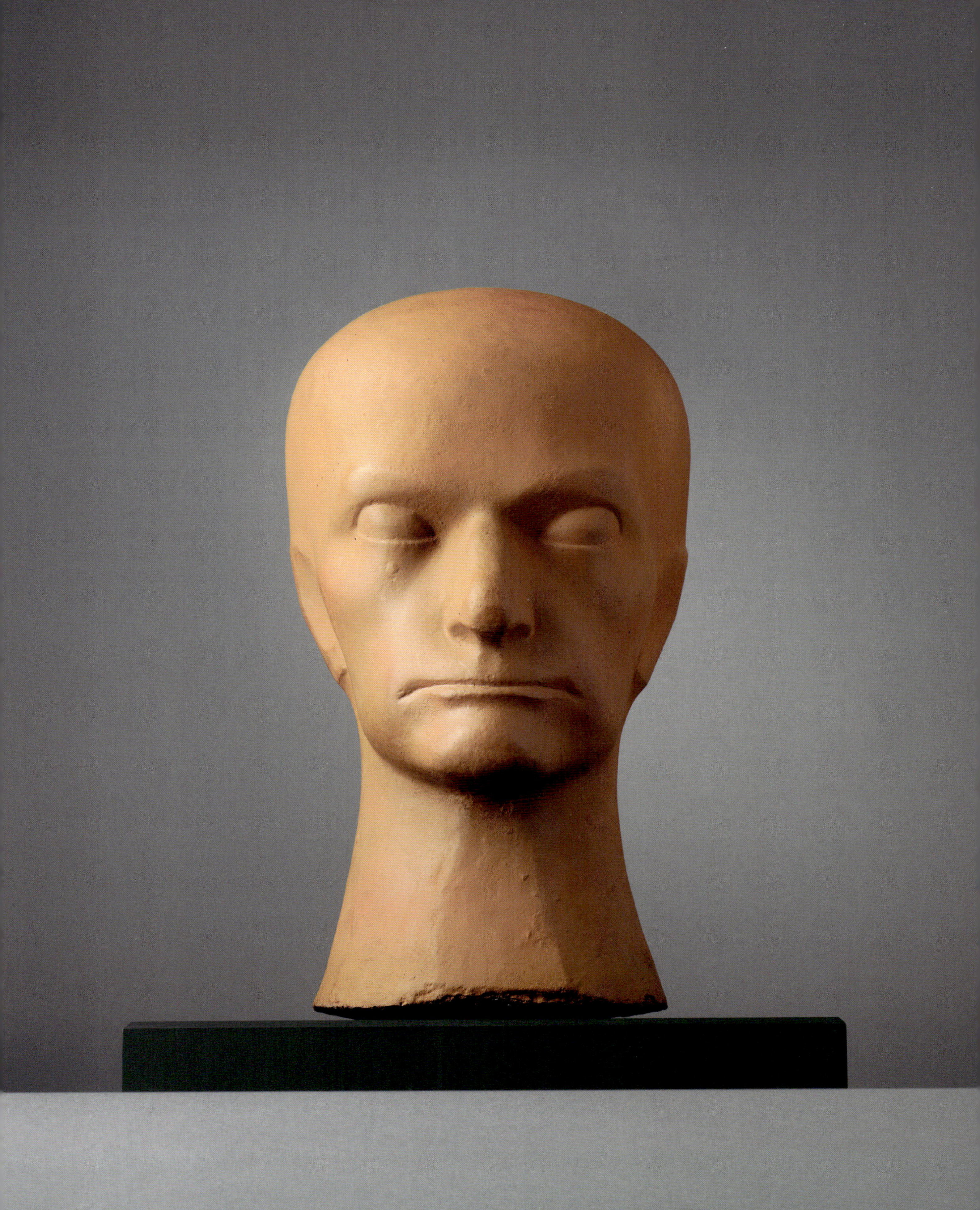

Umberto Boccioni
1882 Reggio di Calabria – 1916 Verona

Bronze, Cast from plaster original: 1949
(foundry: Giovanni and Angelo Nicci, Rome)
120 × 40 × 90 cm

Inv. no.: S7T
Acquired 2000

04 Umberto Boccioni
Forme uniche della continuità nello spazio
1913

Forme uniche della continuità nello spazio (Unique Forms of Continuity in Space) was created with the objective of making the movements and dynamics of the human body visible in space. Marcel Duchamp, like Umberto Boccioni, explored the same concern around 1912, which Henri Bergson had already attempted to capture in philosophical terms. Duchamp remarked in an interview that no one had ever before thought about introducing actual movement into a work of art. The fact that he and the Futurists had both addressed that potential indicates that the idea was in the air at the time thanks to the invention of the moving picture. He was particularly taken with the idea of capturing the movement of a nude walking down a flight of stairs within the confinement of a static image. Duchamp painted his *Nude Descending a Staircase* (1912) the same year in which Boccioni started working on his sculpture *Forme uniche.* Duchamp had been inspired by chronophotography, a medium he had discovered in physiologist Etienne Jules Marey's textbook *Le Mouvement* (1894). Boccioni was also familiar with the photographic sequences of the human body in movement reproduced in this book. As a sculptural counterpart to Duchamp's *Nude Descending a Staircase, Forme uniche* moves into the third dimension but it is still a static visual image. This sculpture is thus unlike all of its art historical precedents inasmuch as it does not merely represent a human body in movement but actually shows the continuum of movement, specifically the way in which it affects and changes the shape of the human body. It is almost as if Boccioni had skinned the body in order to show even more clearly, chronophotographically as it were, how muscles are stretched and elongated by movement. The artist has created the quintessential "futurist image of man" by showing how the body is affected by the "speed of modern life", which was enthusiastically embraced by the Futurists and by Boccioni as one of the movement's main proponents.

To explore the effect of movement on the human body, Boccioni created three other sculptures in 1913, none of which has survived. Ever increasing reduction of his sculptural material ultimately led to *Forme uniche,* which he executed in plaster, as he had the three preceding sculptures. Authorized bronze casts of the original, preserved at the Museu de Arte Contemporânea da Universidade de São Paulo, were not made until after the artist's death.
UW

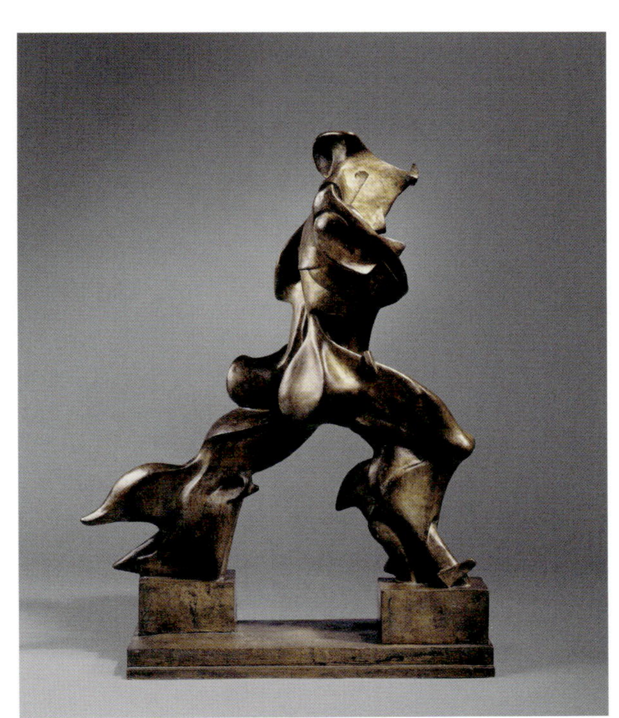

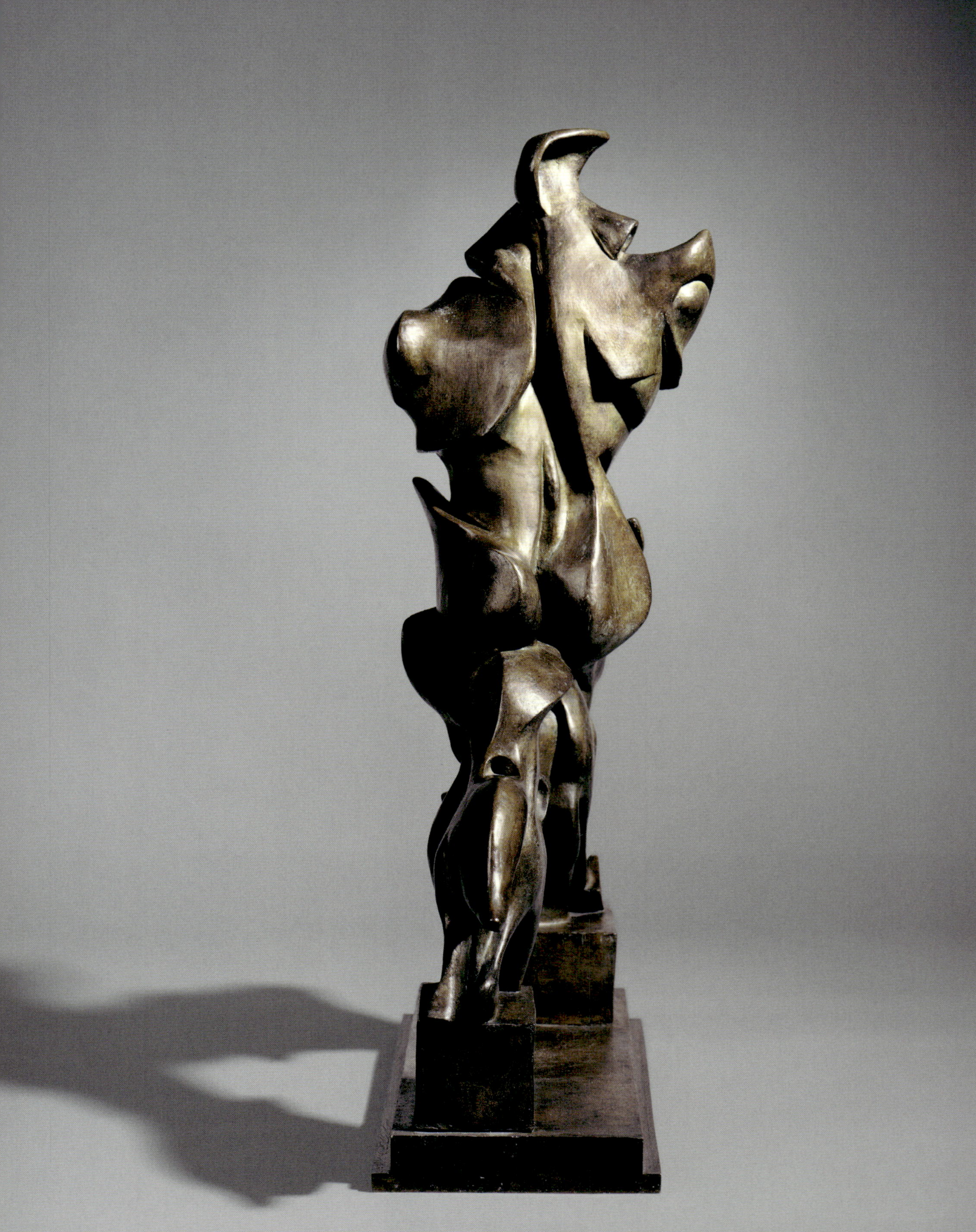

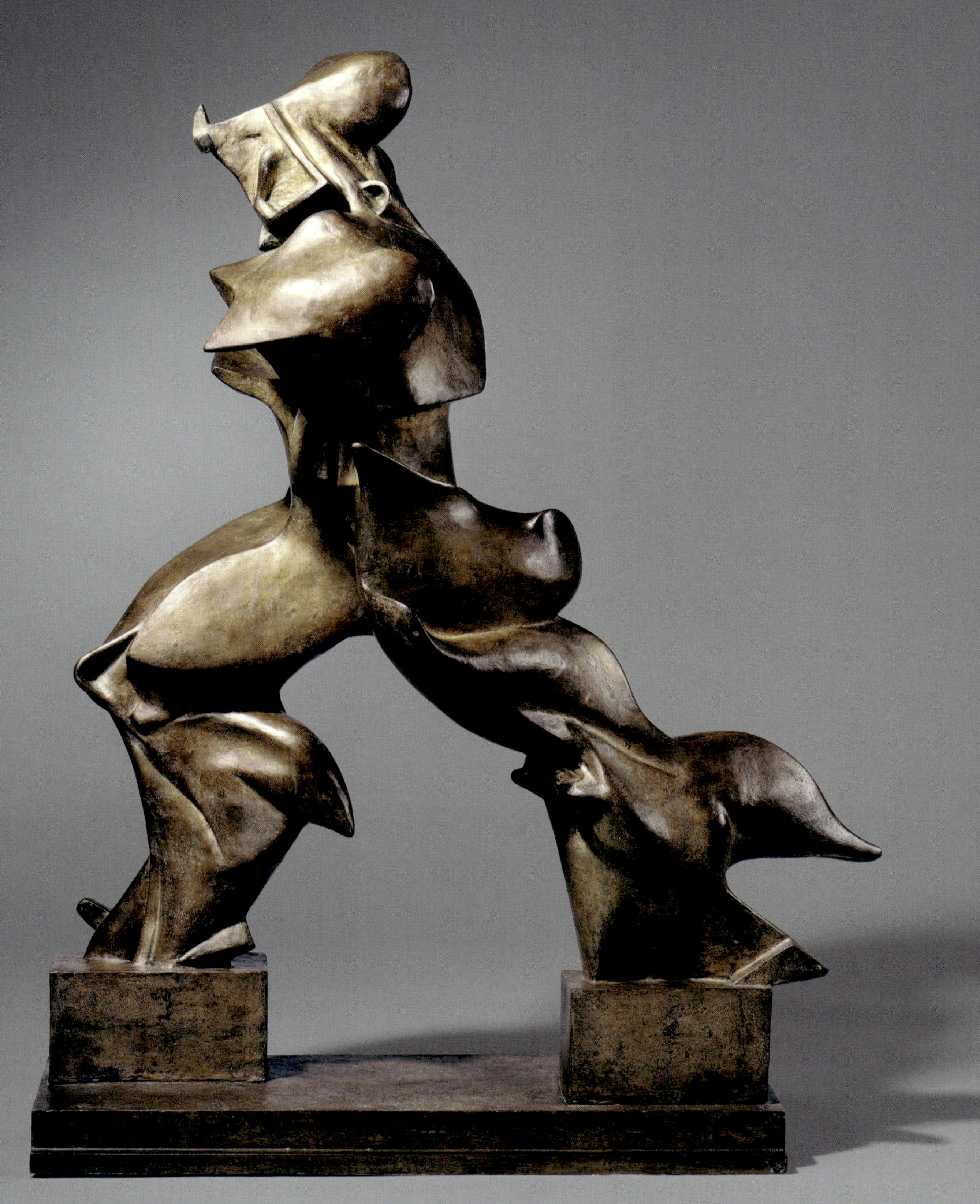

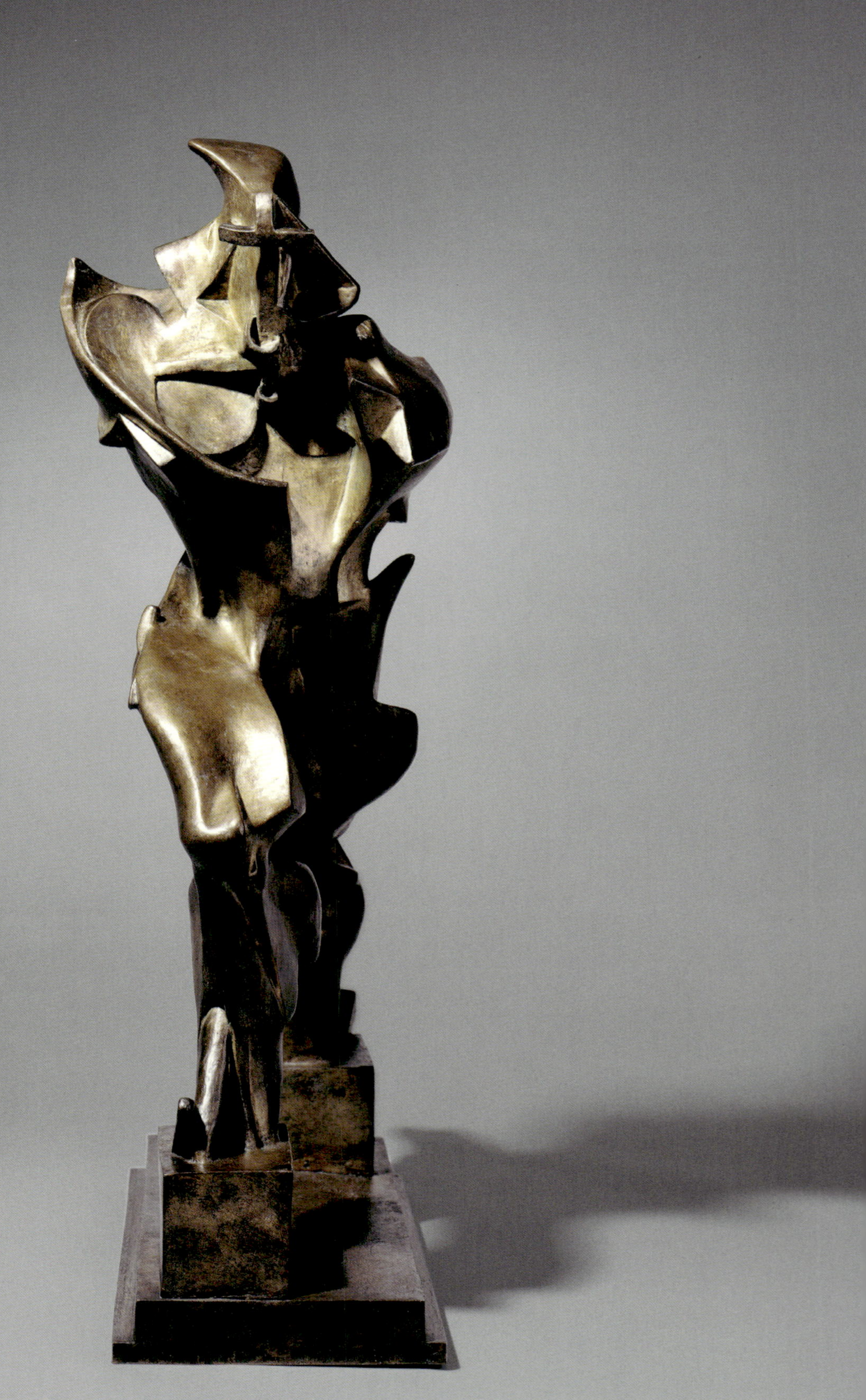

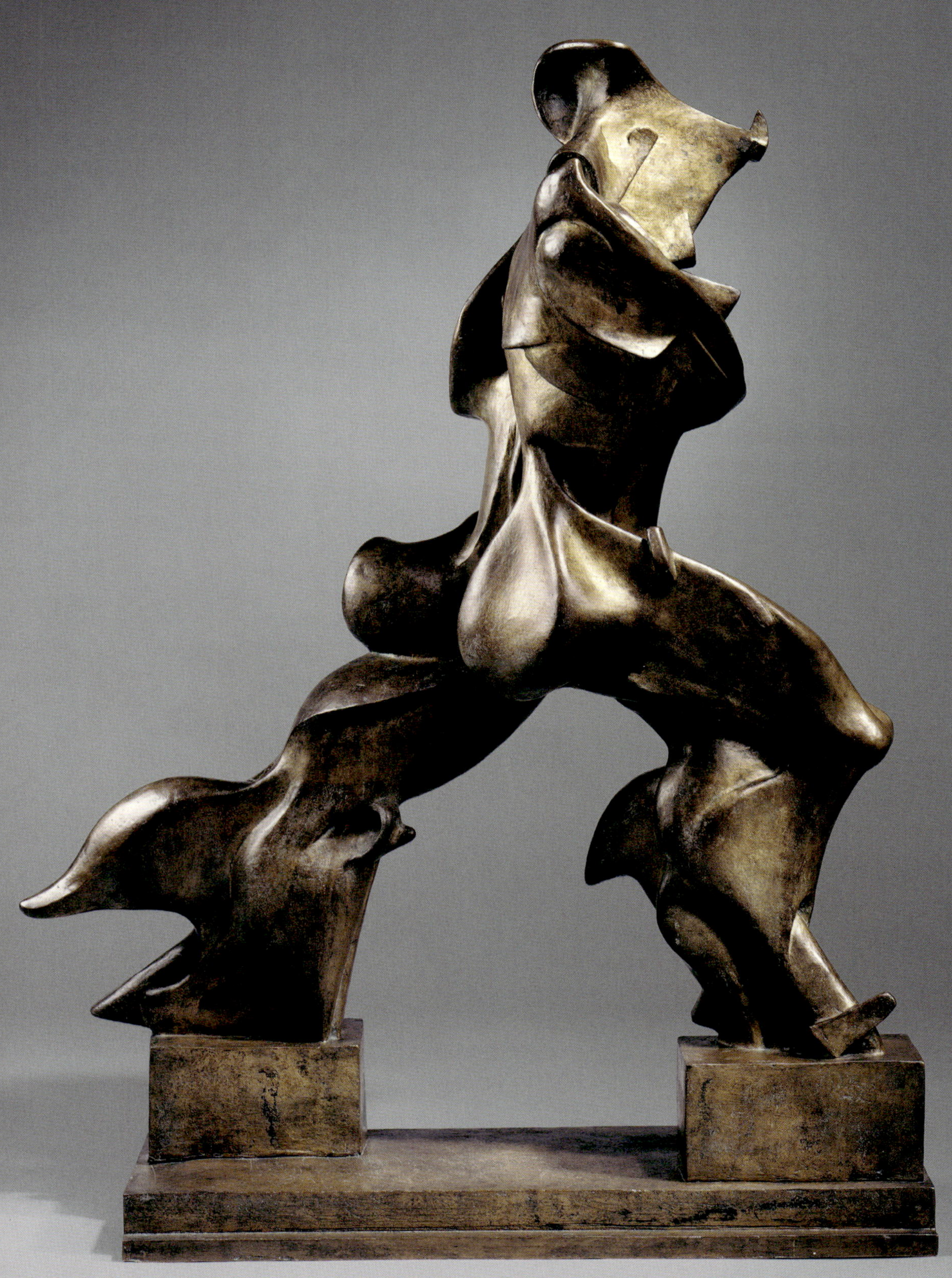

Pablo Picasso
1881 Málaga – 1973 Mougins, Cannes

Oil on canvas
Signed and dated lower right: Picasso XXXII
Inscribed and dated on verso:
Boisgeloup, 14 Août XXXII
92.1 × 73 cm

Inv. no.: P25T
Acquired 2003

05 Pablo Picasso
Femme dans un fauteuil
1932

In 1931–32 Picasso painted several pictures of a young blonde woman, usually seen sitting and in some cases sleeping. In some of these paintings, the model that inspired Picasso can clearly be identified as Marie-Thérèse Walter. Her perfectly aquiline nose, giving her the look of an ancient Greek sculpture, made a profound impact on Picasso at their initial and now legendary encounter in front of the Lafayette department store in January 1927. Her youthful face first appeared in a few drawings and her entire figure came to dominate many paintings in the years that followed. Through the hand of the artist, Marie-Thérèse's body undergoes virtuoso transformations from a blossoming Venus and a sleeping saint to an archaic sculpture.

Picasso painted this work, dated 14 August 1932, in Boisgeloup, the castle near Gisors northwest of Paris that he had purchased the year before. Marie-Thérèse is sitting in the nude in a Spanish armchair against a light yellow and off-white background, as if the wall were bathed in sunlight. The sitter, and in fact everything in the painting with the exception of the chair, is rendered in soft, rounded, and at times biomorphic shapes. The essentially static motif of a seated figure is animated by sweeping curves, obviously connoting femininity, in explicit contrast to the angular, "masculine" linearity of the chair. The movement is generated by the arrangement of the interrelated circular shapes and is heightened by the additional movement within the picture of the overlapping colours and shapes that mark the sitter's head and torso.

Variations in painterly composition are seen, for instance, in the patches of spontaneous and expressive brushstrokes that alternate with "cool" smoothly painted sections. Subtle differences between top and bottom, distance and closeness, intellect and eros are combined with formal details, testifying to the artist's relationship to his model. The Spanish armchair, which may well mark the presence of the painter himself, shows a motif of upholstery tacks that is echoed in the pearl necklace and the red fingernails.

The yellow, green, and mauve palette that typifies paintings of Marie-Thérèse alludes to her "natural" complexion, her blonde hair and blue eyes. The pertinent literature has also drawn attention to an artistic predecessor, Paul Gauguin's painting *Spirit of the Dead Watching* of 1892, which Picasso had seen in 1901 at the gallery of his Parisian dealer Ambroise Vollard. As in Picasso's *Femme dans un fauteuil,* the ghostly ancestor sitting next to the bed is pictured in profile with both eyes facing front. Despite her unmistakably erotic presence, Marie-Thérèse's "magic" eyes ultimately give her an aura of unattainability, characteristic of many other paintings by Picasso as well. AS

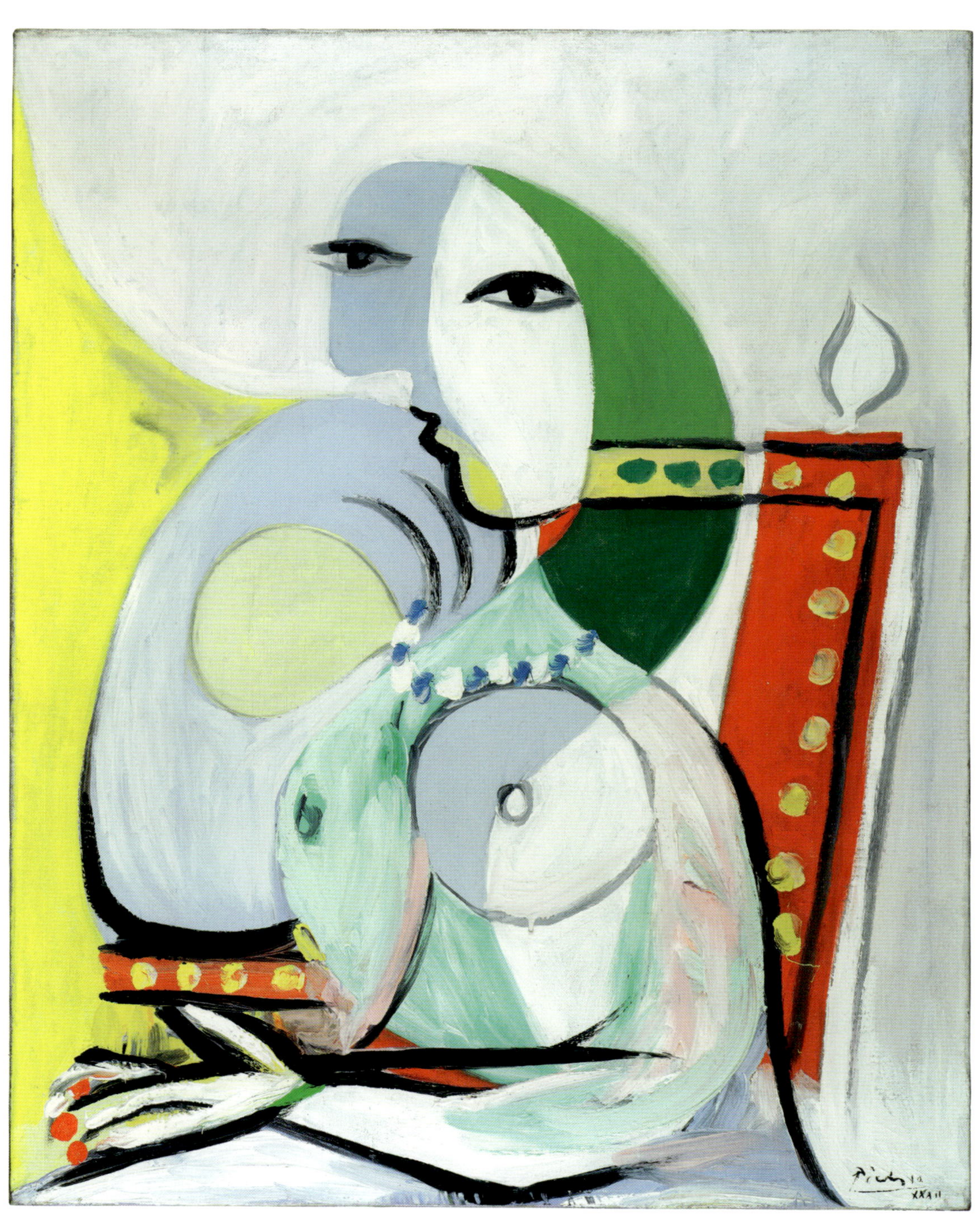

Max Beckmann
1884 Leipzig – 1950 New York

Oil on canvas
Inscribed lower right in German script:
Beckmann B. 36
110.2 × 64.4 cm

Inv. no.: P62T
Acquired 2014

06 Max Beckmann
Selbstbildnis mit Glaskugel
1936

In the course of his artistic career, from his youth until his death, Max Beckmann repeatedly portrayed himself in drawings, prints, paintings, and sculptures. Like the self-portraits of other great artists, these works bear witness to the physical appearance and mental state of a creative person within the context of ever-changing life circumstances. Reflecting these circumstances, marked by artistic success as well as private and social recognition, but even more so by two world wars, professional banishment, exile, and emigration, Beckmann depicts himself in a diversity of attitudes: self-confident or vulnerable, sublime or devastated, argumentative or melancholic, clear-sighted or gloomy. But no matter how he related to the "Lord's great, eternally changing world theatre" with all its passions and longings, conflicts and miseries, his interest in the "mystery of being", which always included himself, never waned.

When he painted his *Selbstbildnis mit Glaskugel* (Self-Portrait with Crystal Ball) in 1936, Beckmann was still living in Berlin but considering emigration to the United States. Three years earlier, shortly after the Nazi party had come to power in Germany, he had been relieved of his teaching post at the Art Academy of the Städel Museum in Frankfurt. He was slandered in the press for his "degenerate" art and his paintings were removed from the walls of Berlin's Kronprinzenpalais, a section of the National Gallery of Modern and Contemporary Art.

He did not succeed in immigrating to the United States. But in 1937, immediately after Hitler's radio speech in Munich on the opening of the *Grosse Deutsche Kunstausstellung,* Beckmann and his wife fled Berlin and settled in Amsterdam, which was occupied by German troops in 1940. After ten years of oppressive exile, they finally immigrated to the United States on 19 August 1947.

This brief biographical sketch reveals the circumstances under which Beckmann painted his *Selbstbildnis mit Glaskugel.* What would follow the extremely bleak present? To investigate the future the artist uses a crystal ball, an instrument of divination, turning himself into a seer and a soothsayer. Beckmann had always been responsive, across eras and cultures, to anything that would further knowledge and insight into the various guises of reality. His reading encompassed, religion, philosophy, mythology and belles lettres. Esotericism and occultism captivated him. Anything of significance could become the subject matter of his art.

The crystal ball quietly rests in his hand, gently pressed against his chest. Light falls on his face and on his high forehead, but his eyes are deep in shadow. His grave, pensive gaze looks both inwards and out into the dark room that fades into infinity and uncertainty beyond the looming figure of the artist and the open door behind him, which frames his head like a nimbus. By eliminating all narrative detail, Beckmann, seen only with the attribute of a seer and soothsayer, appears suspended from the reality of the times. He has devoted his painting to the timeless subject matter of the unswerving recognition of truth with both mind and eye. This challenging work of art lends the artist a near prophetic aura. Hölderlin, one of the many writers in Beckmann's library, once wrote, "Yet in the man a god has his dwelling, too, so that he sees what is past and to come." This thought reverberates in Max Beckmann's paintings.
UW

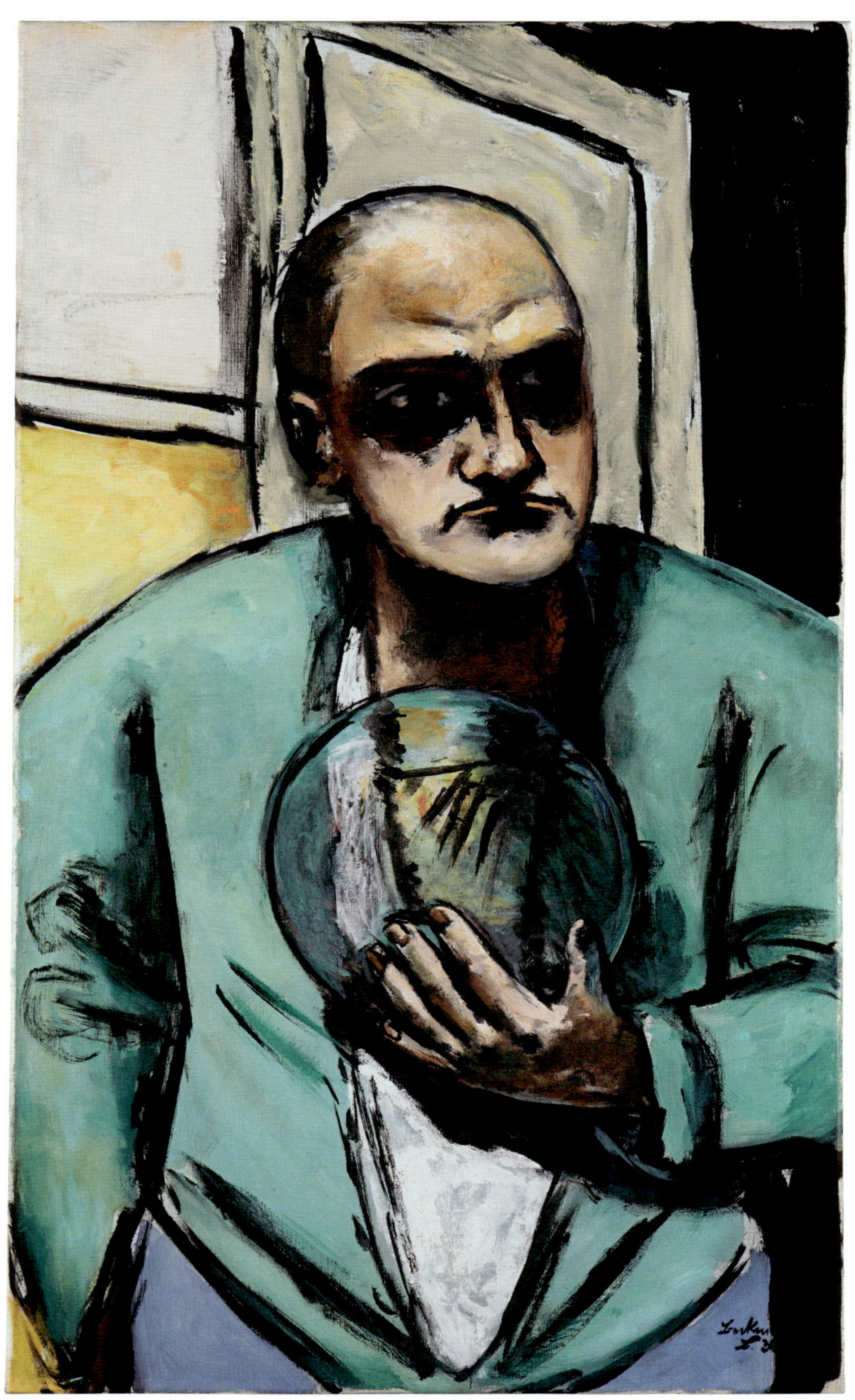

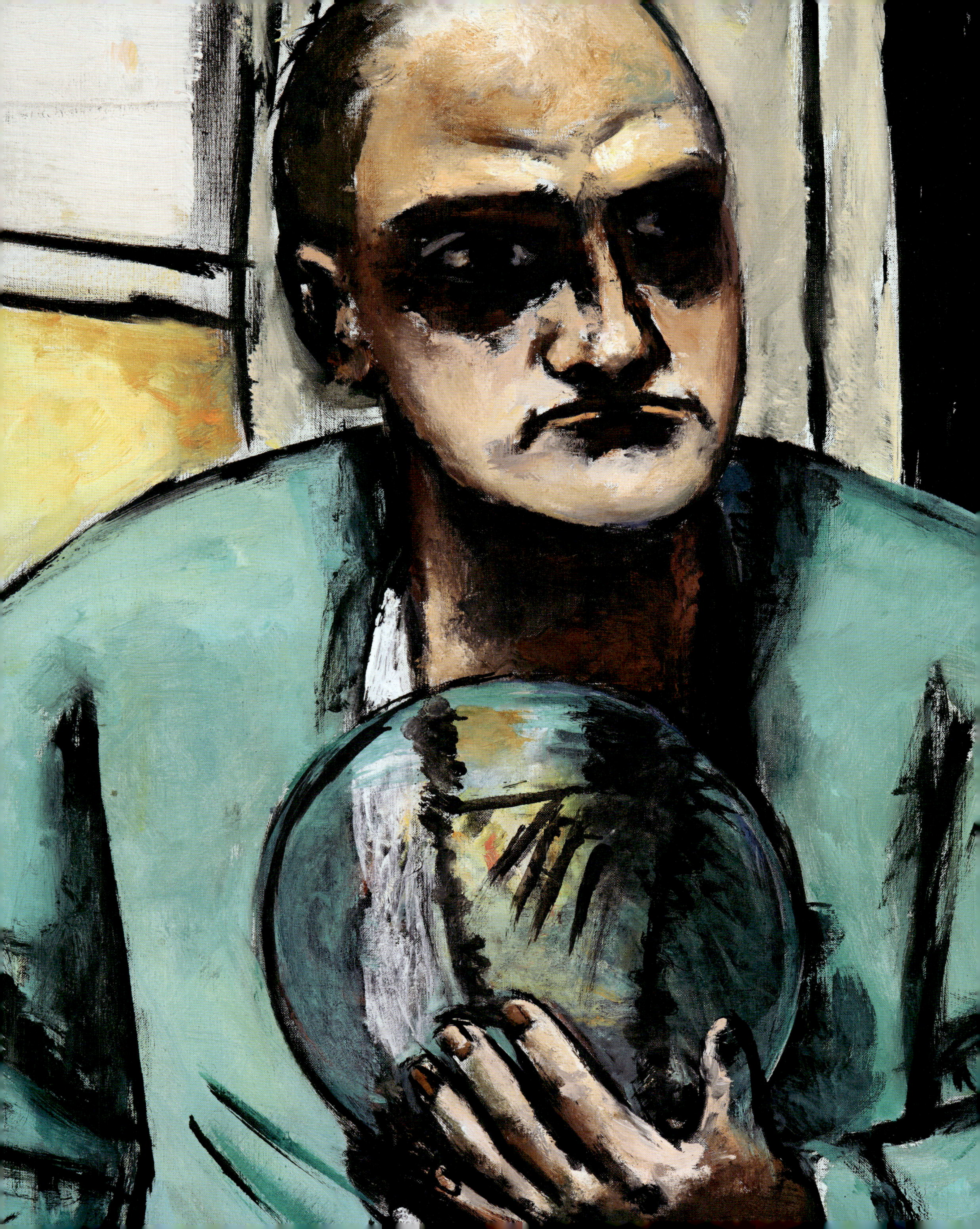

Max Beckmann
1884 Leipzig – 1950 New York

Bronze
(Cast between 1958 and 1968)
56.7 × 28.5 × 18 cm

Inv. no.: S179M
Acquired 2007

07 Max Beckmann
Mann im Dunkeln
1934

In the spring of 1933, the Nazis relieved Max Beckmann of his post as professor at the Städelschule in Frankfurt although he had already moved to Berlin in January, hoping that the large, anonymous city would enable him to work undisturbed and in peace. From 1933 to 1937, he created a number of important paintings, including the triptych *Abfahrt* (Departure, 1932/33), *Versuchung des Heiligen Antonius* (Temptation of St. Anthony, 1936–37) and *Selbstbildnis mit Glaskugel* (Self-Portrait with Crystal Ball, cat. 6), as well as six of the eight sculptures that he made during his lifetime. Beckmann may have turned to sculpture for several reasons. His lifelong interest in people and in the philosophical implications of space—its darkness, uncertainty and infinitude but also the home of the gods—may well have played a role. In addition, the physical reality of sculpture lends itself more easily to rendering a message than the complexity of paintings.

The artist created *Mann im Dunkeln* (Man in the Dark) in 1934, the year he turned fifty. It is the first of the sculptures that he fashioned in a small room adjoining his studio in Berlin. His landlord, a trained caster, made the plaster mould for him. The bronze cast was produced posthumously (between 1958 and 1968) at the Roman Bronze Works, a foundry in New York. Measuring fifty-eight centimetres in height, it stands in contrast to the over life-sized, pseudo-heroic figures of official Nazi art. Friedhelm Fischer writes, “Once you have seen *Mann im Dunkeln,* you will not forget him.” The entire energy of the sculpture is concentrated in the figure’s extremities, in the oversized feet and the expressive hands. Although clothed in a toga-like garment, the figure does not evoke antiquity. Holding his hands in front of him, he is protecting himself against the menace of the unknown, which he cannot consciously perceive for his face is turned away and his eyes are closed. Even so, we feel as if the wandering man is looking into an abyss, a sleepwalker, unable or unwilling to confront what he divines.

We know that Beckmann did not think of himself as a political artist but his letters and the entries in his diary clearly indicate that he was acutely aware of the terrible menace of events looming around him. In this context, *Mann im Dunkeln* becomes a devastatingly prophetic commentary on what has now become history. However, Beckmann’s interests were larger: transcending the specific historical moment, he sought to represent the invisible forces that beleaguer humankind. In Amsterdam, in a diary entry from 1940, the artist noted, “One thing is certain, pride and defiance in the face of invisible forces shall prevail regardless of the worst to come.” AS

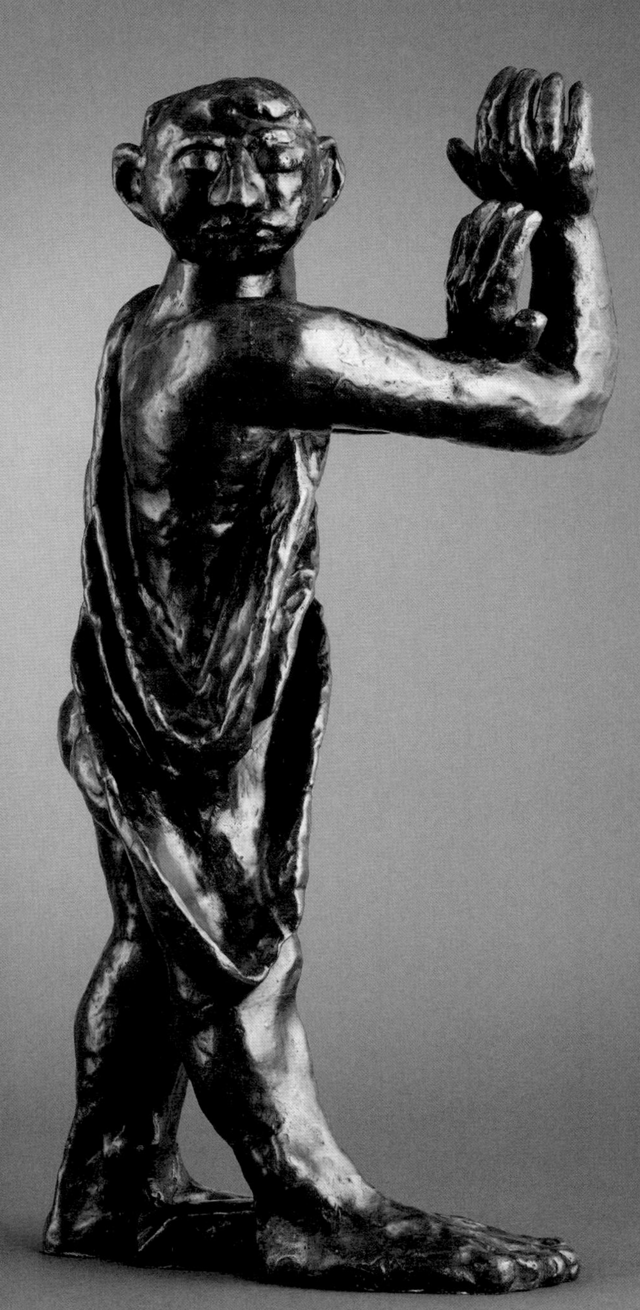

Germaine Richier
1902 Grans, Arles – 1959 Montpellier

Bronze
(Cast: K. Stutz / Kunstgiesserei / Zurich)
Signed on the plinth: G. Richier
89.9 × 38 × 28 cm

Inv. no.: S35T
Acquired 2006

08 Germaine Richier
Juin 40
1940

World War II broke out in September 1939 while Germaine Richier was on holiday in Switzerland with her husband Otto Charles Bänninger, a sculptor from Zurich. As a result, they decided to settle down in Zurich. The following June the German Wehrmacht occupied Paris, where Richier had been living and working. Devastated by these events, the artist created *Juin 40,* a figure of a nude boy cast in bronze. Between 1920 and 1929, Richier had worked with Louis-Jacques Guigues in Montpellier and later Antoine Bourdelle in Paris, experiences that resonate in the making of her sculpture. Both men had studied with Auguste Rodin, so one might say that Richier was a "granddaughter" of this great master of modern sculpture.

Richier's statue invites comparison with Rodin's *Age of Bronze,* which he created in the wake of the Franco-Prussian war of 1870–71. However, the pathos of Rodin's young man is entirely internalized while Richier's boy looks out at the world in anguish with eyes and mouth wide open. His nudity is an expression of his helplessness and vulnerability; the attitude of his arms and hands of suffering and surrender. In contrast to Rodin's young man, the legs of this statue in contrapposto do not offer stable support. As an allegorical figure, *Juin 40* symbolizes human agony and embodies a primal denunciation of the ravages of war.

Initially, Germaine Richier devoted herself primarily to sculptural depictions of the female body. Increasing intensity of expression and figurative deformation led, as of the mid-1940s, to the bizarre hybrids, half-animal half-human, characteristic of the artist's late work, in which she raised essential questions regarding life between nature and civilization, between fate and freedom, between barbarism and humanity. UW

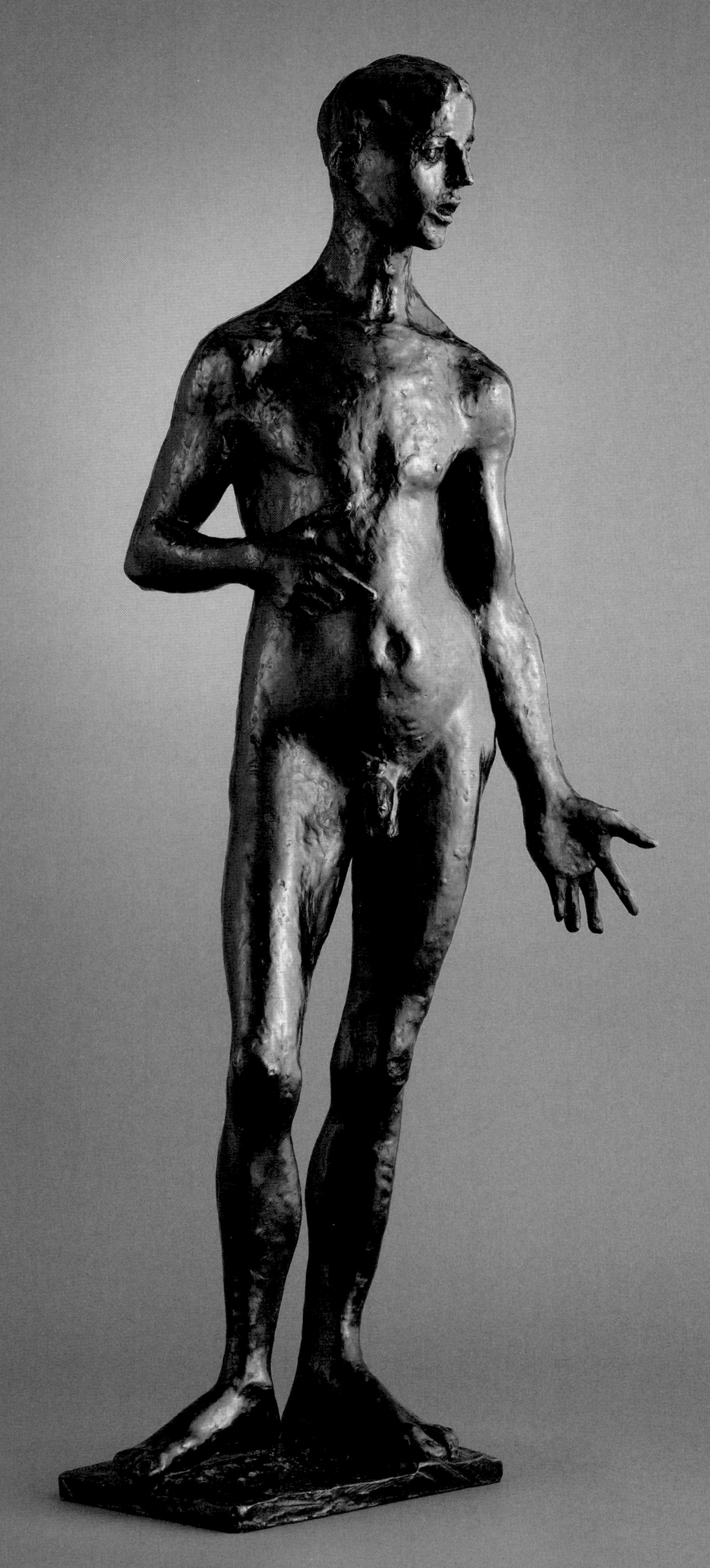

Alberto Giacometti
1901 Borgonovo, Stampa – 1966 Chur

Oil on canvas, mounted on wood
Signed lower right:
Alberto Giacometti 1949–50
74 × 44 cm

Inv. no.: P2T
Acquired 2002

09 Alberto Giacometti
Diego dans un intérieur
1949–50

Although Giacometti considered himself primarily a sculptor, he essentially treated the paintings he made from 1946 until his death in 1966 as equivalent to his sculptural output. Sympathetic to the achievements of Modernism, his father Giovanni already introduced him to painting as a child. Giacometti began his career with a paintbrush in his hand. He painted his first picture in oils when he was twelve years old and his first sculpture followed a year later.

Early on in his career, Giacometti found himself embroiled in the conflict between the perception of visible reality on one hand and its artistic representation on the other. Understanding something as a whole and simultaneously perceiving its countless details was terribly difficult for him. He therefore distanced himself from his subject matter only to the extent that he could see it in its totality, while rendering its overall appearance in untold quantities of the finest brushstrokes. The resulting texture creates the impression of a wealth of detail seen in extreme close-up and converging into the shape of a human body.

Diego dans un Intérieur (Diego in an Interior, 1949–50) shows Giacometti's brother in his studio in Paris. We see only sparing hints of the room itself: a few lines mark a shelf, possibly a couch, and behind it an unembellished wall. Diego, sitting on a chair in the exact centre of the composition, faces the viewer head-on in an attitude of aloof detachment. The picture is more like a drawing than a painting. Using a pointed paintbrush, Giacometti has rendered the contours and shape of the body in black, adding white highlights to the overall grey of the whole so that we seem to perceive light and shadow but barely any colour. The figure looks oddly unfinished like a provisional wire construction—as if flesh and bodily warmth had been mislaid by the simultaneous distance and closeness of Giacometti's gaze, as if in the emptiness of the room Diego were only permitted a fleeting existence between the void out of which he has come and the void into which he will go. Sartre, existentialist and Giacometti's friend, writes that in every one of his images the artist raises the age-old metaphysical question of why anything, rather than nothing, even exists at all.

Giacometti's artistic oeuvre explores single, concrete individuals and at the same time human existence per se. For decades, he made do with very few people as models for his paintings and sculptures: his wife Annette, his brother Diego, friends and others who were close to him. His sitters can always be identified and named, and yet ultimately they are generalized representations of the human species in all its complexity and unfathomability. UW

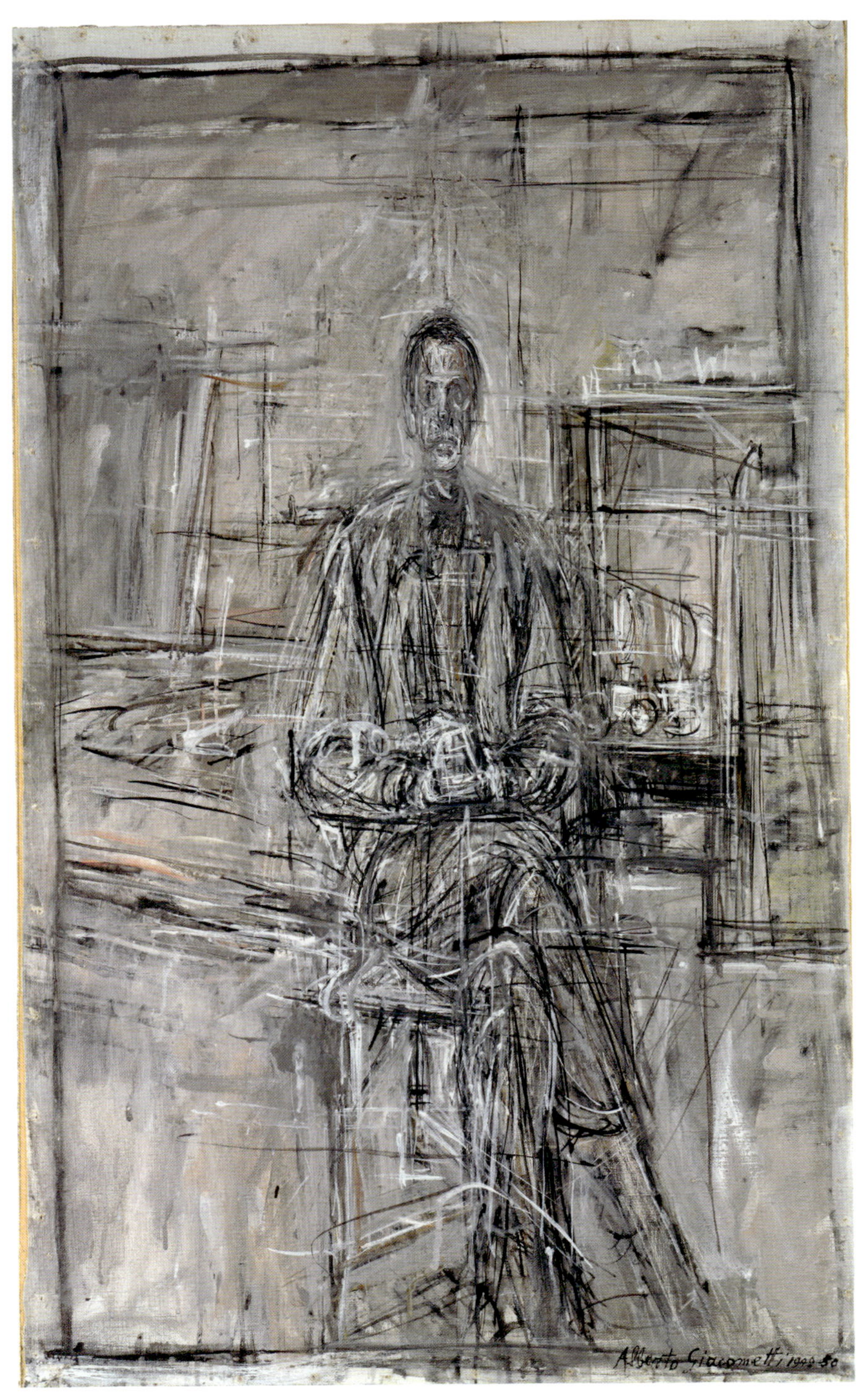
Alberto Giacometti

Alberto Giacometti
1901 Borgonovo, Stampa – 1966 Chur

Bronze
(Cast: Susse Fondeur, Paris 1973)
Signed and numbered on reverse:
Alberto Giacometti 6/8
57.7 × 36.5 × 25 cm

Inv. no.: S54T
Acquired 2012

10 Alberto Giacometti
Buste d'homme (Eli Lotar II)
1964–65

In 1964–65, the last two years of his life, Giacometti fashioned three sculptures of the photographer and filmmaker Eli Lotar. When he died in 1966, the last one, *Eli Lotar III,* was still propped up in his Montparnasse studio. He had completed plaster versions of the first two, *Eli Lotar I* and *Eli Lotar II,* in 1965. All of the bronze casts were produced posthumously between 1968 and 1981.

Giacometti had met Lotar in the milieu of Parisian nightlife. The talented son of a Romanian poet, Lotar wasted his time as an habitué of the bars in Montparnasse, a quintessential example, according to Giacometti's biographer, James Lord, of artistic failure and of the inability to work—issues that always troubled Giacometti as well.

Photographs taken in the studio by Giorgio Soavi show the intensity of Giacometti's relationship to his sitter. He spent the entire year in 1964 working almost daily on the two busts, which took excruciatingly slow and laborious shape in countless sittings. Giacometti wanted to capture every single vibrant moment, every single aspect of his model—an insuperable undertaking.

The bust of *Eli Lotar II,* measuring 57.7 centimetres in height, culminates in a clearly detailed head, pitted against the amorphous mass of the torso with sloping shoulders and arms hanging slack, resembling flowing lava or a craggy mountainside. It bears traces of Giacometti's modelling, of his powerful hands that have animated the inert matter. The sitter's head rises out of this mass like a piece of fruit. All the energy of the work is distilled here, in Lotar's mouth, nose, and above all in his eyes. His gaze pierces reality, peering into the distance with utmost concentration, focusing on an infinitely remote, unnameable goal. In contrast to the transient body, which returns to pure matter, the seeing spirit, physically embodied in this head, survives. AS

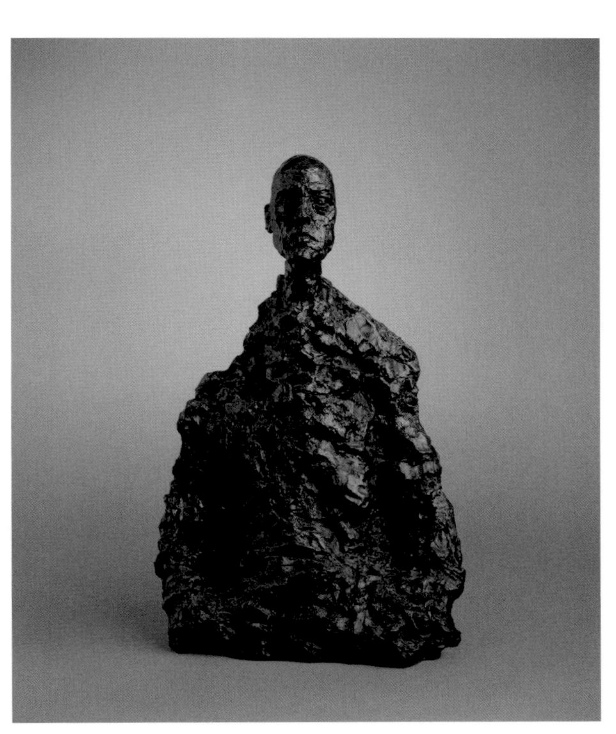

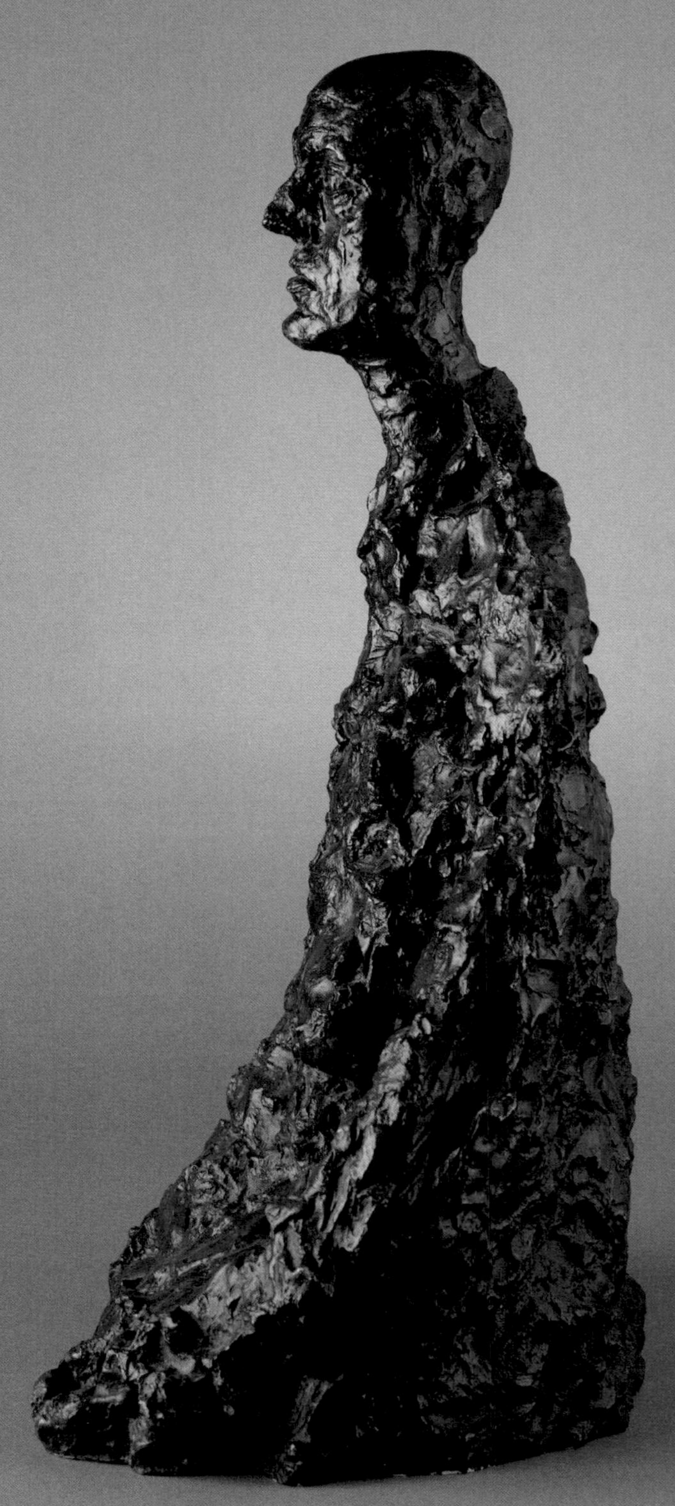

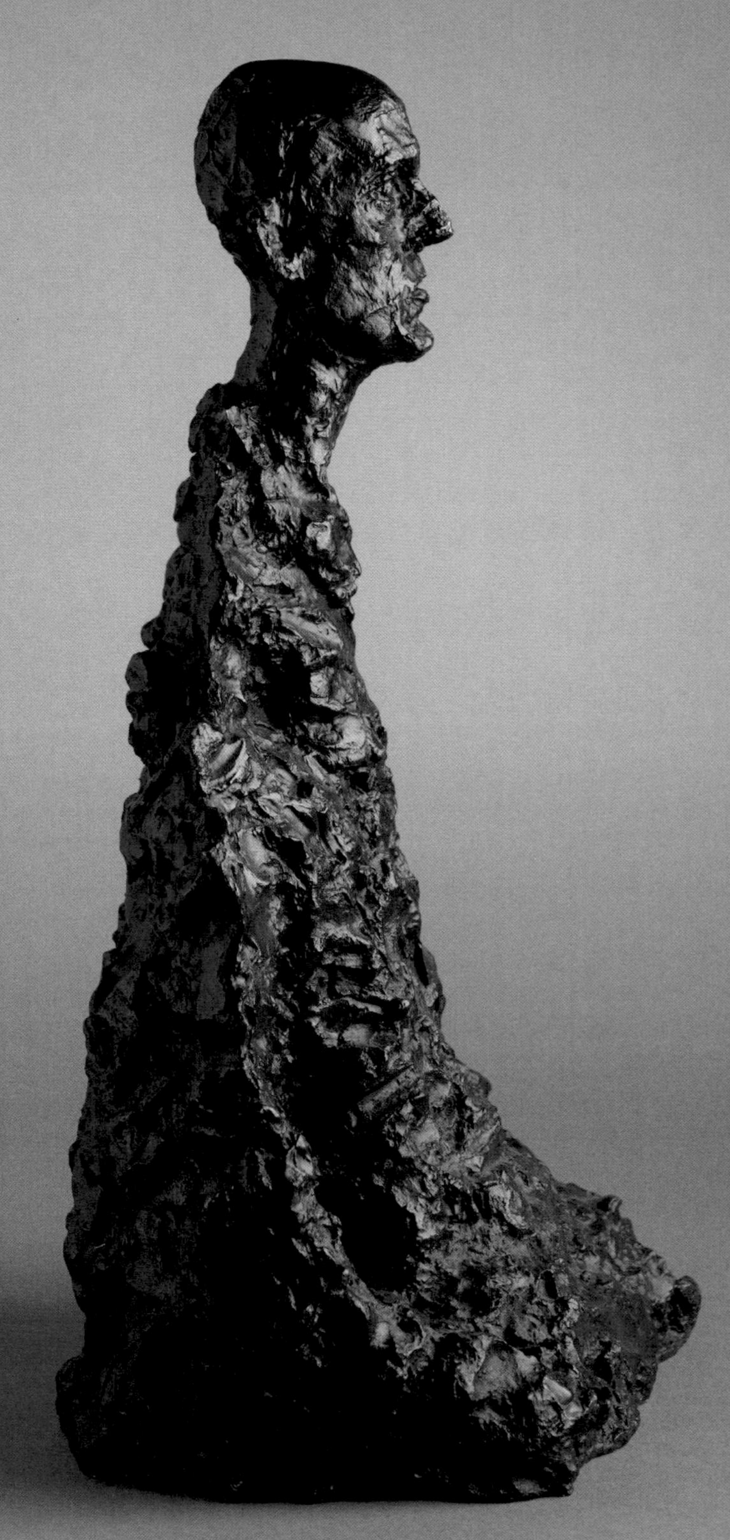

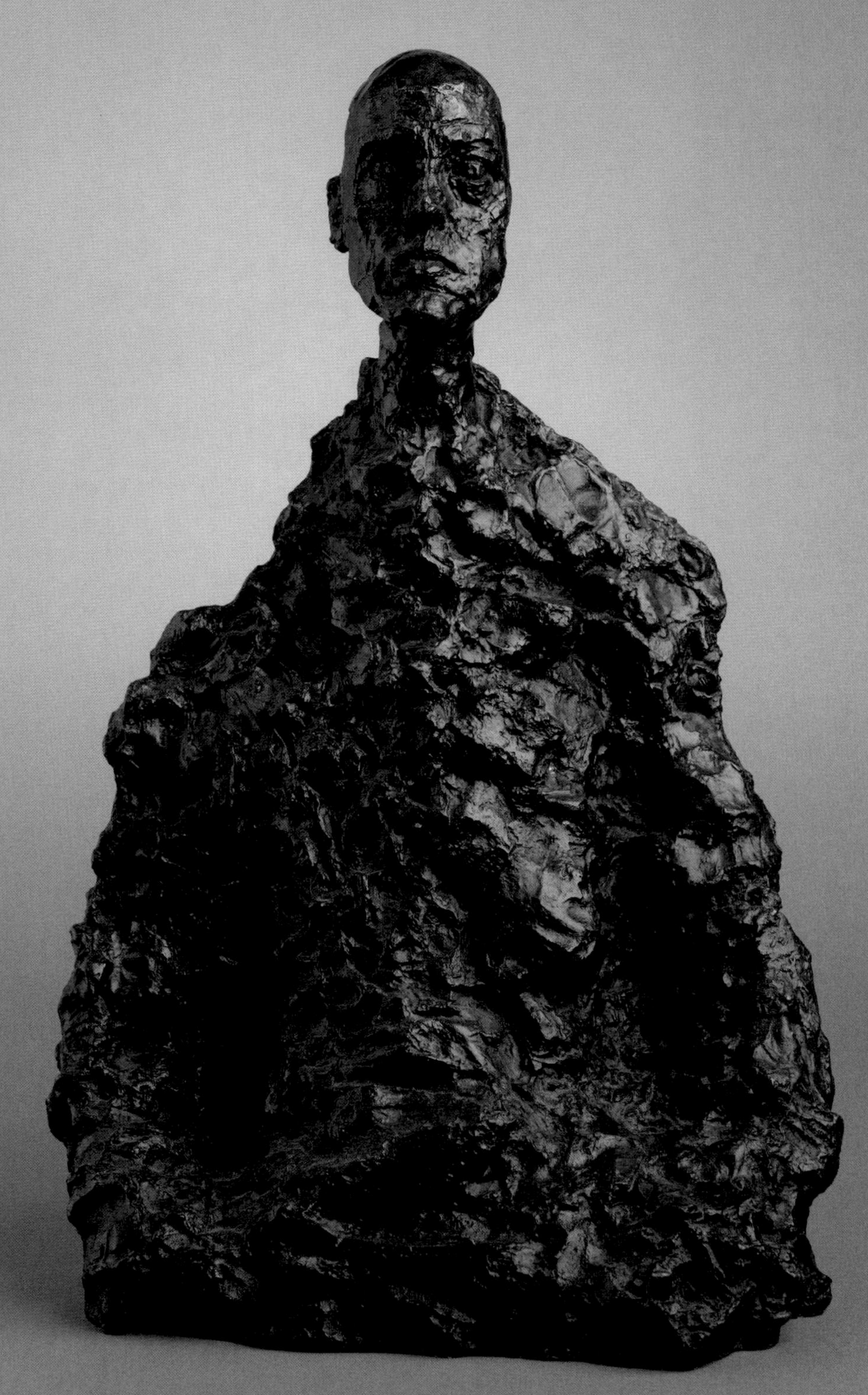

Willem de Kooning
1904 Rotterdam – 1997 Long Island, New York

Bronze
(Cast at Modern Art Foundry, New York)
Signed and numbered on right leg:
W. Kooning A/P I
62.2 × 42 × 42 cm

Inv. no.: S59T
Acquired 2013

11 Willem de Kooning
Cross-Legged Figure
1972

In comparison to his paintings, the twenty sculptures that Willem de Kooning created in the short period between 1969 and 1974 play a relatively subordinate role within his oeuvre as a whole. Nonetheless, the artist, who was deeply interested in the human figure, gave this body of work a compelling shape that is as self-contained as it is significant.

In 1969, De Kooning took advantage of a chance encounter in Rome with a friend, the sculptor Herzl Emmanuel, who gave him the use of his workshop and foundry in Rome where he playfully worked in clay and then cast the results in bronze. He started out making small objects almost like amulets, before moving on to medium-sized and later monumental sculptures, which were basically anthropomorphic in appearance. The striking way in which de Kooning treated his materials led to figures that do not appear to have been worked from inside out in the traditional fashion, starting with a sturdy skeleton and gradually fleshing it out. Instead, they trace the action of the hands, working from outside in: we do not see the hands following the logic of the figure, but rather the figure following the logic of the hands and their direct impact on the clay. Often shaped with his eyes closed, the works quite literally incorporate the flow of the artist's movements and sensations, yielding results that are analogous to the iridescent nature of de Kooning's expressive painting between figuration and non-figuration.

Structurally, some of the sculptures, like *Cross-Legged Figure* of 1972, cannot stand on their own; they are presented lying down or require a support to appear more or less stably suspended in space. The works draw attention to primary, fundamental aspects of sculpture, to the initial creative impulse in handling materials. This impulse, which relies primarily on the sense of touch, is motivated by the artist's search for origins, immediacy, and vitality. The floating dynamics of this particular sculpture evoke a dancing figure, for instance, the Indian god Shiva, a medieval Morris dancer, or early modern dance, indeed, dance in general with its both standardized and ecstatic forms of movement. *Cross-Legged Figure* inspires other associations as well, its raw existence possibly representing an early stage of natural history, a creature that embodies all the immanent potential of the development of matter and spirit, or, quite the opposite, an end state of civilization, in which catastrophe has exhausted that potential, leaving behind nothing but deformed, lifeless matter. UW

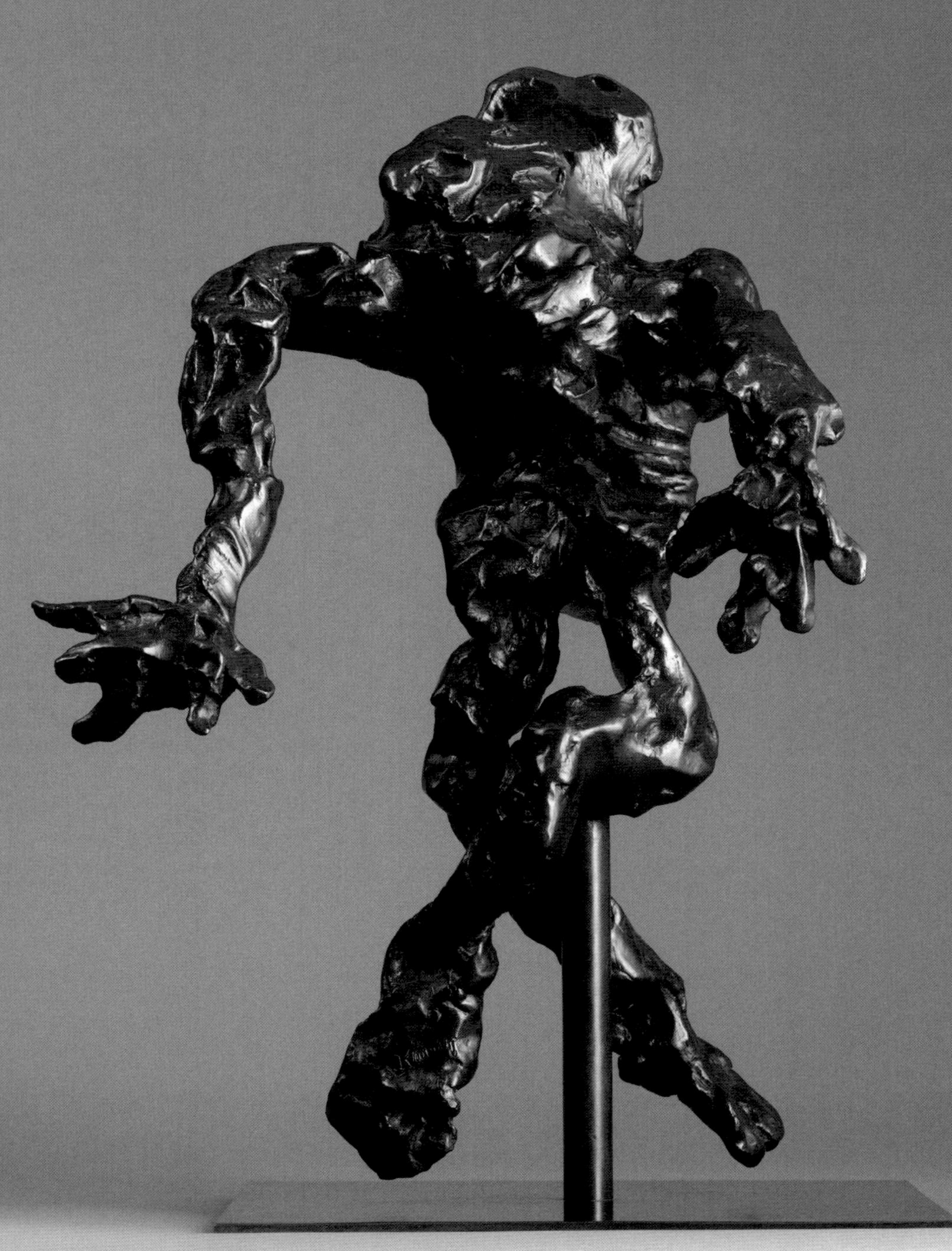

Experiment and Existence

Georges Seurat
1859 Paris – 1891 Paris

Oil on canvas
33.2 × 41.3 cm

Inv. no.: P44T
Acquired 2010

12 Georges Seurat
Le tas de pierres
1882–84

A man wearing dark trousers, a white shirt, and a straw hat is stoutly hacking away at stones in the earth. A second person is picking up the stones and putting them in a pile. Green vegetation provides the backdrop to this tightly framed scene. Seurat observes people hard at work in rural surroundings with the eye of an impressionist and, by the look of it, directly on-site. For he has rendered the relatively small format and therefore easily portable painting entirely in the style of Impressionism, that is, with rapidly executed brushstrokes, allowing the colours to blend before the paint dries and imbuing the whole with the sense of a moment arrested. The contours are blurred in the bright light and shimmering air; the shadows are coloured and the contrasts complementary. The two people are depicted without individualizing features.

Seurat was already familiar with Barbizon painters like Corot and Millet, as well as Courbet, whose works depicted natural environs and human labour. But when he saw the work of Manet and Pissarro at the Fourth Impressionist Exhibition of 1879 in Paris, he was so deeply impressed that he gave up studying at the Academy and, from then on, sought out the motifs of his art in the real world, in both city and country. In the early 1880s, he was drawn to the outskirts of Paris, in particular Le Raincy, where his father lived. There he observed people at work, capturing them in drawings and small oil studies that would later provide source material for the execution of larger paintings in the studio.

Early on, Seurat studied the phenomenon of colour. Insights gleaned from reading Charles Blanc's *Grammaire des arts du dessin* (1867) and Michel-Eugène Chevreul's *De la loi du contraste simultanée des couleurs* (1839) led in the mid-1880s to an increasingly systematic application of colour in his paintings. Seurat was particularly interested in the "optical blend" generated by the side-by-side of very small dabs of pure, unmixed pigments, which blend in the eyes of beholders so that they perceive the desired colours. Through this method, for which art criticism invented the terms Pointillism or Neo-Impressionism, Seurat underpinned Impressionism with theoretical and rational foundations—and simultaneously surmounted them. The method was to exert an exceptionally great influence on many contemporaries and successors of Seurat and was to rank him among the trailblazers of modern art next to Cézanne, Gauguin, and van Gogh. Although Seurat did not yet apply his new method to *Le tas de pierres* (The Stone Heap), the painting does exhibit the qualities that would characterize his greatest and most enduring creations—a serene, detached, and occasionally witty faculty for observation that subtly registers the constantly changing appearances in nature and modern civilization. UW

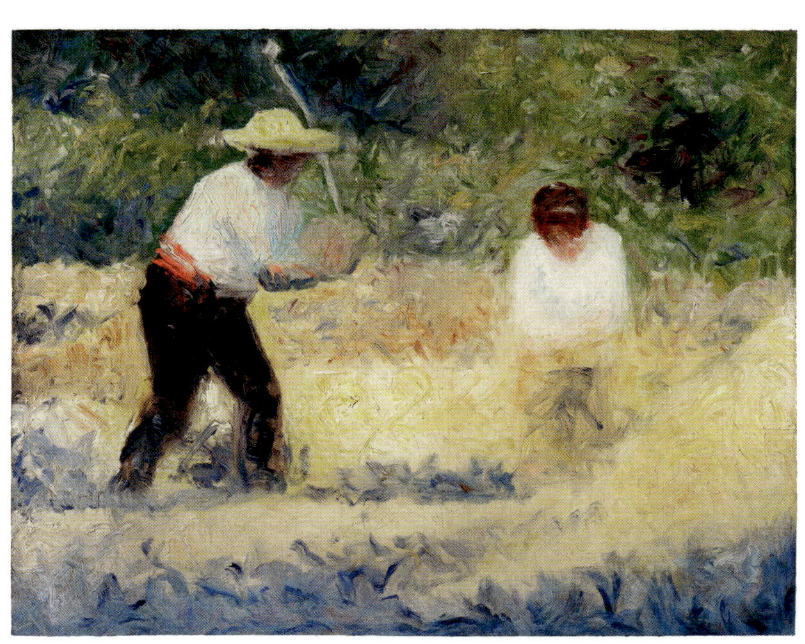

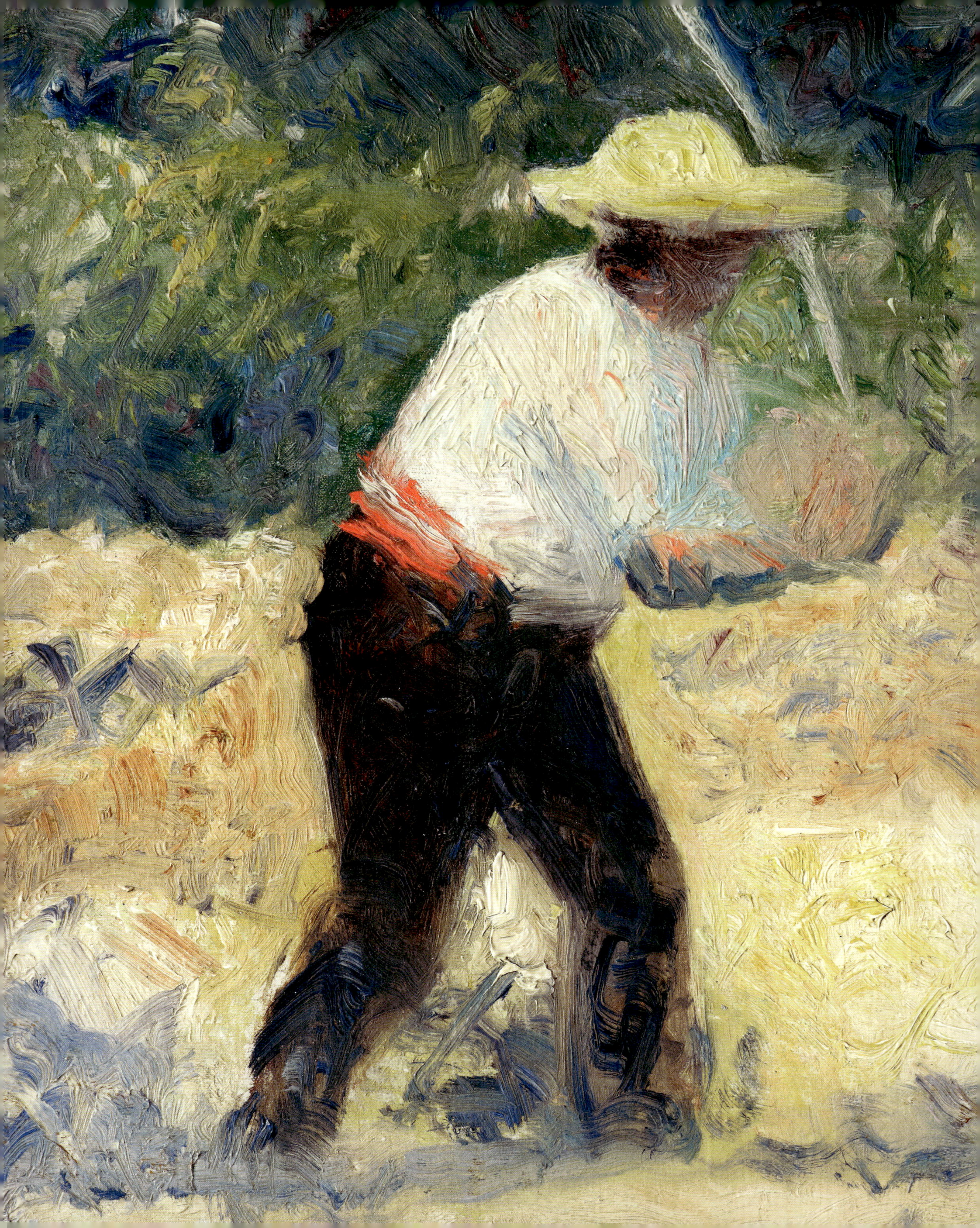

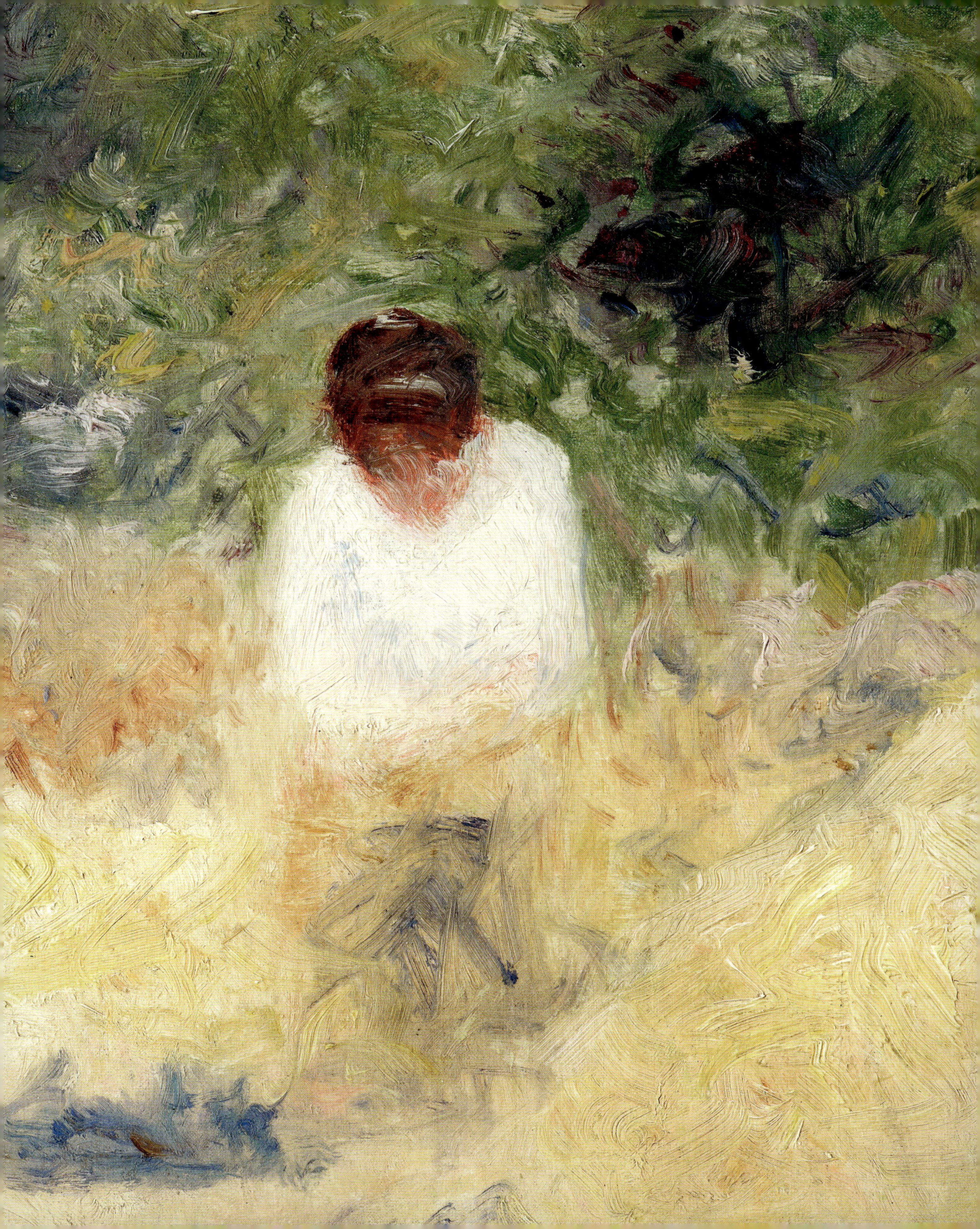

Paul Gauguin
1848 Paris – 1903 Hiva Oa, Marquesas Islands

Oil on canvas
Signed and dated lower right: P Gauguin 89
92 × 73.5 cm

Inv. no.:P19T
Acquired 1997

13 Paul Gauguin
Entre les lys
1889

When Gauguin moved to Brittany from Paris in 1886, he encountered the primal life *("la vie sauvage")* that he had always longed to find and that ultimately took him to the South Seas. In the nineteenth century, Brittany was a remote region, untouched by urban civilization, where women wore traditional folk dress and still embodied the ancient myths. Life was inexpensive there and soon attracted an international colony of diverse artists with Gauguin at its core, first in Pont-Aven and later in Le Pouldu.

Gauguin painted *Entre les Lys* (Among the Lilies) in the year 1889, when he had tired of the tourism in Pont-Aven and was commuting between the two villages. Although it cannot be unequivocally identified, the landscape he chose to paint in *Entre les Lys* shows the low-lying hills and slate-roofed houses typical of the region. A curious procession—a dog looking back at two girls in Breton folk costume—is on its way out of the village, which the artist has framed and partially hidden behind a few trees. The dog is a nod to the great realist painter Gustave Courbet, who gave the animal pride of place in the foreground of his history painting *A Burial at Ornans* (1849). Whether the motif of a procession is also indebted to Courbet or rather motivated by Paul Gauguin's quest for a Symbolist visual idiom, which was gaining prominence in his work at the time, is a moot question.

The dog acquires special significance in comparison to a work painted shortly afterward, *The Loss of Virginity (The Awakening of Spring),* 1890–91, in which a fox plays the role of seducer. In *Entre les lys,* Gauguin presents the dog not only as protector but also suggests the animalistic drive that lures the still innocent girls out into world, passing by white lilies, the Christian symbol of purity, and away from the village flourishing in the warmth of summer. AS

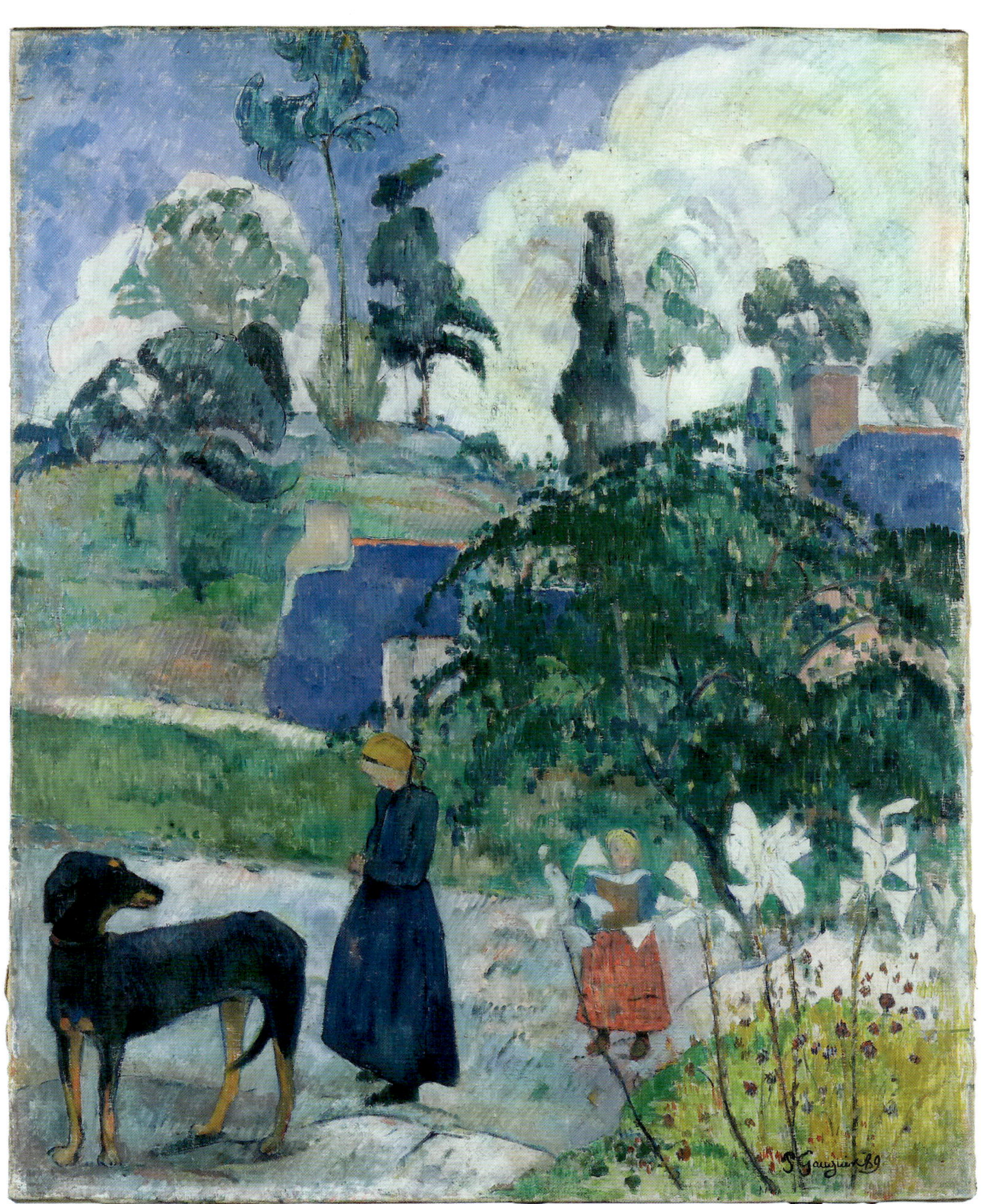
P Gauguin 89

Pablo Picasso
1881 Málaga – 1973 Mougins, Cannes

Clay, shellac
Signed on verso: Picasso
36.3 × 25 × 25 cm

Inv. no.: S1T
Acquired 2001

14 Pablo Picasso
Tête de femme (Fernande)
1906

Picasso's sculptural oeuvre encompasses 664 works. Although much less familiar, apart from a few exceptions, than his body of paintings, it is similarly characterized by ceaseless change in form, content, and expression. The artist created *Tête de femme (Fernande)* in the first half of 1906 during a time of artistic upheaval. He had just abandoned his blue and pink periods to devote himself to "primitivism", Gauguin and early Iberian sculpture.

Tête de femme is the first full sculpture made by Picasso of the head of his then lover Fernande Olivier, who shared with him the years he spent at Montmartre in the Bateau Lavoir. In 1904–05, the sensual young woman with almond-shaped eyes began making frequent appearances in drawings and paintings. Fernande, said to have had a weakness for perfume and furs, gazes at us head on with elegant noblesse. Her hair frames her face and falls loosely to her shoulders. This face, accentuated by a narrow, slightly curved nose and a distinctive mouth, is composed of two different halves. The right side is rougher, less finished, and the tactile surface appeal of the material emphasized. Picasso presumably achieved this effect by pressing gauze into the damp plaster. The right eye engraved in the surface appears to be blind, at least in the bronze version, in contrast to the sculpted and clearly seeing left eye. The asymmetry of the two halves is more than a formal distinction. It demonstrates the fact that the two sides of our faces are dissimilar by nature and refers, of course, to that same phenomenon in the sitter's face, where they might be described as clear and diffuse. The principle of uneven facial features was to play a prominent role in Picasso's oeuvre and recurred with great virtuosity in the decades that followed.

The painterly version of *Tête de femme* echoes the tradition of Auguste Rodin and Medardo Rosso, whose sculptures Picasso had seen in 1904 and 1905. The windblown hair around Fernande's face establishes her as a "creature of nature", redolent of the melancholy mood that marked the turn of the century. AS

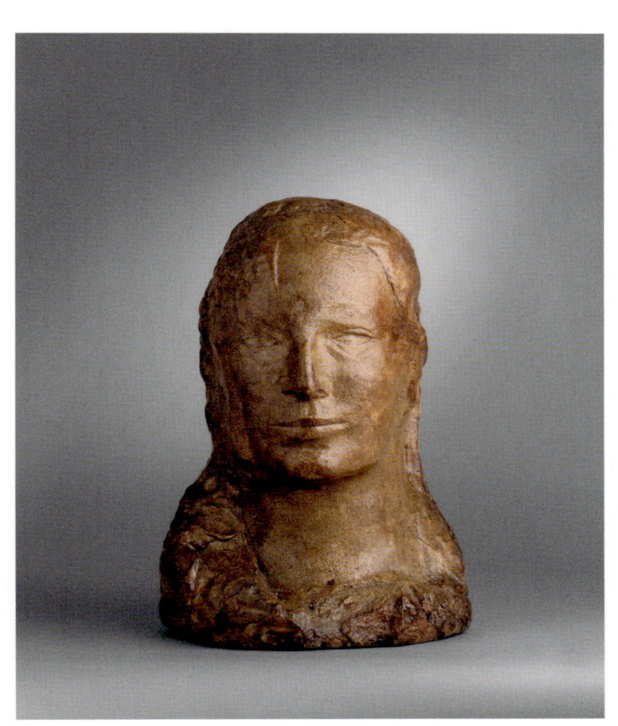

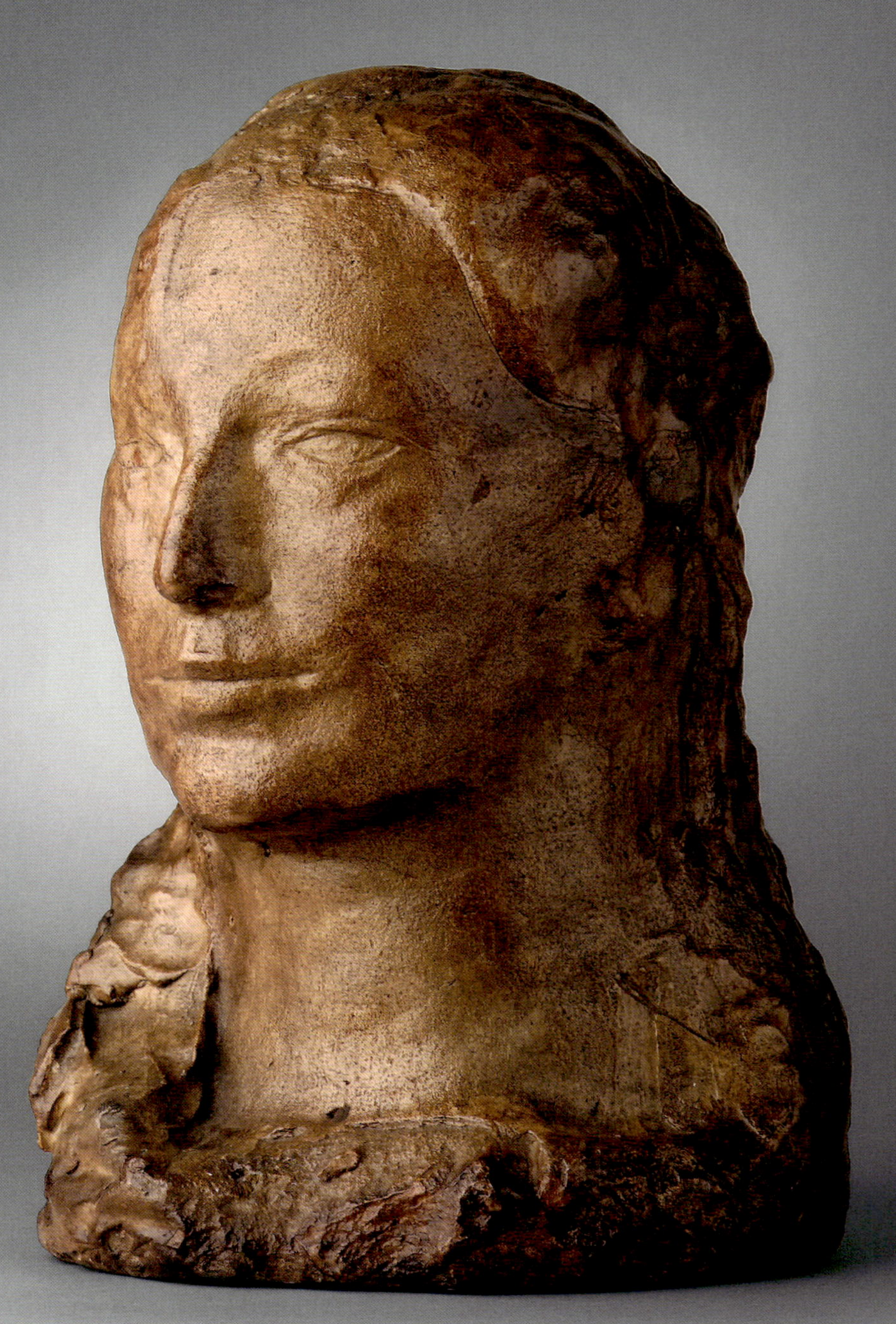

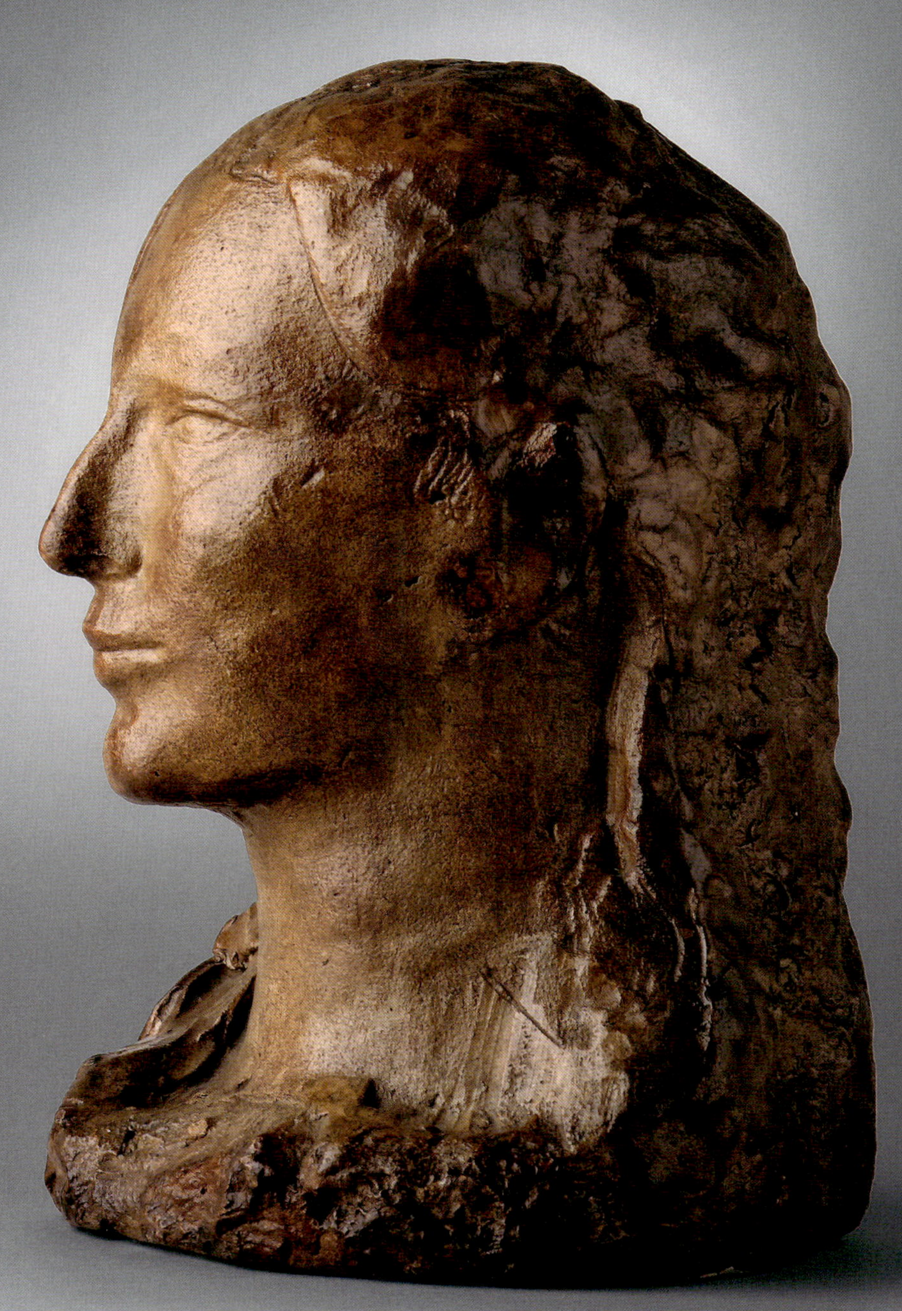

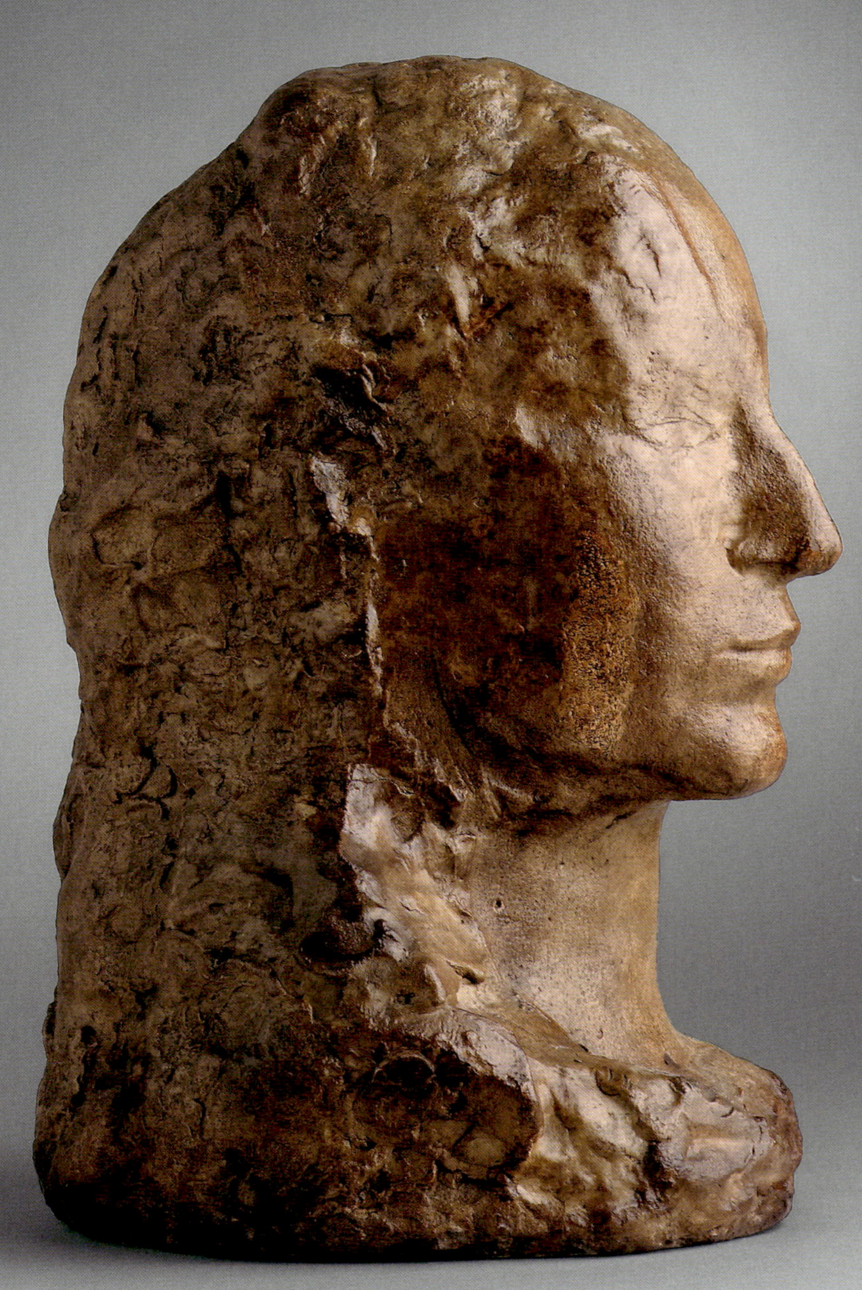

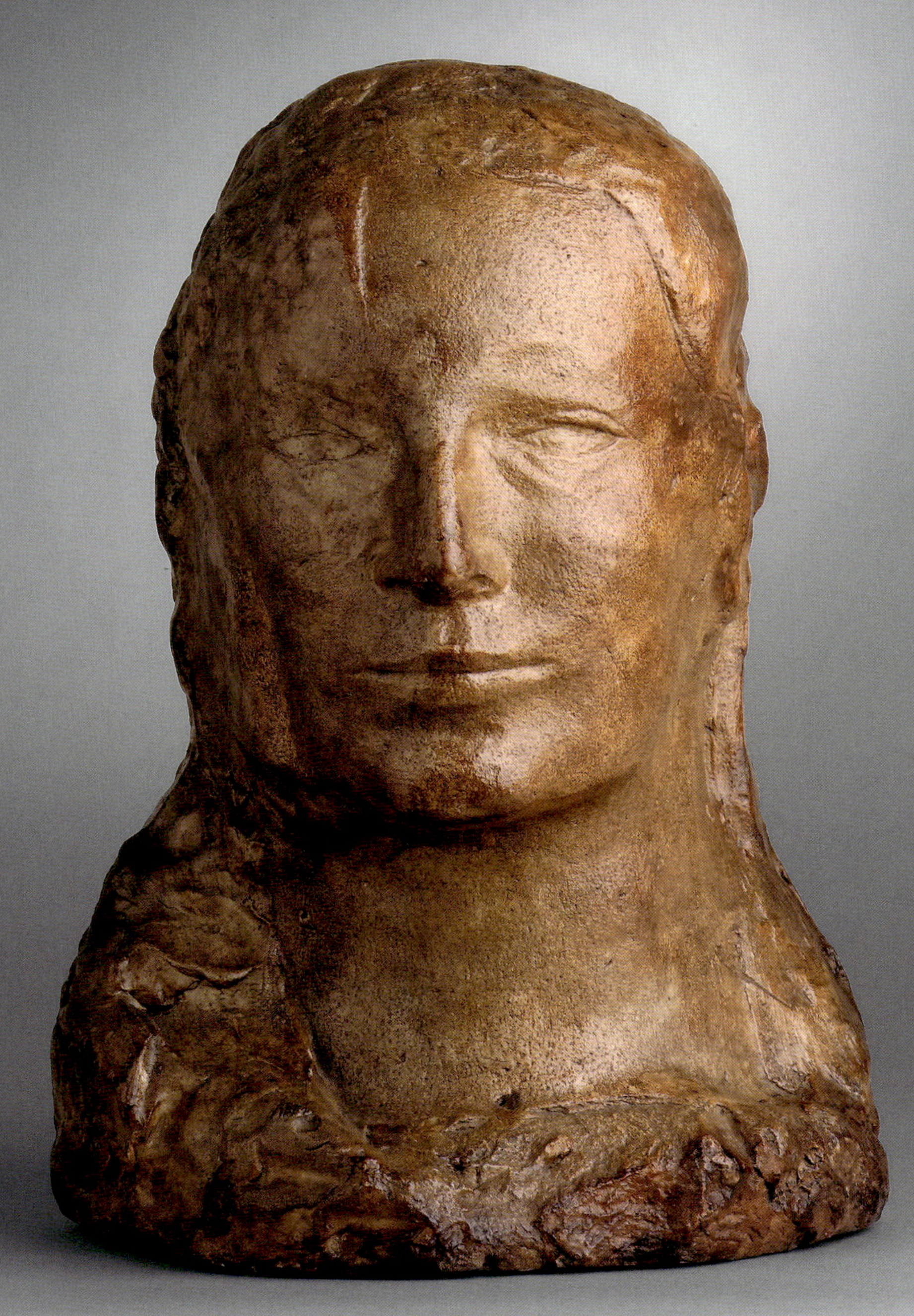

Karl Schmidt-Rottluff
1884 Rottluff, Chemnitz – 1976 Berlin

Oil on canvas
Signed and dated lower right:
S. Rottluff 1911
77 × 85 cm

Inv. no.: P3T
Acquired 2001

15 Karl Schmidt-Rottluff
Die Lesende
1911

On 7 June 1905, Fritz Bleyl, Erich Heckel, Ernst Ludwig Kirchner, and Karl Schmidt-Rottluff founded the artists' group Die Brücke in Dresden. In their brief and emphatic manifesto, the artists, once students of architecture, declared, "Anyone who depicts, with immediacy and candour, that which compels him to create belongs to us." Although they each clearly represented a distinctive artistic temperament of their own, they shared developments during their first years in Dresden that by 1910–11 had led to the flatness that distinguishes Die Brücke paintings.

It was during this period that Schmidt-Rottluff painted *Die Lesende* (Woman Reading). He depicts his young sitter with expansive and monumental gesture. The extreme close-up, essentially a photographic device, is achieved by cropping the figure and squeezing it into the rectangular picture plane. The woman, probably seated on a sofa and engrossed in her book, does not establish eye contact with the viewer. She keeps her distance despite the proximity and informality of her attitude. Her eyes are lowered in full concentration on the book that she is holding in her slender, plant-like hands. The composition converges in this part of the canvas; the shapes are more complex and smaller as opposed to the large flat fields of colour that characterize the rest of the painting. Instead of being placed seamlessly side-by-side, the colours are outlined in the nature of a preliminary sketch. Schmidt-Rottluff borrowed the device from woodcutting, a medium of great interest to him. The colours, clear cut at first sight, radiate an inner luminosity that stems from subtle combinations of primer and superimposed layers of paint, such as green on yellow or petrol on red. The tension and excitement generated by the strong yellows and reds heightens the casual, relaxed pose of the reader.

Die Lesende is one of Schmidt-Rottluff's first large-format works. The sitter cannot be conclusively identified. It may be Nelly, one of the three black models along with Sam and Milly, who were frequent guests at Ernst Ludwig Kirchner's studio in Dresden, where they used to dance. The work shows similarities in physiognomy with a lithograph *(Drei Negerakte/Three Black Nudes)* and a portrait *(Nelly),* both made by Kirchner that same year in 1911, and with a photograph of Nelly and Siddi Riha dancing in Erich Heckel's studio, 1910–11. The mask-like countenance of the young woman with her pointed chin and full lips is reminiscent of West African tribal art, specifically the sculptures made by the Fang people. *Die Lesende* exemplifies the "primitivism" practiced by Die Brücke artists, whose interest in the art of Oceania and Africa was initially inspired by visits to the Dresden Museum of Ethnology. The treatment of plane and the atmosphere of Schmidt-Rottluff's painting evokes Paul Gauguin's paintings of the South Seas while the countenance of his sitter references the heritage of Africa. AS

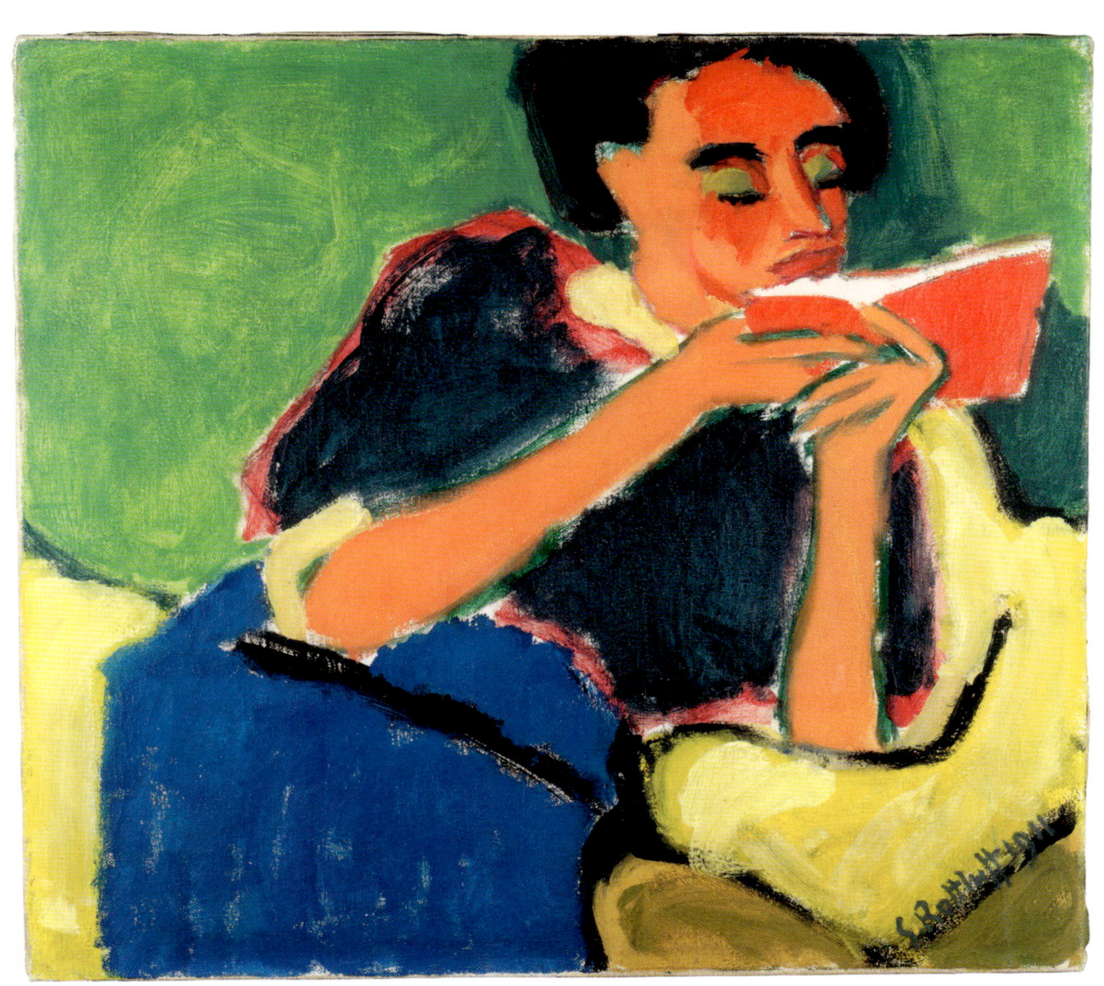

Ernst Ludwig Kirchner
1880 Aschaffenburg – 1938 Frauenkirch-Wildboden, Davos

Oil on canvas
Signed lower right: E. L. Kirchner
100 × 75.5 cm

Inv. no.: P37T
Acquired 2007

16 Ernst Ludwig Kirchner
Paar unter Japanschirm
1913

Kirchner painted *Paar unter Japanschirm* (Couple under Japanese Umbrella) in 1913 during extremely productive years, beginning when he moved to Berlin from Dresden in 1911 and drawing to a close in the spring of 1915 when he was called up for military duty. The year 1913 was devoted in particular to the large works painted on the Baltic island of Fehmarn and to the artist's important street scenes, culminating in *Der Potsdamer Platz* (Potsdam Square, 1914). Paar unter Japanschirm belongs to a third complex of works that is central to Kirchner's oeuvre: paintings of friendship and conversations in his studio.

There is a hint of Arcadia in the relatively tight framing of the composition, picturing the painter Otto Mueller with his wife Maschka, also a painter. We cannot tell at first sight if this is an interior or a scene on the Baltic Sea, but a 1912 photograph of Kirchner's first studio in Berlin at Durlacher Strasse 14 provides the answer. The painted wall hanging as well as other items can be clearly identified. They testify to Kirchner's avid interest in other cultures. The umbrellas illustrate the great popularity of Japanese fashions that spread from Paris to the rest of Europe; the tablecloth is of Coptic origins; and the leopard stool, on which Mueller is sitting straight as a ramrod, reflects the artist's interest in "primitive" art. The stool, already among the furnishings of Kirchner's studio in Dresden, was probably brought back from Africa by Erich Heckel's brother Manfred.

The picture is painted in the graphic style cultivated by Kirchner in the years 1913–14. The nervous brushstroke applies not only to the contours of the figures and objects but to the entire painting, its vibrant rhythm an artistic equivalent to the hectic urban climate that prevailed prior to World War I. In contrast, the subtle, understated palette of blues, greens, and a matt pink reference nature and are no doubt indicative of an intentional link between indoors and outdoors, underscored by the fact that the wall hanging resembles an arcade. In the blue segments under the arcades—they might be interpreted as sky or sea—we see nudes, as in Arcadia, which feature in many of Kirchner's paintings. The joyous mood in *Paar unter Japanschirm* evokes not only the happy times spent with the Muellers on Fehmarn, but also the summertime mood in the works of the Impressionists and Matisse. It is quite possible that Kirchner had seen Manet's painting *In the Winter Garden* (1879) at the National Gallery in Berlin. **AS**

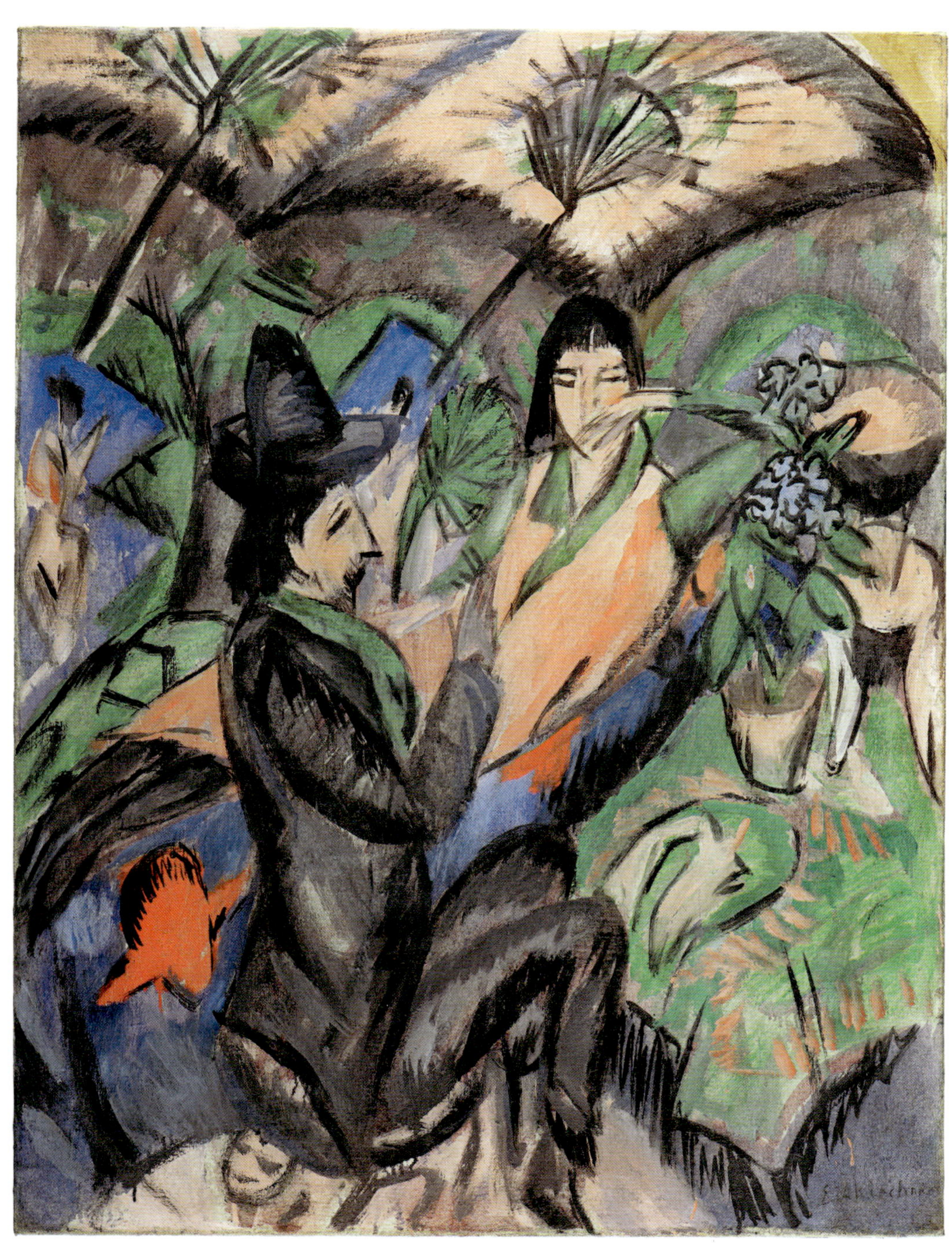

Ernst Ludwig Kirchner
1880 Aschaffenburg – 1938 Frauenkirch-Wildboden, Davos

Wood (Swiss stone pine)
Initialled on stand: ELK
21.6 × 9 × 6 cm

Inv. no.: S56T
Acquired 2013

17 Ernst Ludwig Kirchner
Kniende, nach links gewandter Kopf, rechte Hand auf der linken Brust
1912

Some 80 of the 140 sculptures definitively attributed to Kirchner have survived. With few exceptions, they are made of wood and carved directly out of the tree trunk, so that marks left behind in the wood allow us to trace the development of the works. Forty of these sculptures, showing active and often unusual poses, were made while Kirchner was living in Berlin. In his own words, they make no reference to antiquity. This includes the small, kneeling woman of 1912, one of the few sculptures with a monograph. She is not only pictured in a photograph that Kirchner took in 1913; she also appears in a painting of 1912, *Stilleben mit Plastiken and Blumen* (Still Life with Sculptures and Flowers).

The small, unquestionably regal figure with the aloof gaze of a Sphinx is reminiscent of Egyptian statuettes and commands respect. The uneven, convoluted arrangement of her arms and legs yields completely different views of this squatting figure. She may, for instance, appear to be in movement or at rest, one of many impressions inspired by the artist's study of nature and, as he himself wrote in retrospect, by his "experience of the figures of contemporary life". Transposing that experience into art led to what Kirchner termed a hieroglyph.

In addition to the vibrancy and lifelike intimacy expressed by the *Kniende* (Woman Kneeling, Head Facing Left, Right Hand on Left Breast), one can identify diverse references to art history, as in many of Kirchner's works. While the tribal art of Africa reverberates in the choice of material and the kneeling pose—Kirchner's interest in the sculpture of Cameroon is well documented—the inspiration of French nineteenth-century painting is also unmistakable, for instance, Delacroix's *Women of Algiers,* Degas's paintings of women bathing, or Gauguin's squatting women in his paintings of the South Seas. The conspicuously asymmetric position of the legs does not typically feature in African tribal art but is occasionally seen in works by the above-mentioned painters, referring in turn to life forms outside of Europe. However, the right hand of the *Kniende,* resting on her left breast, echoes the traditional gesture of a Venus pudica, a chaste Venus covering her breasts and private parts. Revealing and concealing, seducing and rebuffing: these are ancient modes of female existence. AS

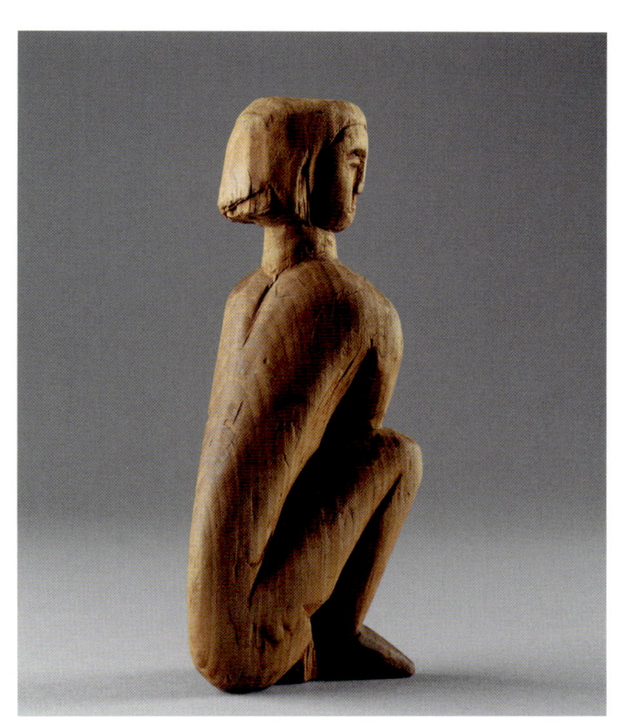

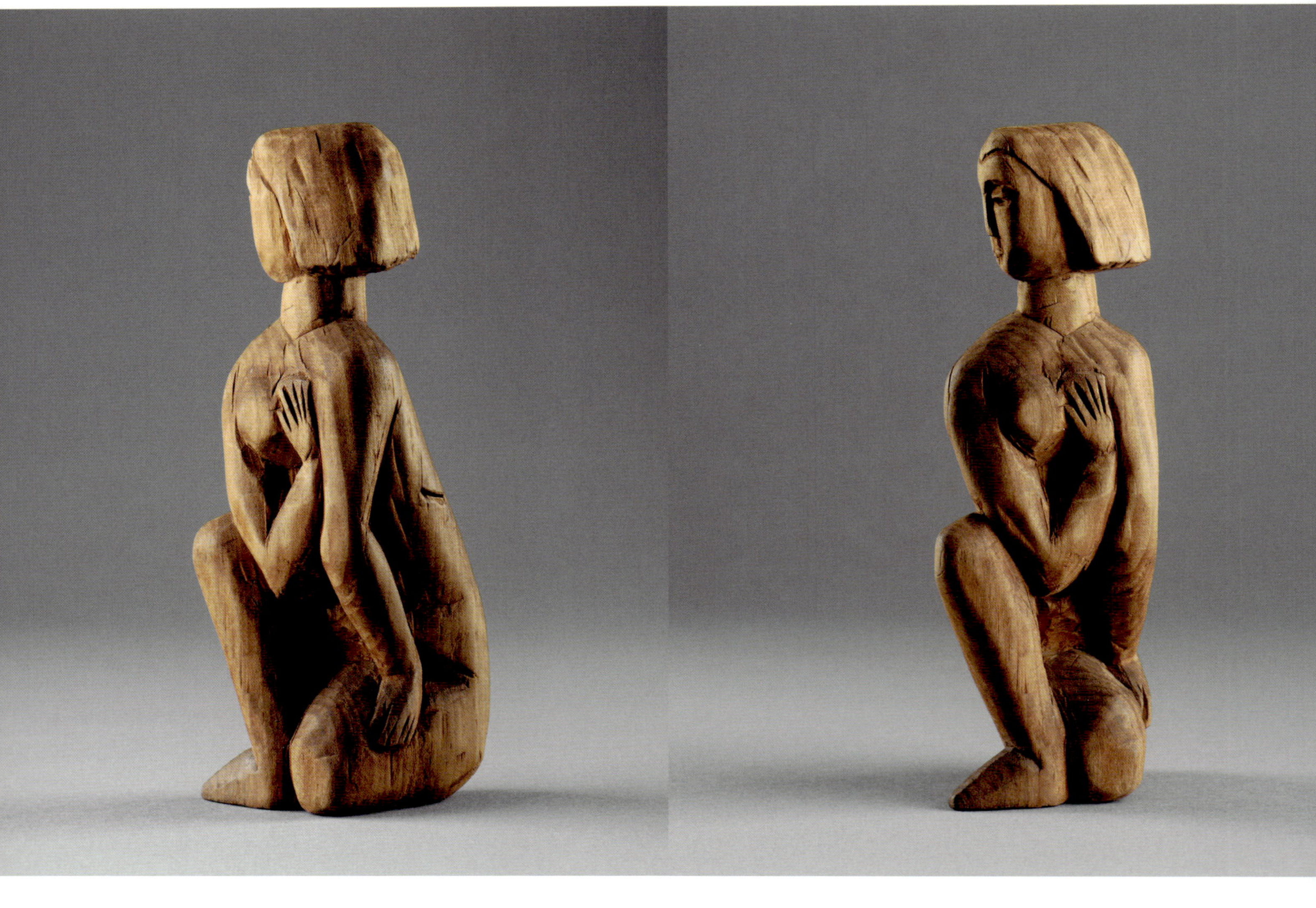

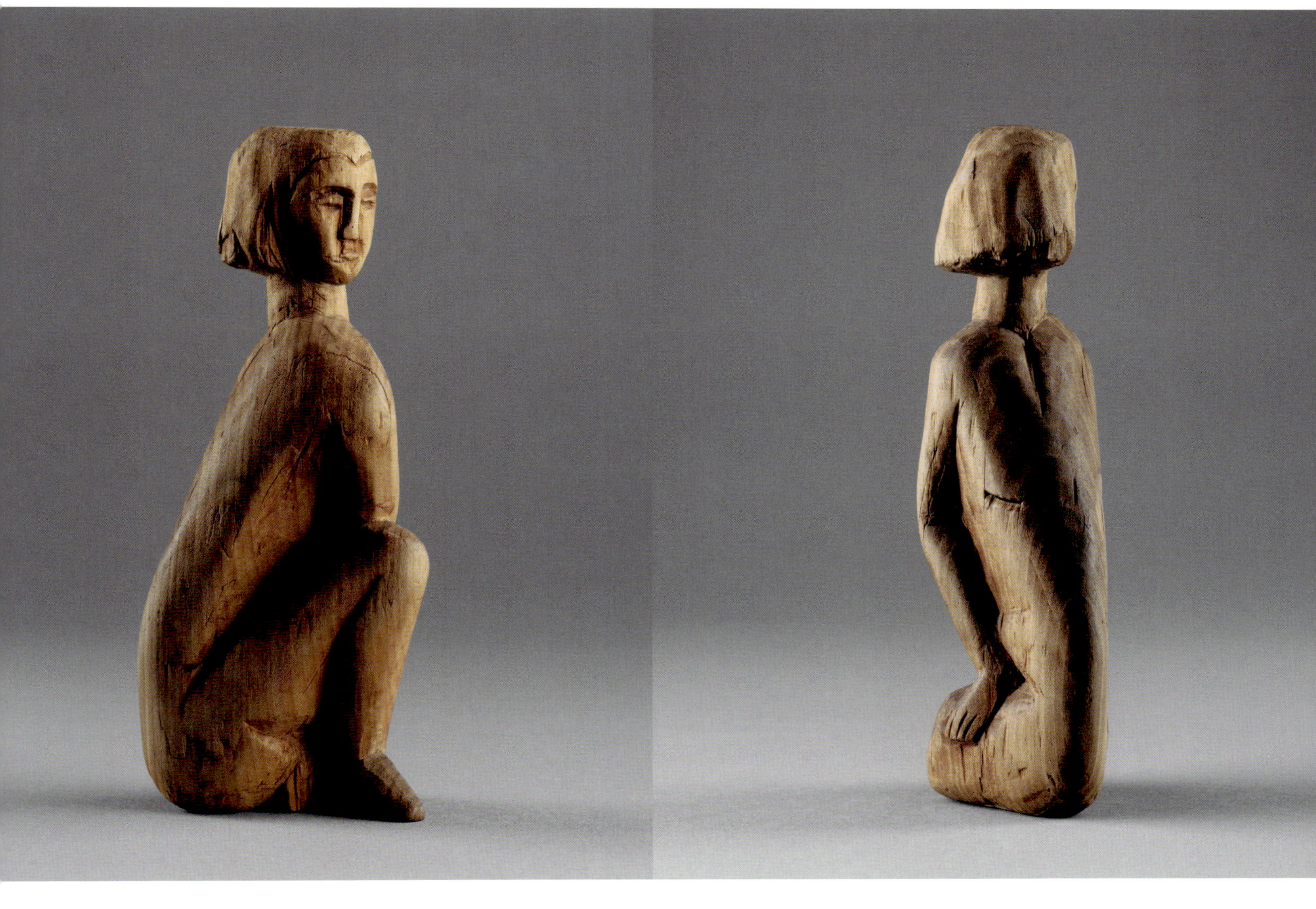

Franz Marc
1880 Munich – 1916 Verdun

Oil on canvas
Signed upper right: Marc
58.5 × 84.2 cm

Inv. no.: P33T
Acquired 2006

18 Franz Marc
Schweine (Mutterschwein)
1912

Franz Marc's basically pantheistic worldview was based on the unshakable conviction that all living creatures share a mutual affinity in the constant flow of space and time, and all creation participates in the "organic rhythm" of nature. Since he felt that animals were more beautiful and purer than human beings, since he could "still hear them speak", as the writer Else Lasker-Schüler once said, he devoted his attention to them and their "misunderstood souls". Despite perceiving a certain "anti-sentiment" and "ugliness", the artist felt they were purer because they led more instinctive lives, unlike humans who had been alienated from nature by the applied sciences and technology. Correspondingly, diverse animals populate Marc's paintings, domestic and exotic, above all cats, dogs, cows, swine, horses, and deer but also elephants, tigers, lions, and monkeys. Animals embody the longing for an originary existence in harmony with nature, even when they are a mutual menace. Occasionally, human beings, as if dreaming, become part of the natural creation that inhabits the imagery of this nearly untouched universe.

In visualizing the "animalization" of art as a means of spreading a new spirit, Marc adopted stylistic features of Cubism, Orphism, and Futurism to create works of crystalline transparency and radiant colouring. A profound glow marks the palette of *Schweine* (Pigs, 1912); it suffuses the hilly landscape and its vegetation. The sow, painted a pure white, dominates the centre of the composition, while patches of black on her skin and in the background stand in significant contrast. Tenderly, the mother protects her young. Pigs frequently feature in works of art as animals to be hunted, slaughtered and exploited, as useful antagonists or companions of humankind. Marc, in turn, represents them in formal and atmospheric harmony with the open natural environment, emphasizing their original dignity.

1912 marks a highlight in the art of Der Blaue Reiter, a loose association of like-minded artists, initiated by its main exponents, Wassily Kandinsky and Franz Marc, who issued a programmatic almanac that same year. They invoke a "mystical inner construction" of the world and seek to mirror it as a parable in painting—objectives that ultimately led both artists to devote themselves to pure abstraction. UW

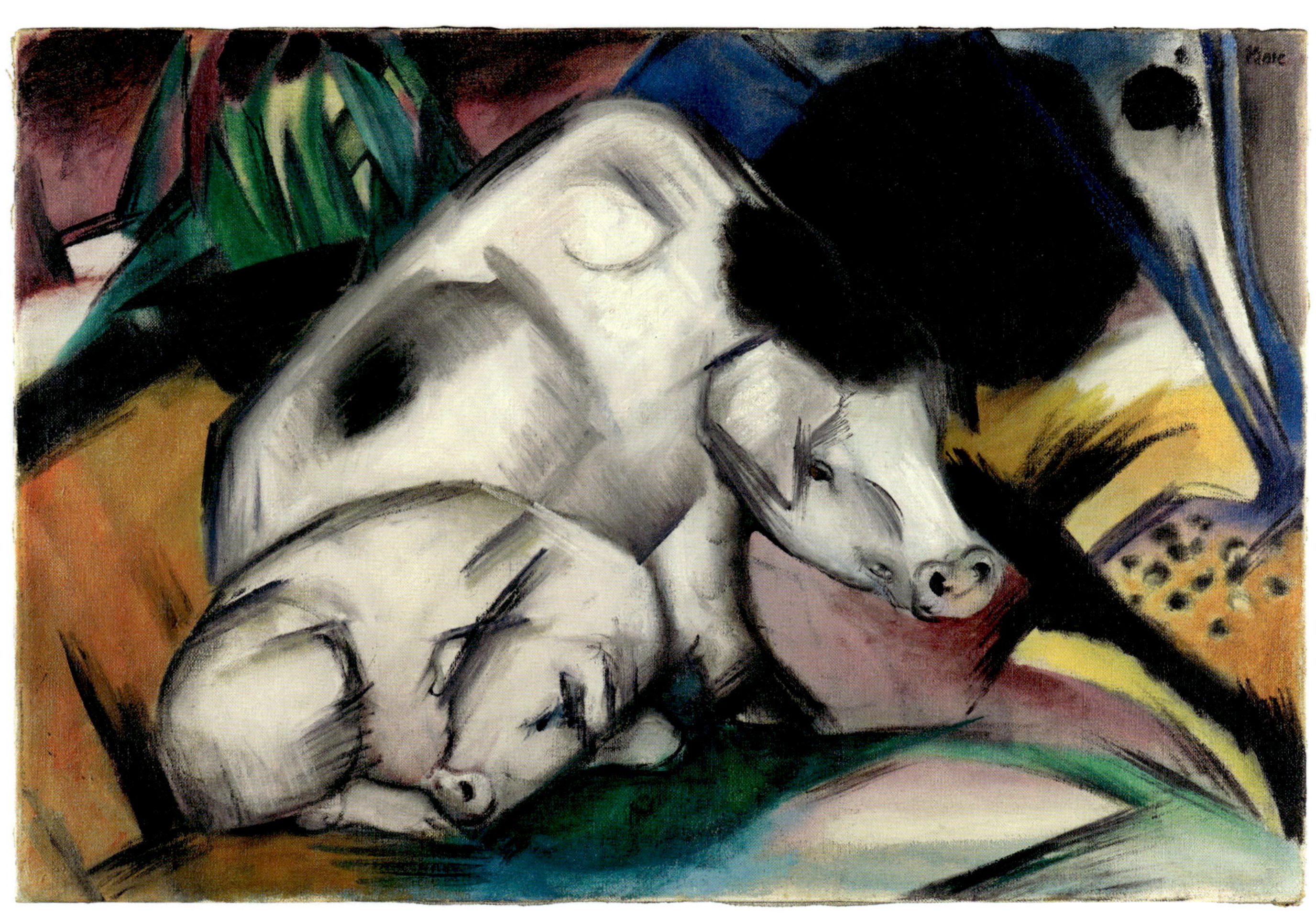

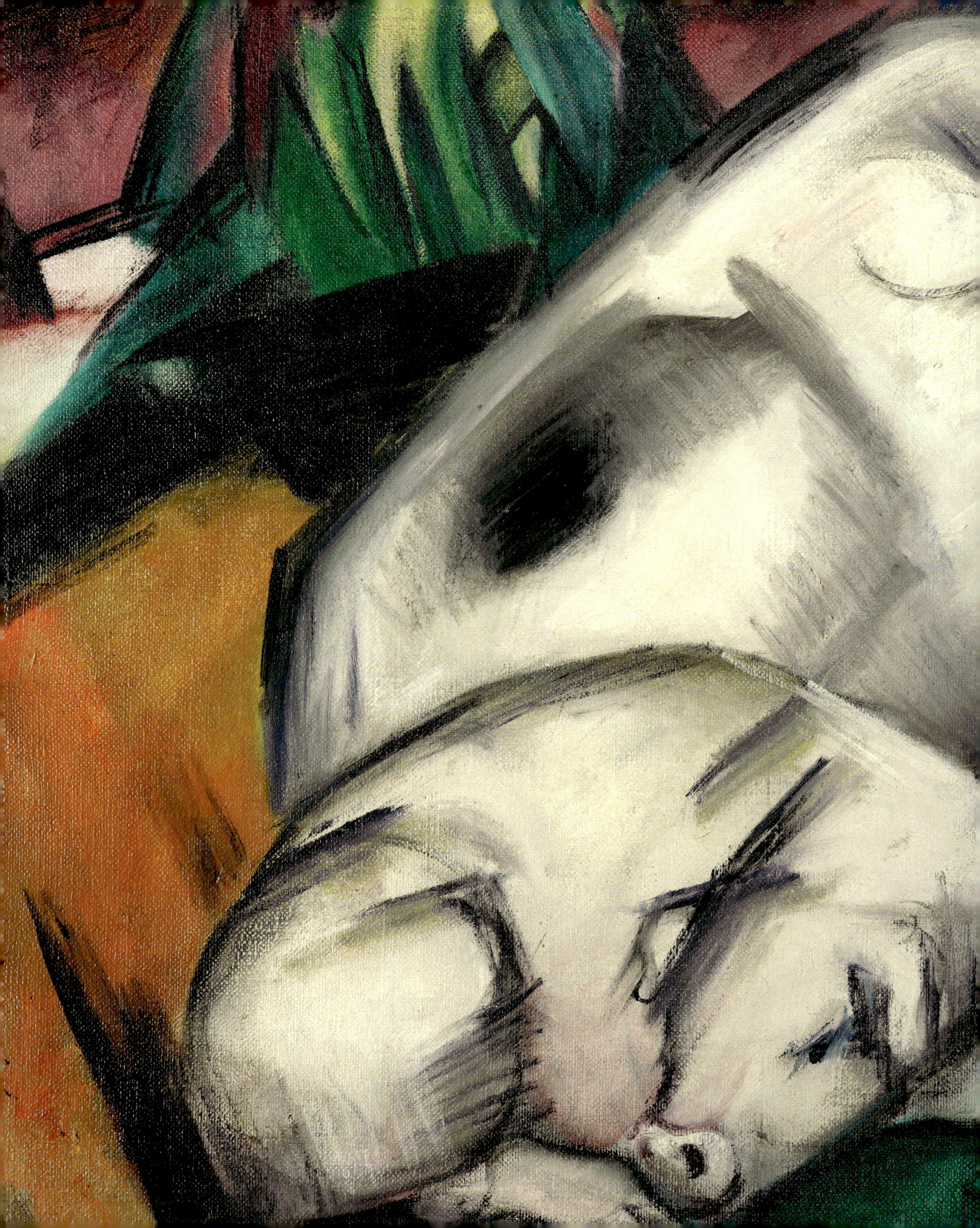

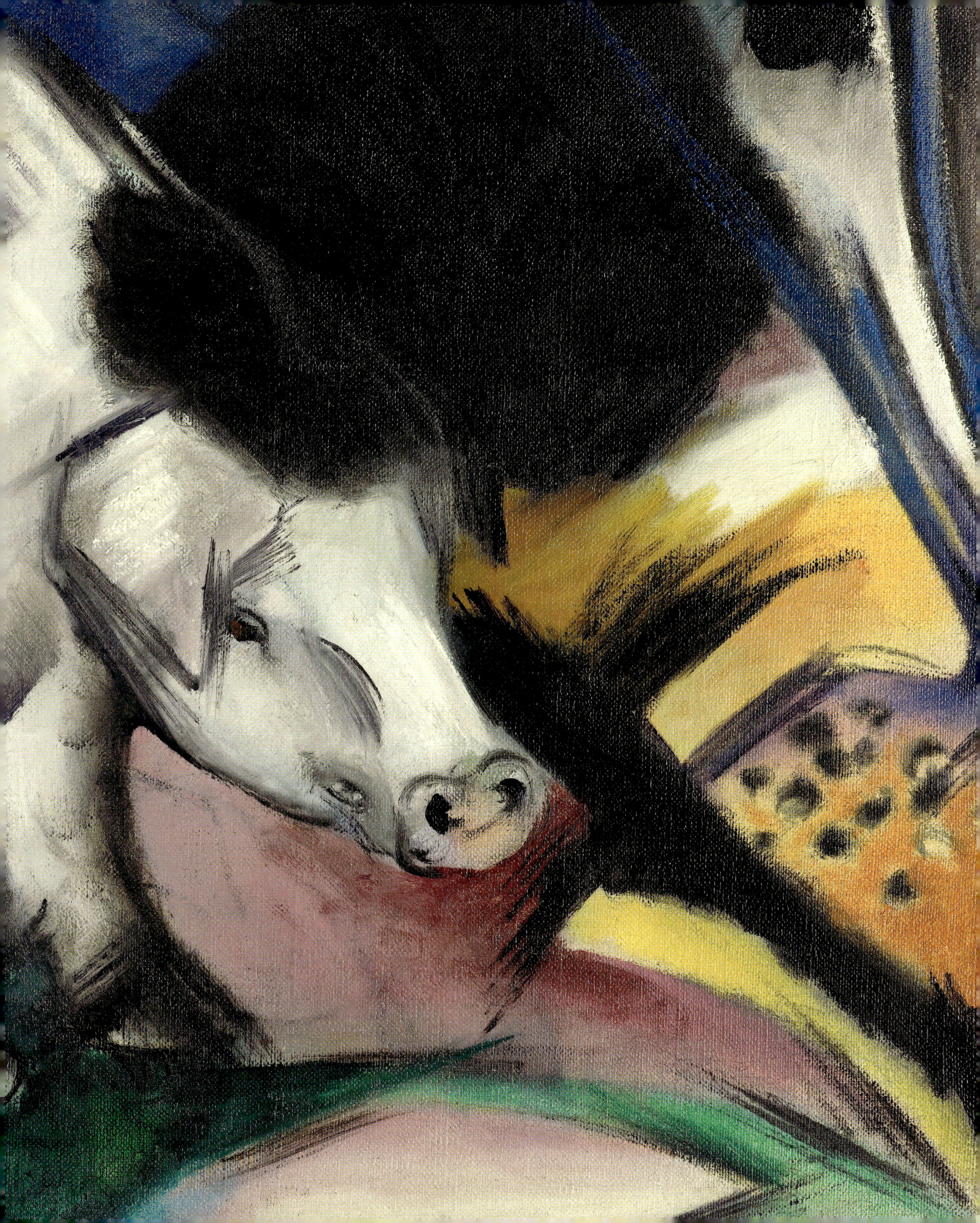

August Macke
1887 Meschede – 1914 Perthe-les-Hurlus

Oil on board
Signed lower centre: A Macke 13 (pencil)
23.8 × 18.7 cm

Inv. no.: P222M
Acquired 2010

19 August Macke
Badende Mädchen
1913

August Macke often spoke of his indebtedness to French painting in the development of his own art. He was drawn to Paris repeatedly between 1907 and 1912 and enthusiastically wrote to his future wife Elisabeth, "When I have been to the Louvre … and encounter Manet, Degas, Pissarro, and Monet in the Luxembourg, I have the feeling that I am coming out of a crater and into the sunlight." And in 1913, he wrote to the Berlin collector Bernhard Koehler about the Delaunay exhibition in Cologne, "That these pictures, above all others, are capable of showering one with a positively heavenly delight in the sun and in life…."

Macke's treatment of light as a supra-temporal, elementary substance, as the art historian Volker Adolphs observes, and his view of form as a parable of life took their cue from his profound knowledge of Impressionism, the Fauves, Cubism, and Orphism. Manet, Monet, Cézanne, Matisse, and Picasso were inspiring and indeed seminal models for him. Artistically he was especially close to Robert Delaunay, whom he met in 1912.

Radiant, like stained glass, the *Girls Bathing* were painted in Hilterfingen on the lake of Thun, where Macke had retired in 1913 after an extremely busy year. Three young women are seen gambolling at the lake under sun-drenched trees, an idyllic scene on a warm summer day. Despite the difference in motif, the subject matter references Manet's *Luncheon on the Grass* (1863), Cézanne's *Bathers* (1899–1906) and Matisse's *Pastorale* (1906). The sense of timelessness, of liberation from the mundanities of life makes one think of Arcadia and nymphs, young and beautiful, though mortal beings who live near waters and in the woods.

The young women are protected by the trees that form an arch of leaves above them. The sun breaks through the foliage, a flickering light that illuminates parts of the trees and the bodies of the girls. The vibrant brushstrokes seem dynamically charged, enabling viewers to trace the act of painting. They invest the picture as a whole with movement that underscores the sense of a captured moment in time. Our gaze wanders back and forth, unable to come to rest. Thus, in spite of the idyllic atmosphere, this wonderful little painting, with no fixed vantage point, is clearly anchored in the twentieth century.
AS

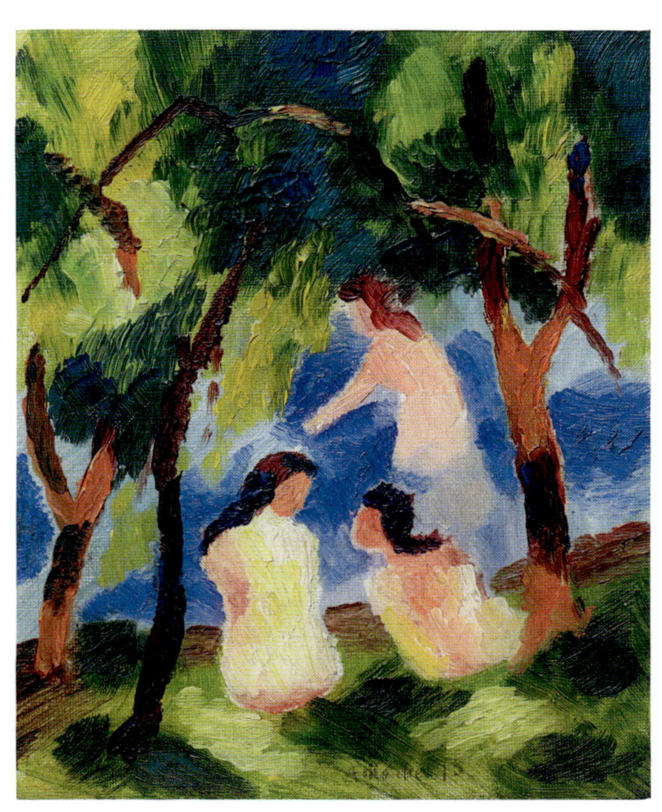

Juan Gris
1887 Madrid – 1927 Boulogne-sur-Seine

Collage, pencil, and gouache on cardboard
Signed and dated lower right:
Juan Gris 1914
39.9 × 39.4 cm

Inv. no.: G40T
Acquired 2010

20 Juan Gris
Le verre
1914

While Pablo Picasso and Georges Braque advanced the "analytical" facet of Cubism, it was Juan Gris who contributed substantially to the "synthetic" elaboration of that movement, which has had an enduring influence on painting and sculpture in the twentieth century. When Gris moved to Paris from Madrid in 1906, he immediately sought out his Spanish compatriot. However, by c. 1912–13, he had abandoned the analytic treatment of the world with its uncompromising division into basic geometric shapes and devised a distinctive idiom of his own: synthetic compositions of clearly outlined, abstract planes to which he assigned subject matter and material only afterwards in response to the requirements of the composition as a whole. Gris once commented that Cézanne, whose works and statements were admired by Cubists, had made a cylinder out of a bottle, while he himself had made a bottle out of a cylinder. Working with elements of the imagination rather than empirical perception, he did not proceed inductively from the specific to the general but deductively from the general to the specific, attempting, as he said, to anthropomorphize the general, or rather, the abstract.

The artist's deductive method is quintessentially revealed in the composition of his still life, *La Verre* (The Glass, 1914). Out of different types of paper cut into varying shapes, he has created a thoughtfully balanced but purely abstract collage with a reduced palette in which that of "analytical" Cubism still clearly reverberates. In a second, basically intuitive step, Gris drew and painted forms derived from this non-figurative composition, evoking the idea of a drinking glass placed on a wood-grained table against a background of patterned wallpaper and seen from several viewpoints. The use of actual wallpaper as a pictorial element is indebted to the technique of collage, invented in 1912 by Braque and Picasso. Their use of newspaper clippings, labels, tickets, and other real objects did not result in an analytical visual reality but rather a synthetic one in the sense of a higher unity created by the ordering spirit. In contrast to Braque and Picasso, Gris's Platonic spirit surfaces primarily in the guise of a classicism and serenity entirely devoid of subjectivity. UW

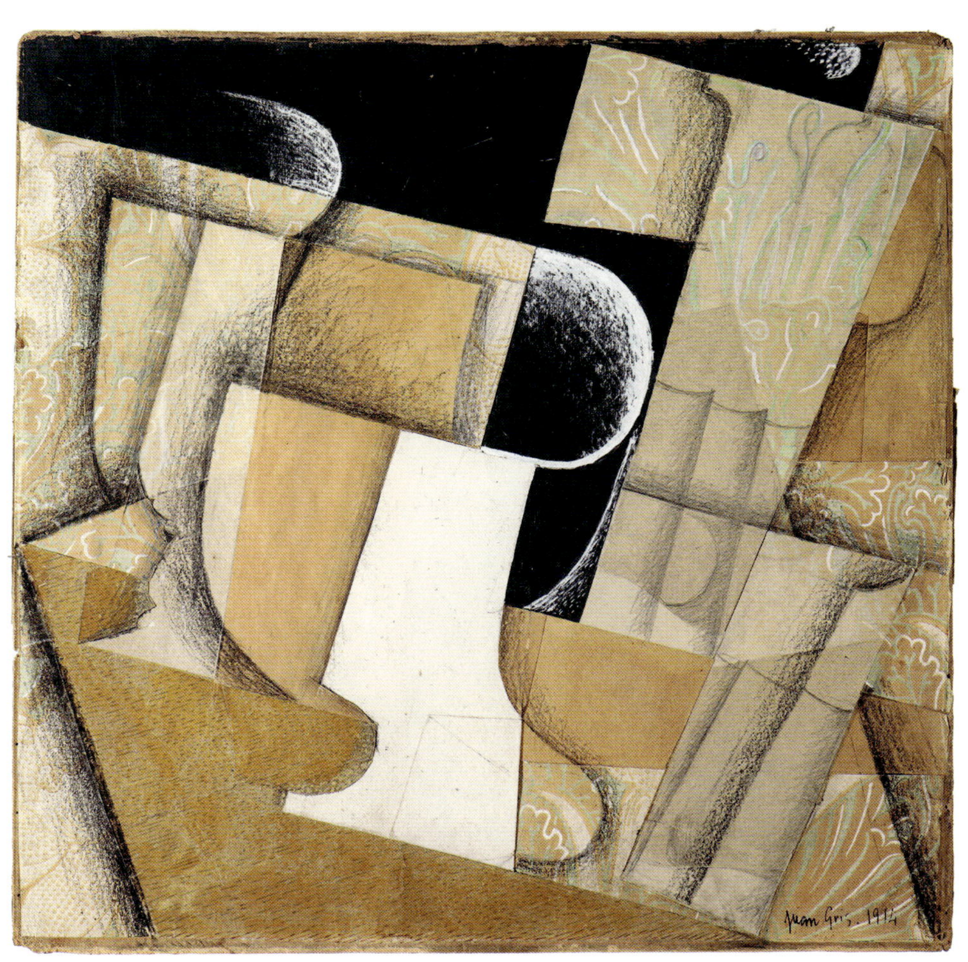
Juan Gris. 1914

Fernand Léger
1881 Argentan – 1955 Gif-sur-Yvette

Oil on canvas
Initialled and dated lower right: F.L 14
61 × 50 cm

Inv. no.: P11T
Acquired 2000

21 Fernand Léger
Contraste de formes
1914

The paintings and gouaches that Léger titled *Contrastes de formes* were created between 1912 and 1914. In them, the artist made the transition to non-figuration, or rather to non-imitation inasmuch as the forms in these works are entirely without mimetic ambition. However, they do still resonate with the memory of objects reduced to their elemental shape in the sense of Cézanne—cylinder, sphere, and cone. Léger did not actually paint abstract works; instead, he briefly used abstraction as a radical means of coming to terms with the "three basic elements of visual composition, line, shape, and colour" and their "simultaneous mutual arrangement" (Léger).

In the present painting, Léger arranged a number of truncated cones of varying sizes as the central figure rising up through a largely vertical structure of lines. Although these truncated cones are interlocked and stacked on top of each other, they are not governed by any structural or perspectival logic. The composition is entirely autonomous—an achievement of Cubism—and obeys only the intent of the artist who is fully aware that the workings of contemplative reason rather than sensual feelings can produce a complete, self-contained image of abstract shapes. In addition to line and shape, this work also makes use of the third "basic element of visual composition"—colour—in order to flesh out the structure. The colouring, clearly a feature that has been added, does not slavishly follow the outlined shapes but rather seems to float in a state of suspension. Yellow, blue, and pale purple hues accentuate contrasting reds and dark greens. White highlights on the truncated cones heighten the sense of space and depth, while occasional patches of unpainted, primed white canvas indicate that Léger was not interested in a subtle blend of colours. One might in fact say that his palette is as rudimentary as the shapes into which it is inscribed. The combination yields an image that is both planar and spatial, structural and dynamic, graphic and painterly, robust and fragile—in other words, a composition of many beautifully balanced contrasts.

To Léger, contrast means dissonance. The social and technological upheavals of his time were "dissonant" and he registered the "short-lived, multifarious bustle" of modern life that "shunts us back and forth and threatens to tear us apart" with seismographic sensitivity. Léger's artistic response to such trials, on the eve of the World War I, might almost be read as a parable, for his *Contrastes de formes* are couched in an abstract idiom that reconciles opposites without neutralizing tension. UW

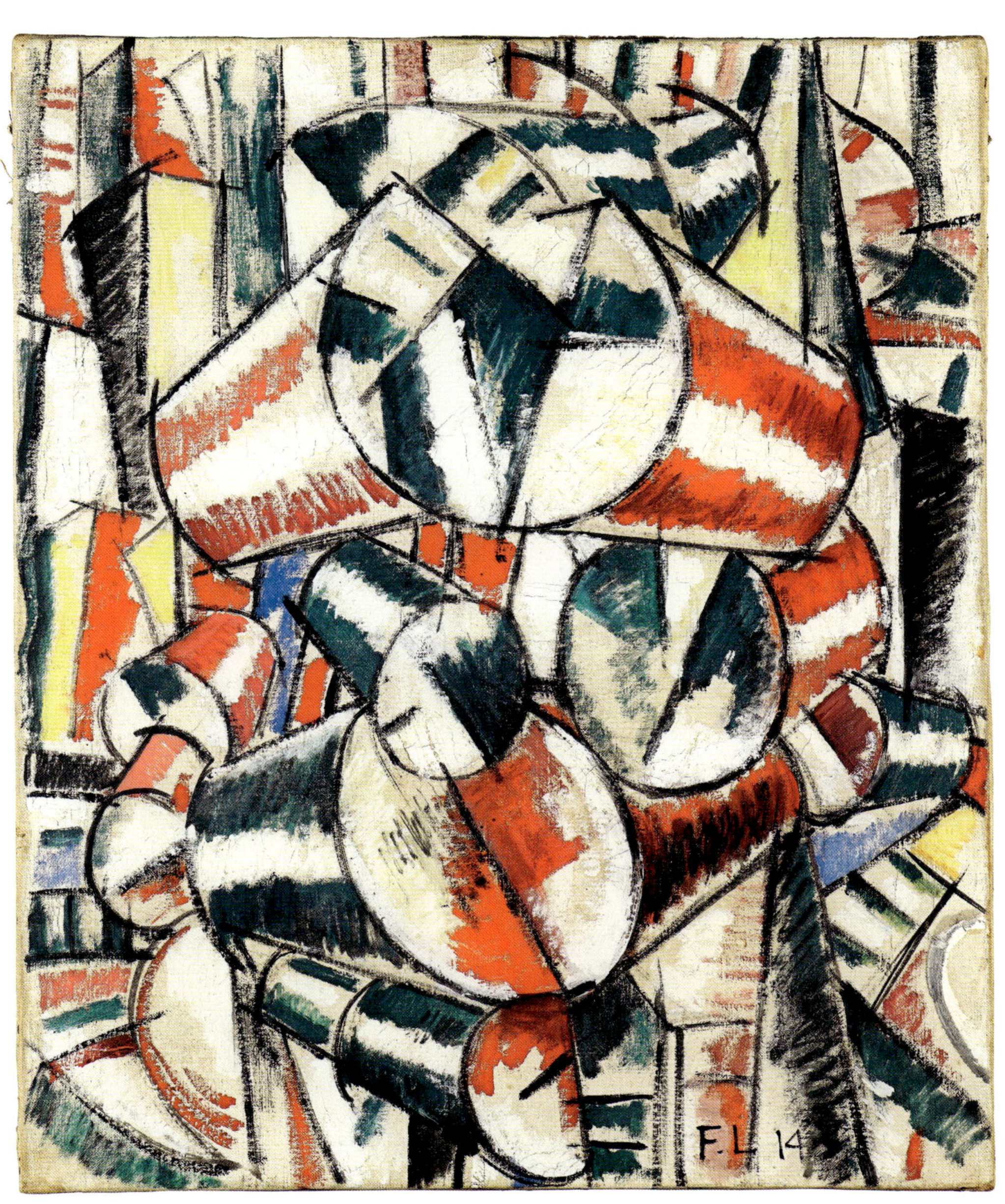
F.L 14

Piet Mondrian
1872 Amersfoort – 1944 New York

Oil on canvas
Initialled and dated lower right: 25 PM
53.2 × 46.2 cm (incl. frame, not original)

Inv. no.: P23T
Acquired 2002

22 Piet Mondrian
Tableau No. VIII with Yellow, Red, Black and Blue
1925

Mondrian wanted to express universals in his art, which he felt were veiled in nature: "Nature reveals everything, truth as well as beauty, but it expresses both under the veil of natural appearances, and this veil that lies in front of the truth is tragic." He came to the conclusion that the universal as the unity of truth and beauty could not be expressed through the illusionist depiction of natural objects but "only through abstract-concrete composition". In consequence, Mondrian reduced his visual vocabulary to line, plane, and colour and he did so with such uncompromising rigour that he allowed for lines only as verticals and horizontals, planes only as rectangles, and colours only as primary colours. On the other hand, he did not aspire to rigid formalism but instead worked to achieve a lively balance of line, plane, and colour. Taking his cue from Hegel's dialectics, he was convinced that all being becomes "real" only in connection with its opposite: the universal through the individual, the spiritual through matter, active through passive or masculine through feminine. The liberation of form from accident or chance was to culminate in what he called Nieuwe Beelding (new plastic art or neo-plasticism)—a term that formed the theoretical core of the artists' group De Stijl, founded in Leiden in 1917 and to which Mondrian, Theo van Doesburg, and others belonged.

Only in small steps did Mondrian achieve his objective of creating compositions that establish a dialectical balance among elements extracted from the diversity of nature's forms and colours. The realization, for instance, that the juxtaposition of yellow, red, and blue planes of colour produces an impression of depth contradicted his concept of painting as a strictly two-dimensional phenomenon. To neutralize that impression, he embedded his colours in a strict grid of vertical and horizontal black lines. But since the static structure of this grid undermined his wish to lend the compositions a lively order, he began varying the play of lines, planes and colours, combining them into finely balanced "Compositions".

Tableau no. VIII of 1925, which belongs to Mondrian's "classic" phase (c. 1920–32), shows all the features of his artistic convictions. It is one of the "peripheral" *Compositions,* in which a large white rectangle (not a square!) takes up so much room that it pushes the smaller planes of colour to the margins of the painting. All of the colours he permitted himself to use each occur only once. As in all of his paintings, Mondrian avoided centring and symmetry, achieving a balanced composition not by applying mathematical rules but intuitively, through playful combination. By placing the canvas in front of the frame, he additionally gave the painting the status of an object. UW

Joan Miró
1893 Montroig, Barcelona – 1983 Palma de Mallorca

Pencil, oil and gouache on wood
Signed and dated lower right: Miró 13·8·24
23.5 × 19 cm

Inv. no.: P46T
Acquired 2011

23 Joan Miró
Untitled
1924

The small, untitled drawing in oil is one of three works Miró created in Montroig on 13 August 1924. The family's farmstead, near Tarragona not far from the sea, appears in a number of Miró's paintings. It was a place of creative retreat, where the artist regularly spent the long summer months in order to work undisturbed. After his first exciting visit to Paris in 1920, he wrote to Ricart, a friend of his youth, "At long last, never back to Barcelona again. Paris and the countryside to the end of my life." The decision may well have been reinforced by Picasso's words, "Believe me, if you want to be a painter, then don't stray far from Paris." And so it was that Paris and Montroig became the focal points in Miró's artistic development.

He set up his studio at Rue Blomet 45 in Montparnasse, where the painter André Masson was his neighbour. The poets Georges Limbour and Robert Desnos as well as the writer and ethnologist Michel Leiris were among his close friends. They would converse, for instance, about Nietzsche's philosophy and spend long nights reading poems to sharpen their appreciation of various poetic forms. Later, Masson was to write in a letter that "poetry in the broadest sense of the term was crucial for Miró and for me." And it did, indeed, exert a seminal influence on Miró's creativity. His work underwent an extraordinary metamorphosis from the post-Cubist, hyperrealistic, and exceptionally disciplined paintings, such as *The Farm* of 1920–21, to the open-ended and fanciful, enigmatic figurations of his *Catalan Landscape (The Hunter)* of 1923–24.

The oil drawing of 1924 belongs to this period. The artist has outlined a figure resembling a gourd with three objects, shaped like insects or onions, placed around it as on a coat of arms. The colouring is tenuous. Shown against a white, basically empty ground, the central figure looks like a transparent emblem. The curved contours, drawn with delicacy and ease, describe a biomorphic, supple, almost nimble, and no doubt ambivalent figure. The pipe-shaped horn that crowns it might be interpreted as a stamen, a cornucopia, or a phallus, indicative of a subtle eroticism. The gourd is embellished with yellow, red, green, and black dots and lines, resembling siurells, clay whistles from Mallorca in the shape of little devils, farmers, or animals, designed to chase away evil spirits and winds. Probably from Crete or of Phoenician origins, they have become symbols of good luck and omnipresent souvenirs in Mallorca.

Miró had such figurines himself and, like many Surrealists, he was particularly fascinated with their use in magic and ritual. The artist may also have been inspired by Picasso's Cubist works with speckled planes, especially the *Glasses of Absinthe,* painted bronze casts made in 1914. AS

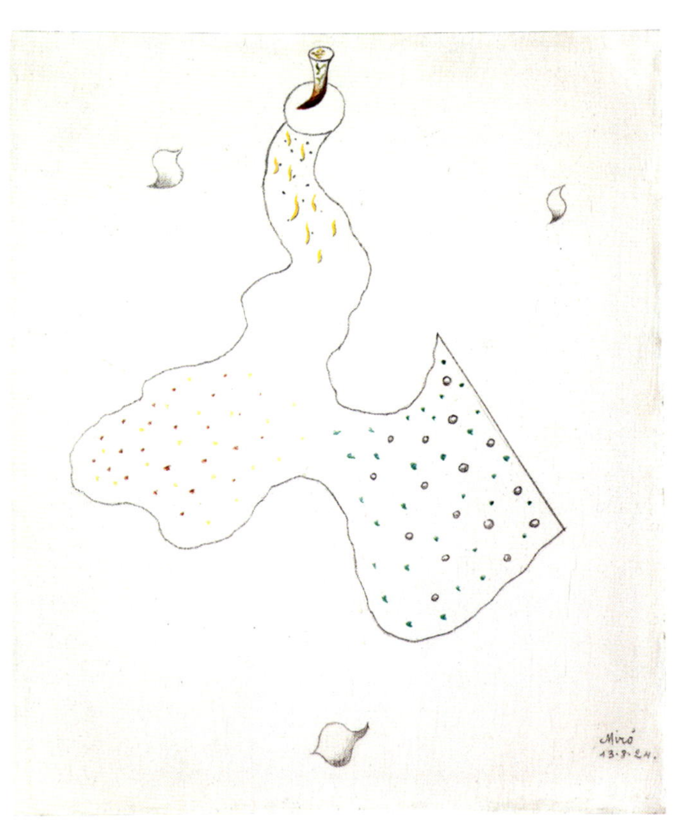
Miró
13·8·24.

Hans Arp
1887 Strasbourg – 1966 Basel

Painted wood
61 × 53.3 × 21 cm

Inv. no.: S43T
Acquired 2010

24 Hans Arp
Kopf-Stabile
1926

Arp's many talents were recognized and fostered at an early age. His subsequent academic training in Weimar and Paris with a bias for classical mimesis held little interest for him. It was not until he discovered Kandinsky in 1912 and Cubism in 1914 as well as becoming involved with Dada in Zurich in 1916 that his creative powers as a poet and fine artist came to full flower.

Dada did not stand as much for a style as it did for an attitude, for revolt against hierarchy. As Arp wrote in his 1958 essay *Betrachten,* "The Dadaists disdained the conventional notion of art and instead enthroned the entire universe as art: that seems to me to be the essence of Dada." In his poetry, Arp juxtaposed and combined old and new words, creating a seemingly nonsensical universe of infinite semantic potential, a challenge for readers to decode and devise ever new interpretations. Arp's poems are no different from the visual arts in their refusal to be reduced to a single, unequivocal message. This new freedom and emancipation from style gave the artist the impetus to construct small wood reliefs out of found materials and colourful pieces of painted wood. Inspired by the principles of chance and play, these whimsical works act as if they were objects of nature. The study of nature and the structural properties of plants, branches, and pebbles polished by water proved to be an inexhaustible reservoir for Arp's inventive spirit. In time, the "moving oval" emerged as the form that was to beget all other forms.

Arp made *Kopf-Stabile* (Head Stabile) in 1926, the year he left Paris only to return two years later, having acquired French citizenship and moving from Strasbourg to Meudon, southwest of Paris. Measuring sixty-one centimetres in height, Arp's *Kopf-Stabile* is larger than life and the first free-standing relief to interrelate different spatial planes. A smaller oval of wood has been applied to the large, irregularly curved oval of the head, whose significant shapes within—eye, nose, and throat—have been cut out of the panel. They are linked to space in keeping with their function: the eye with which we perceive the world, the nose and throat through which we breathe. Art critic and Arp's longtime friend Michel Seuphor remarked in 1966 that the presence of the sky softens the shapes, making everything appear as if it were afloat. The slightly inclined head has been painted white except for the reddish brown oval sections. They could represent the cheeks of an impish yet unfathomable clown face—or a death's mask? The head is seen neither from the front nor in profile, so that our eyes wander back and forth without coming to rest. As Seuphor observed, only Arp can be unmistakably clear and ambiguous at once. AS

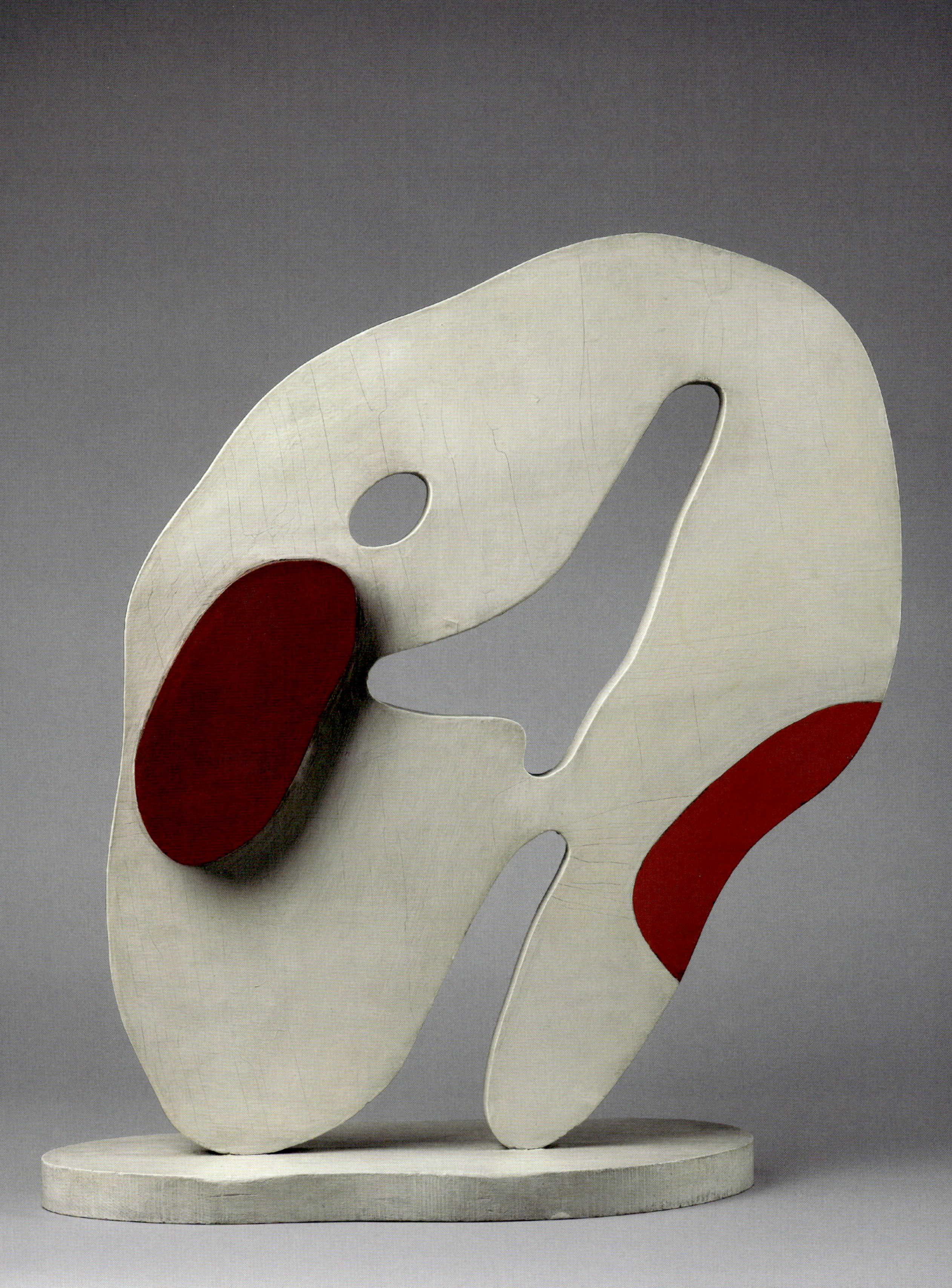

René Magritte
1898 Lessines, Hainaut – 1967 Brussels

Oil on canvas
Signed lower right: Magritte
74 × 65 cm

Inv. no.: P57T
Acquired 2013

25 René Magritte La chambre du devin 1926

Magritte painted *La chambre du devin* (The Seer's Chamber) in 1926. The year is significant, for it was then that the artist joined the musician and poet Édouard Leon Théodore Mesens, the art dealer Camille Goemans, and the biochemist and photographer Paul Nougé to found the Surrealist group in Belgium. The work is an early example of the Surrealist universe that began to evolve as of 1925, particularly through the inspiration of the Italian artist Giorgio de Chirico. Magritte was fascinated by Chirico's "pittura metafisica" and his notion of a "complete break with the mental routine of artists".

In 1927 *La chambre du devin* was on view at Le Centaure Galilean Brussels along with forty-eight other paintings and twelve *papiers collés,* a group of works by the then twenty-eight-year-old artist that was to form the foundations of his entire oeuvre. The exhibition, which opened on April 23, was Magritte's first solo presentation. *La chambre du devin* already shows salient features of Surrealist painting: the form and content of its subject matter, though painted illusionistically, defies the logic of everyday experience. Oscillating between reality and appearance, causality and absurdity, conscious and unconscious, Surrealism equally features a delight in metamorphosis, eroticism, spiciness, play, and originality. Duplication, another common characteristic of the movement, is also typical of Magritte's early work. The present painting shows two largely identical flat figures carved out of wood, standing opposite one another and immovably affixed to a long board. One single pair of shared, straight, stiff arms connects them but also keeps them at a distance. They are placed on a platform that rests on a balustrade with a rear wall, somewhat like a stage, behind which clouds dramatically fill the sky. Rods protrude through the irregular holes in the platform. The figure in the rear stands in a flame-shaped opening cut out of the wall, providing an additional view of the turbulent skies and lending the figure a flickering "aura". Are these two people, possibly a woman and a man, condemned to face one another for all eternity in their raw state, inseparable and yet irrevocably separate? Or is it humankind per se with its alter ego? Or the body of the soul, the substance of the spiritual, the "ether body" or "astral body" on uncertain ground above the yawning abyss of space? The painting is inescapably enigmatic, in the spirit of Surrealism, and its title, more confounding than clarifying, follows suit. This, too, is a strategy that Magritte enlists to subvert the logic of everyday life. UW

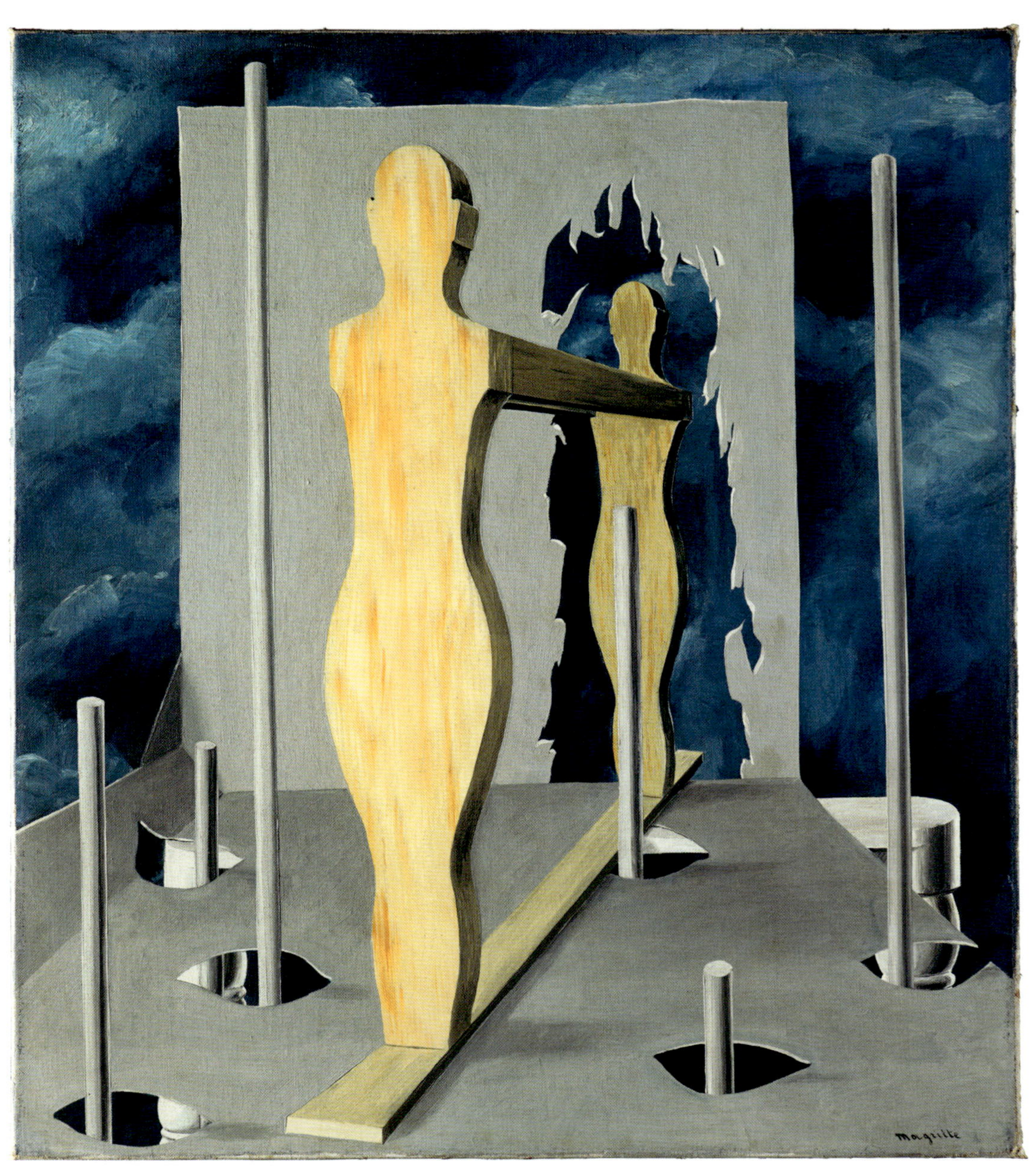
magritte

Max Ernst
1891 Brühl – 1976 Paris

Oil on canvas
Signed lower right: max ernst
60.2 × 92 cm

Inv. no.: P9T
Acquired 2000

26 Max Ernst
Le paradis
1927

The title of the painting, *Le paradis,* draws attention to the fundamental discrepancy between meaning and representation, between word and image, that is one of many bewildering constants in the oeuvre of Max Ernst. When we hear the word "paradise", we are unlikely to envision anything resembling this painting. As if privy to absurd theatre, we are confronted with a frightening, life-threatening scene of animalistic, sexual violence and bondage. The figures we see clearly embody the central themes of Surrealism.

The terrified animal arrested in flight in the centre of the picture might be a cow or a mare. It has been brutally overpowered by a monster almost twice its size that could be anything from a dinosaur to a hyena. As André Breton reports, the Parisian Surrealists used to entertain themselves of an evening by inventing animals and producing unexpected images. The head of the soft, white domestic creature, delineated with the charm of a picture-book illustration, is thrown back to the sky in a desperate plea for help, although it is already in the stranglehold of its tormentor and about to be raped. The demonic figurations sprouting out of the skeletal, snaky body of the bloodthirsty beast also appear in the crowd paintings Ernst made during the same period. The encounter between the two animals takes place at eye level, as it were, their visages converging into a horrific image of abject fright, terror, and animalistic violence. This turbulent scene, which also applies to its formal execution, is the centrepiece of the composition while off to the right a white barn owl, the traditional symbol of wisdom, is perched in a compact, box-shaped cage. Although it is not clearly behind bars, it has been apprehended and robbed of its effectiveness.

The fluid painting style and the bright, quasi-enlightened atmosphere, underscored by a colourful palette of red, yellow, green, blue, brown, and purple, stands in stark contrast to the dismal subject matter of the composition. The luminous green meadow and the light-blue sky are flooded with light. The fine black lines would seem to be fragments of constellations, implying a universe out of joint. The complexity of Ernst's enigmatic imagery is a consequence not only of his intellectual inventiveness but also of his curiosity and mastery in devising new painting techniques. Taking inspiration from the accidental "natural" shapes that emerge when using frottage and grattage, he follows their trail without surrendering control over his compositions.

The title *Le Paradis* is not primarily ironic but rather a description of our paradise on earth. It is also an example of "convulsive beauty", in the words of Breton, who invited Max Ernst to mount his first exhibition in Paris in 1921, shortly after the devastating war. In his foreword to the catalogue, Breton expressed his admiration of Ernst's ability to achieve different realities without abandoning the realm of experience. **AS**

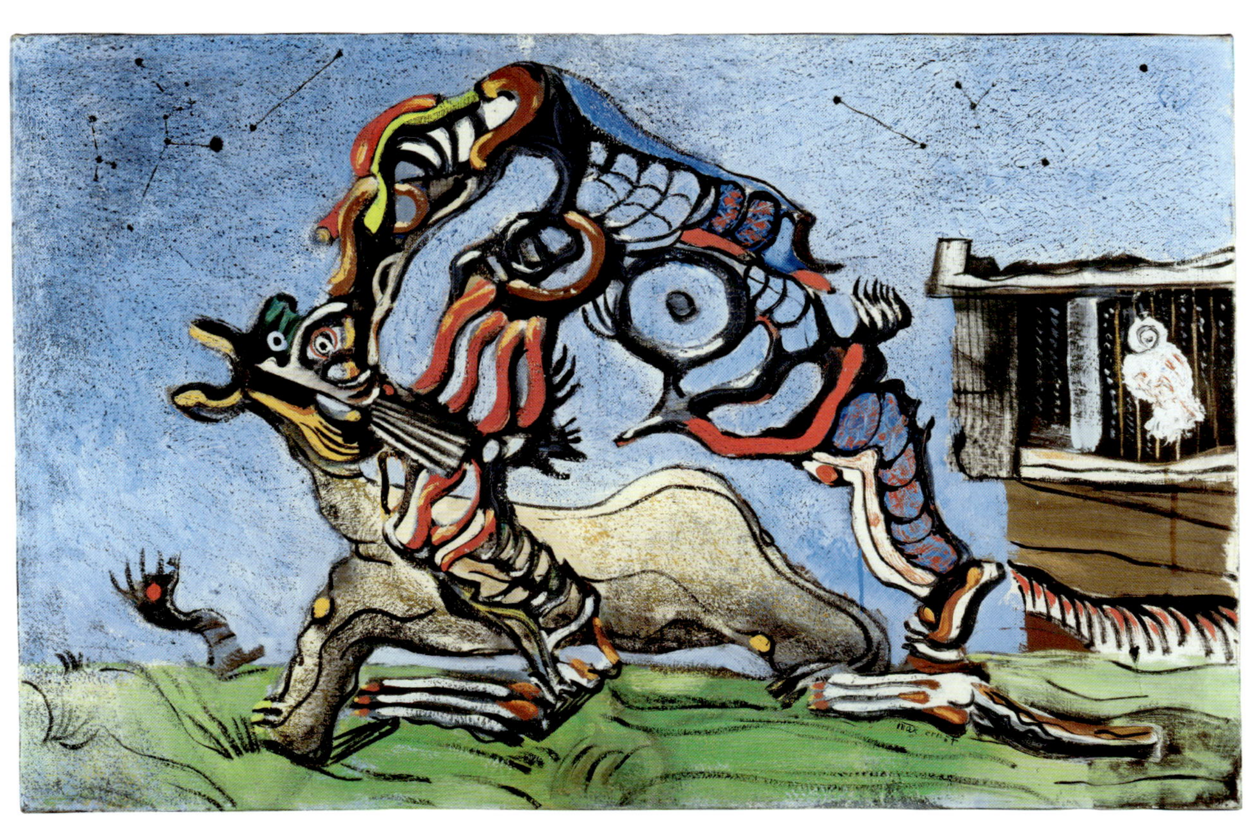

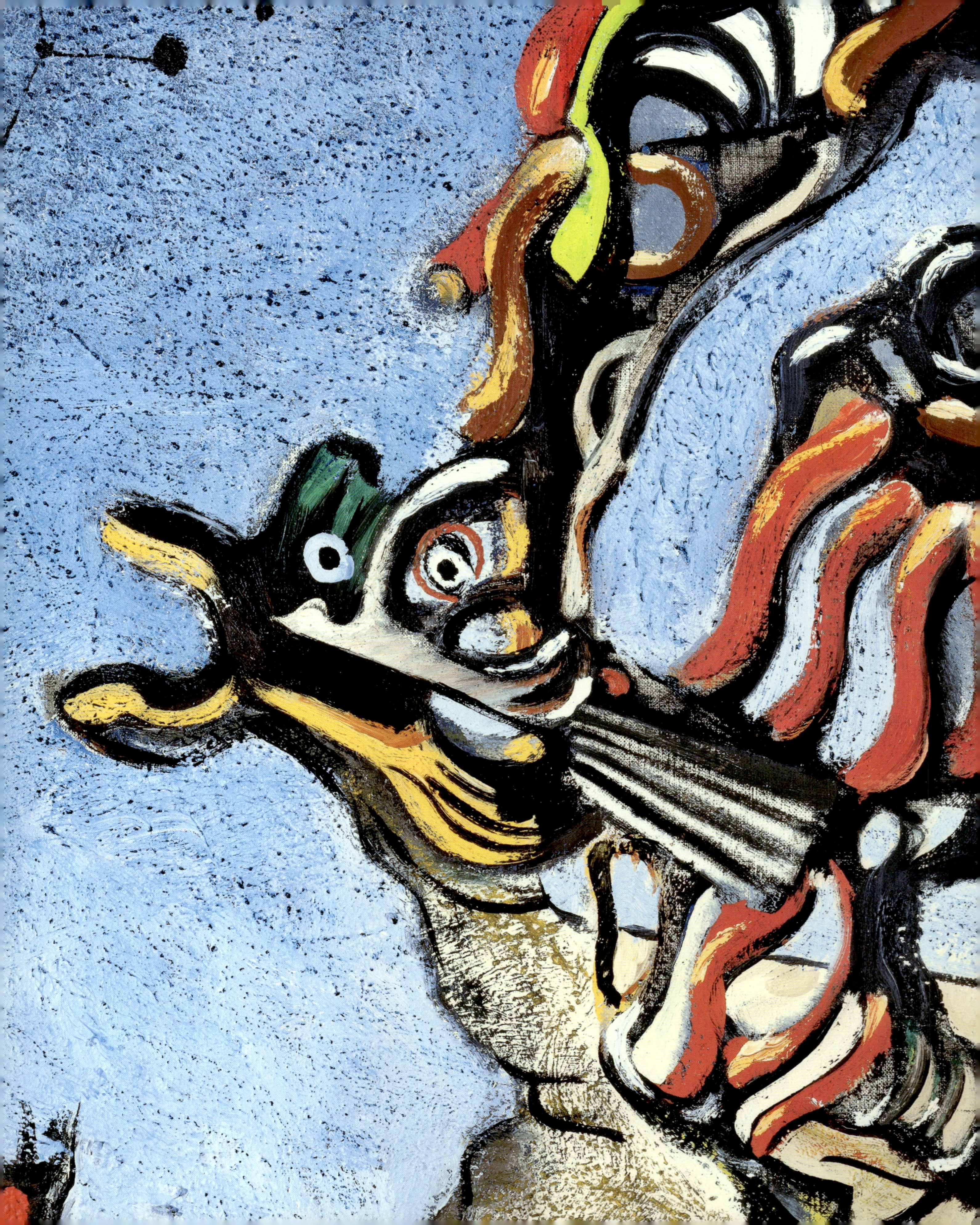

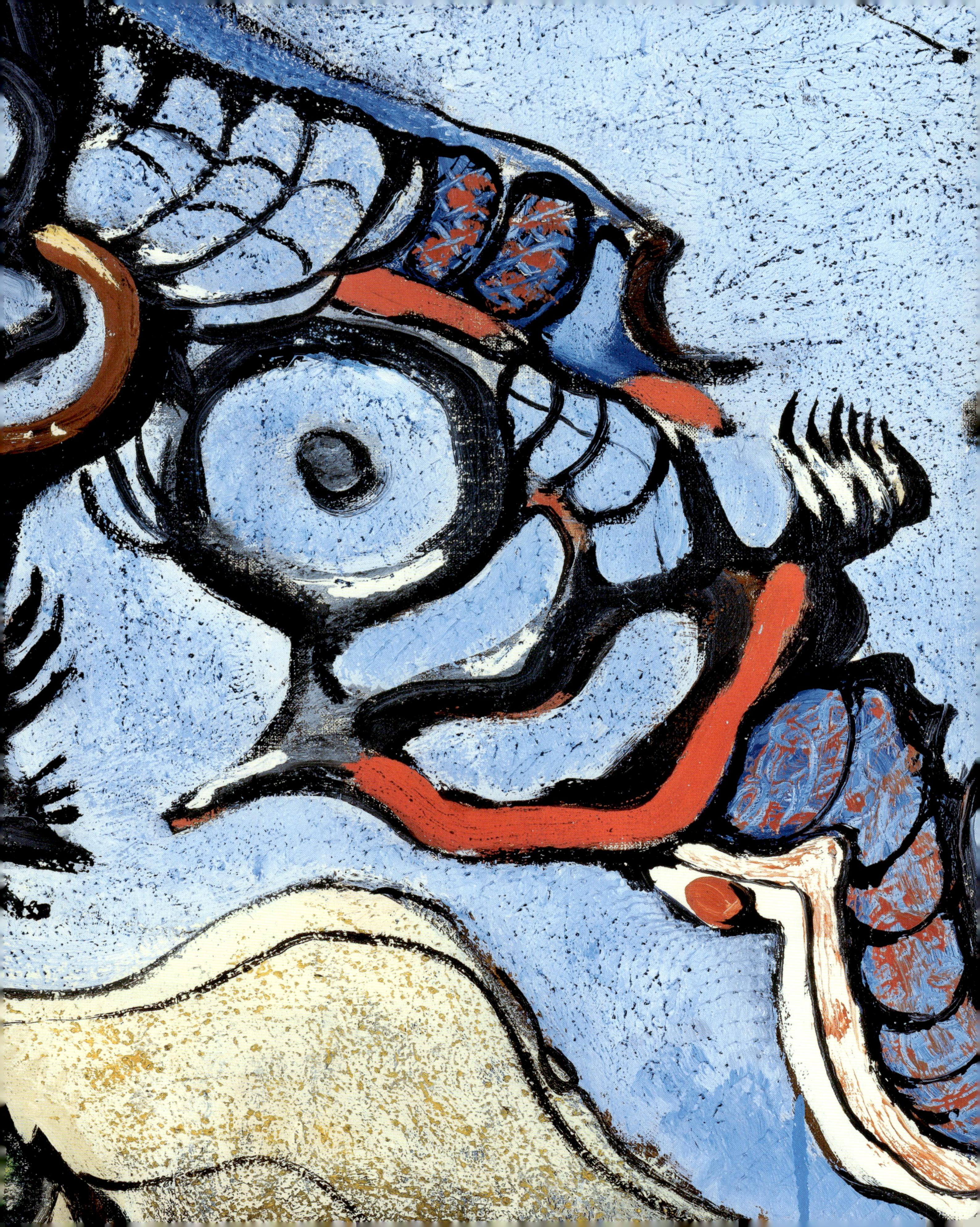

Yves Tanguy
1900 Paris – 1955 Woodbury, Connecticut

Oil on canvas
Signed and dated lower right:
Yves Tanguy 29
92.2 × 73.2 cm

Inv. no.: P61T
Acquired 2014

27 Yves Tanguy
Titre inconnu (noyer indifférent)
1929

According to Yves Tanguy's own legendary testimony, he was so moved on seeing Giorgio de Chirico's paintings in a Parisian gallery at the end of 1923 that he decided to become a painter himself. His early, initially representational work is stylistically indebted to Expressionism, Cubism, and the New Objectivity. In 1925 he became closely involved with the Surrealists in Paris, in particular André Breton, who had penned the Surrealist Manifesto in 1924 and spearheaded the international group of writers, painters, photographers, filmmakers, and object artists. Inspired by Pierre Janet's and Sigmund Freud's investigations into the human psyche, the group devoted themselves primarily to the workings of the unconscious and to the world of dreams. Tanguy's paintings soon began to show the influence of Max Ernst, Juan Miró, Hans Arp, and de Chirico. Increasingly, representation gave way to clearly distinguishable but unidentifiable figurations, suggesting both inorganic and organic origins, coming perhaps from the depths of the oceans, the expanses of the desert, or the infinity of the universe. From now on, these dominate the artist's universe.

Similarly enigmatic, unfamiliar figurations populate *Titre inconnu* (1929), which also dates from Tanguy's early Surrealist phase. The shapes could as easily represent the beginnings of natural history as the catastrophic end of civilization. The four largest of them, casting shadows from an invisible source of light, have congregated around a patch of fog rising in delicate tendrils. Both fog and figurations are seen against a dark ground whose relief-like surface is broken by pallid, white horizontal bands that fade into the immeasurable, pitch-black depths of space. We gaze upon an alien, nonhuman, and yet disconcertingly real universe that is in the process of becoming or of dying away, buffeted by the primeval clash between lightness and darkness. The art of Max Ernst, for instance, *Der Nordpol* (The North Pole, 1922), resonates in this painting as well as the work of Hieronymus Bosch and, as Reinhard Hohl has observed, other Dutch masters of the early sixteenth century.

The Swiss psychiatrist C. G. Jung, who acquired Tanguy's painting the year it was created, discusses it in detail in his book *Flying Saucers: A Modern Myth of Things Seen in the Sky* (1979, first published in German in 1958). He associates it with bleakness, coldness, and human detachment, with cosmic inhumanity and endless abandonment, additionally interpreting it as an example of the loss of beauty and meaning in contemporary art, which has thrown human beings back on themselves as viewing subjects. However, the absence of explicit meaning, as demonstrated by *Titre inconnu,* can also lead to associations and reactions that yield illuminating insights into the world of darkness, very much in the spirit of Surrealism. UW

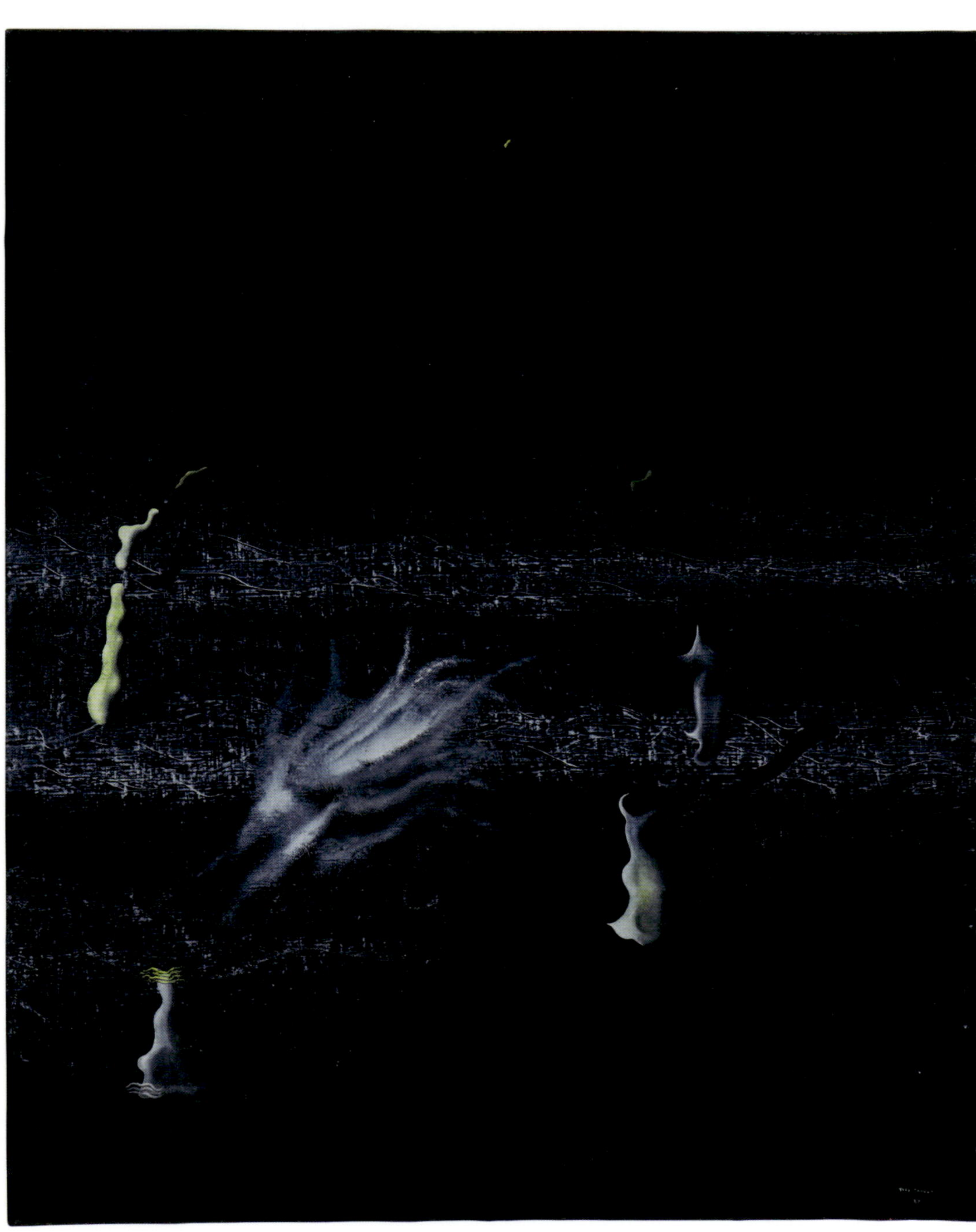

Alexander Calder
1898 Lawnton, Pennsylvania – 1976 New York

Wood and wire
Signed and dated on stand: Calder 1935
102.4 × 60 × 19 cm

Inv. no.: S53T
Acquired 2012

28 Alexander Calder
Untitled
1935

We associate the art of Alexander Calder primarily with large and small mobiles that playfully keep forming new configurations and in turn reconfigure space and time. He is equally well known for the towering, imposing stabiles that have invested numerous public spaces with life since the 1950s.

With the exception of his famous *Cirque Calder* (1926–31), the works that he made in the days of Surrealism are not as well known although they are seminal to his subsequent oeuvre. While living in Paris in the early 1930s, Calder frequently met with such artists as Joan Miró, Jean Arp, Fernand Léger, Piet Mondrian, and the uncompromising head of the Surrealists, André Breton, though without ever joining the group himself. Chance, play, magic, and eroticism were not only of interest to the Surrealists; they also feature significantly in Calder's work. It was Marcel Duchamp who coined the term "mobile" for the kinetic sculptures, and Jean Arp who in turn came up with the term "stabile" for the stationary ones.

In 1933, Calder returned to the United States for a few years, where he purchased a small farmhouse in Roxbury, Connecticut, some 100 kilometres north of New York. He later built a studio extension to the farmhouse. The present work from 1935 was made during this period, using items that happened to be in his studio at the time. The pieces of wood in different colours have not been worked in any way but were left instead in their original, raw state. Such objets trouvés, which first appeared in the Cubist collages made by Braque and Picasso, establish a link between art and real life. They are relics of daily life, testifying to unknown stories now embodied in the work of art.

The present work consists of a precarious wood construction placed on a slender square pedestal. A board lies at a slant on a narrow, semi-circular piece of wood, possibly from the back of a chair or an armchair. On the board, Calder has balanced an undulating piece of wood tapered to a point at one end and an oval wooden shape mounted on a metal wire at the other. The two objects are related and communicate with each other; they resemble parts of a plant. The leaf growing upwards and the nut-shaped fruit represent the cycle of nature, in visual tribute to processes of growth and transience. The phallic shape of the board and the female, ovular shape of the wood represent in turn the male and female elements and the fragile balance between them, for it seems that they could collapse at any moment. AS

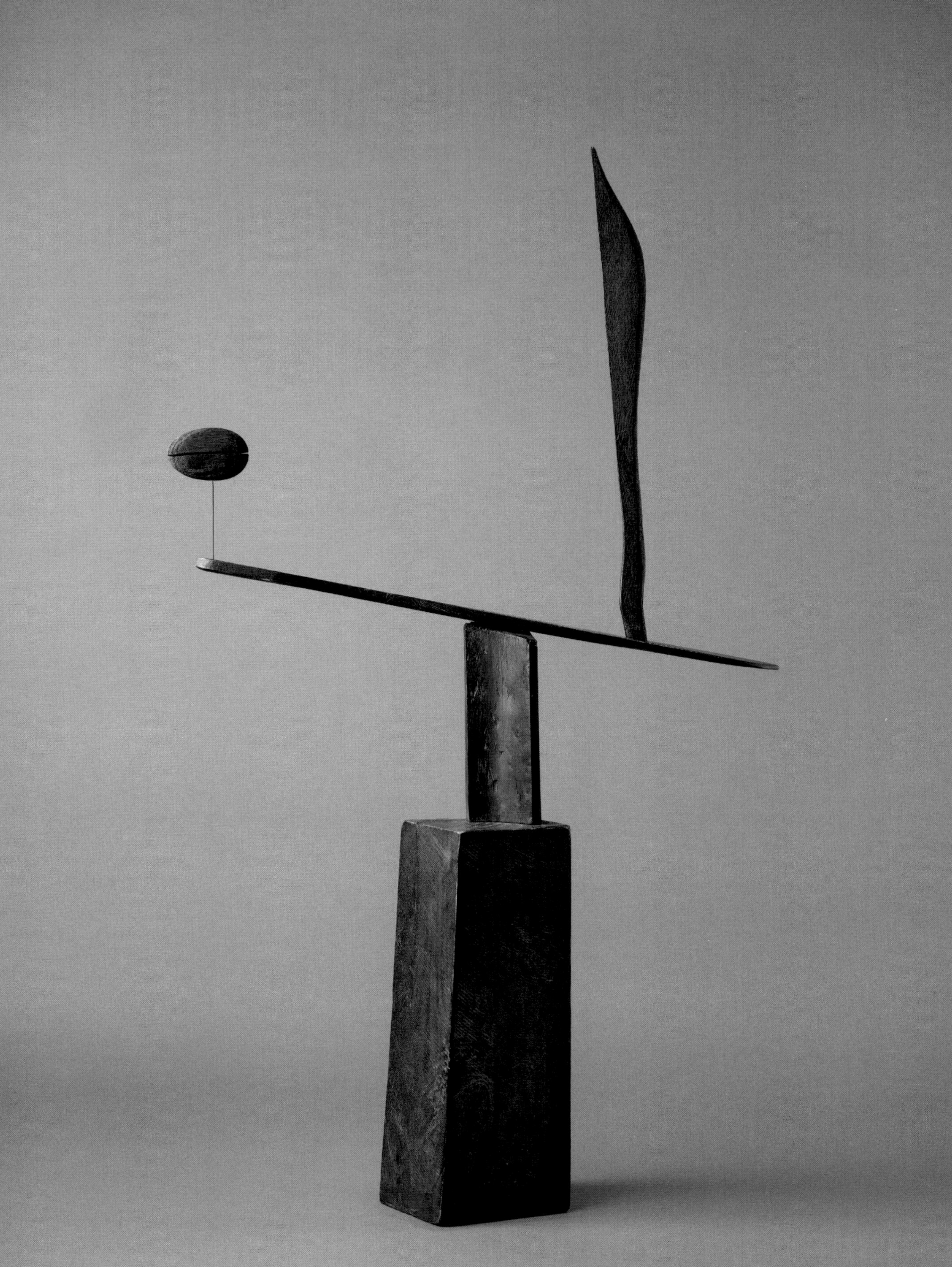

Paul Klee
1879 Münchenbuchsee, Bern – 1940 Muralto-Locarno

Oil on canvas
Signed lower right: Klee
68 × 50.5 cm (original framing)

Inv. no.: P5T
Acquired 2002

29 Paul Klee
Clown
1929

The medium of the stage, particularly the theatre and opera but the circus and puppetry as well, fascinated Klee all his life. Frightening masks, grotesque comedians, tightrope walkers and fools, fairground musicians and clowns appear in his drawings and paintings since his early years in Munich. As society's outsiders, they populate a motley universe, comic at times, at times ironic, that occasionally seems to be thrown entirely out of joint. *Clown*—Klee always titled his pictures himself and kept a meticulous record of them—was painted in 1929 when he was teaching at the Bauhaus in Dessau. Offered a position by Gropius in 1920, he had essentially outgrown the Bauhaus by 1929 and was looking for an occupation that would give him more time for his painting. In 1931 he took up a position at the Art Academy in Düsseldorf, from which he was dismissed as a degenerate artist in April 1933 shortly after the Nazis came to power.

Clown is a statuesque work and relatively large in comparison to most of the paintings from the Bauhaus period. The matt layers of paint almost give the expansive and clearly structured composition the appearance of a fresco. Although so very different in content and form, the inner monumentality and the regal gaze of the bust bring to mind likenesses of the early Italian Renaissance. This impression is reinforced by the framing, which is part of the composition and firmly anchors the clown's egg-shaped head within the picture plane. Instead of the inscriptions used in the Italian likenesses to provide information about the sitter, Klee has drawn a zigzag line that might be interpreted as extremely sparing indication of the clown's ruffle or perhaps as the ups-and-downs that mark the life of a clown. The clown's head is like the *manichini,* the jointed dolls from which Carlo Carrà and Giorgio de Chirico drew inspiration in creating their mechanical figures. Above all, however, Klee's oeuvre itself contains a diversity of clearly structured egg-shaped heads or moon faces, articulating another demonized, desperate, and driven aspect of humankind. Examples include *Köpfe* (Heads, 1913), *Selbstporträt* (Self-Portrait, 1919), *Wissen, Schweigen, Vorübergehen* (Knowledge, Science, Passing, 1921) and *Orientierter Mensch* (Oriented Man, 1927).

The clown's head, boldly filling the picture plane, shows a countenance that links profile and frontal view, as in many paintings by Picasso, whose work Klee had studied with great intensity. The face consists of two halves that are distinct in colour and form, with the left side resembling a child's drawing of a moon. The little turquoise hat and ball still reference the attributes of a clown, but the eyes gazing into the distance, one of which resembles an embrasure, suggest that the portrait might also be read as a seer, shown against a fiery, blood-red background from which he looks out at a world that remains hidden from us. AS

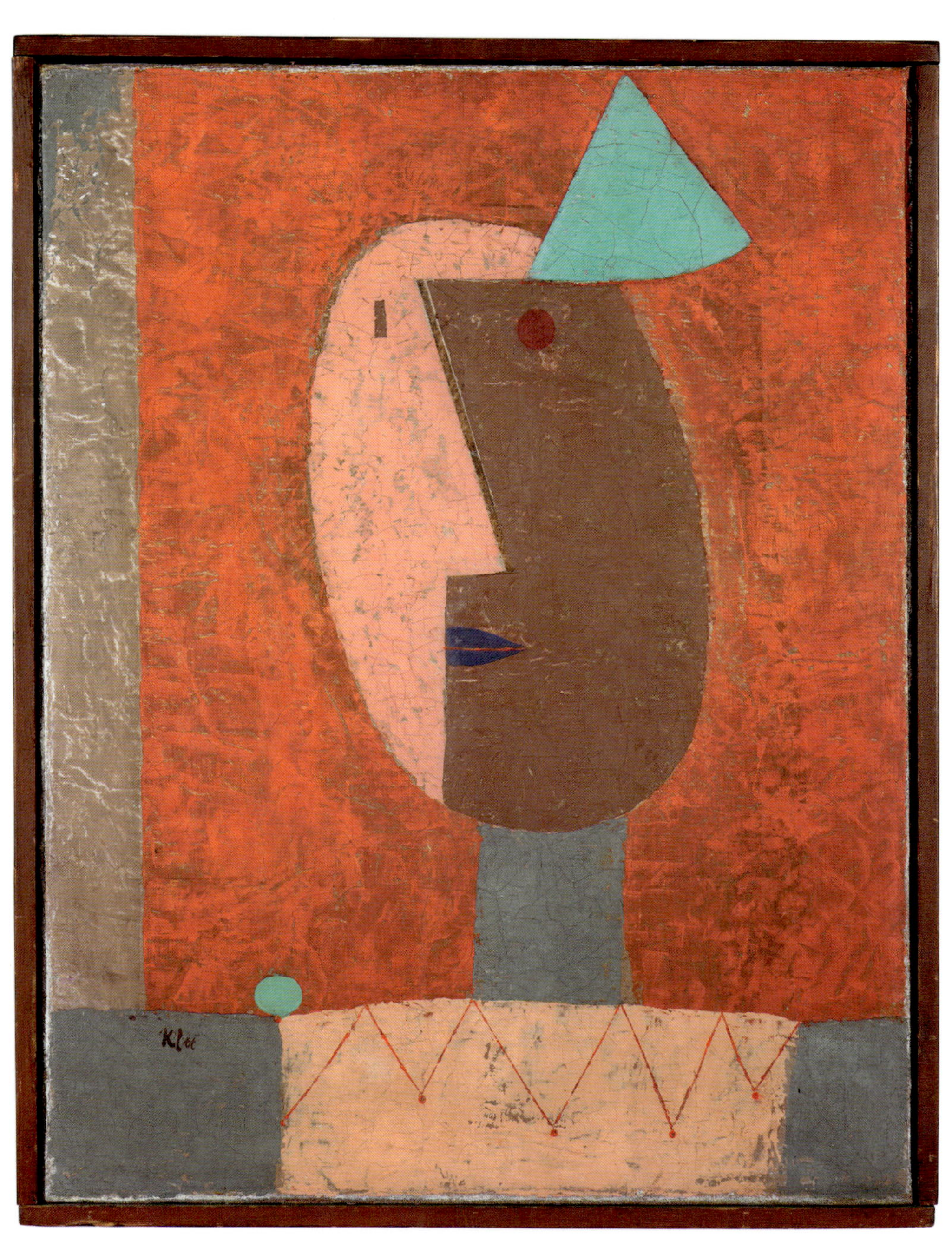

Max Beckmann
1884 Leipzig – 1950 New York

Oil on canvas
Inscribed centre lower right
in German script: Beckmann A 43
90 × 145 cm

Inv. no.: P36T
Acquired 2007

30 Max Beckmann
Traum des Soldaten
1942/43

On 19 July 1937, the day after Hitler had given his speech to open the *Grosse Deutsche Kunstausstellung* in Munich, Max Beckmann left Germany to go into exile in Amsterdam. What was meant to be a temporary measure proved to be a ten-year stay and he did not move on to the United States until 1947. In spite of the war and German occupation, the years in Amsterdam were extraordinarily fruitful. Beckmann painted six triptychs, two major cycles of illustrations of the apocalypse and Goethe's Faust, and a number of iconographically and stylistically important pictures.

Traum des Soldaten (Soldier's Dream) was painted in 1942 (dated 1943) when the murderous war of Nazi dictatorship had swept across Europe. By speaking of a soldier's dream in his title, Beckmann refers to the war. But a dream also implies the discontinuity of space and time, the fragmentation and displacement of memory, images of desires and fears and ultimately a description of the world that was in many ways visually crucial to Beckmann's compositions.

The dark subject matter of the painting unfolds like a drama. The trim young soldier, his uniform resembling that of a page, is almost wedged in between two seductive and disconcerting beauties. Both attracted and repelled, he is lying down next to the snake-like redhead in a birdcage, onto which a plant is falling like a heavenly missile as if targeting three shrunken heads. The extremely attractive blonde, sitting on the floor next to the cage in the same attitude as the figure to the right in Delacroix's *Women of Algiers,* has a touch of Marlene Dietrich about her; she is scantily attired in white lingerie that reveals her left breast. Her enamel-white skin is radiant in the bright light; the yellow lilies, traditionally symbols of vanity and pomposity, enhance her enchanting allure. She demonstratively holds up a large clock, its hands set at shortly after 11:30. Resembling a wheel, it shows time running out. Thus, in addition to her role as an allegory of time, the seductive young woman can also be seen as Fortuna, the fickle goddess of fate.

This unusually fragile and ambivalent idyll is surrounded by harbingers of doom: the small, birdlike man with eagle's claws, presaging calamity with his bugle, his clothing marking him as the soldier's alter ego; the horned, apocalyptic monsters rising up out of the sea under a moonlit night; the dark, beaver-like animals in the foreground, desperately gasping for air at the bottom of the painting. In counterpart to this apocalyptic scenario, presumably taking place on a ship, a mirror is seen, in which the planks of the ship fade into the infinite blackness of space. It is the "Ein Sof", a Kabbalistic sign, whose circular shape is divided in half, symbolizing the horizon of infinity in the sense of the absolute, the divine, the infinite, and the highest form of knowledge. Its impact transcends the great *theatrum mundi* of humankind.
AS

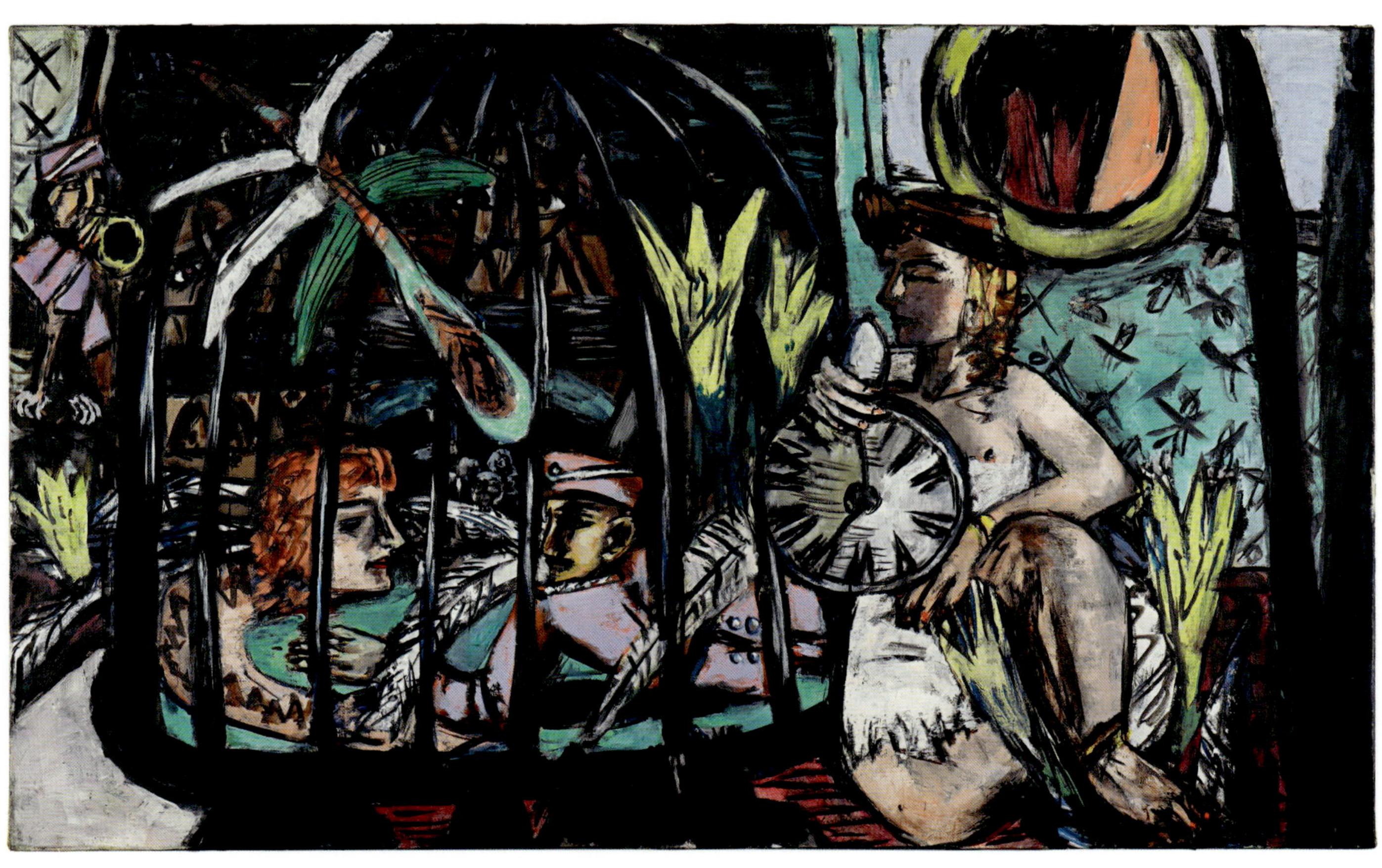

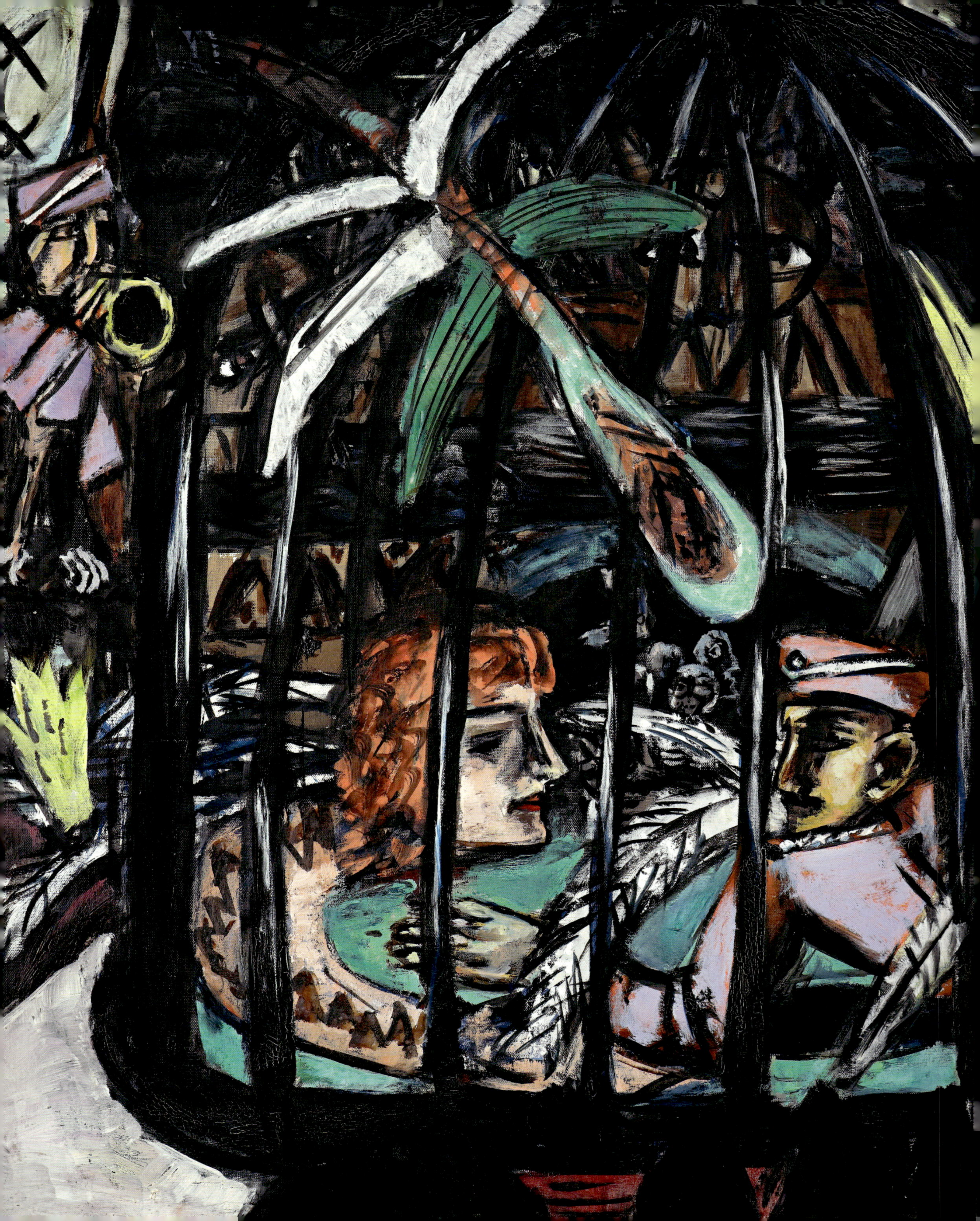

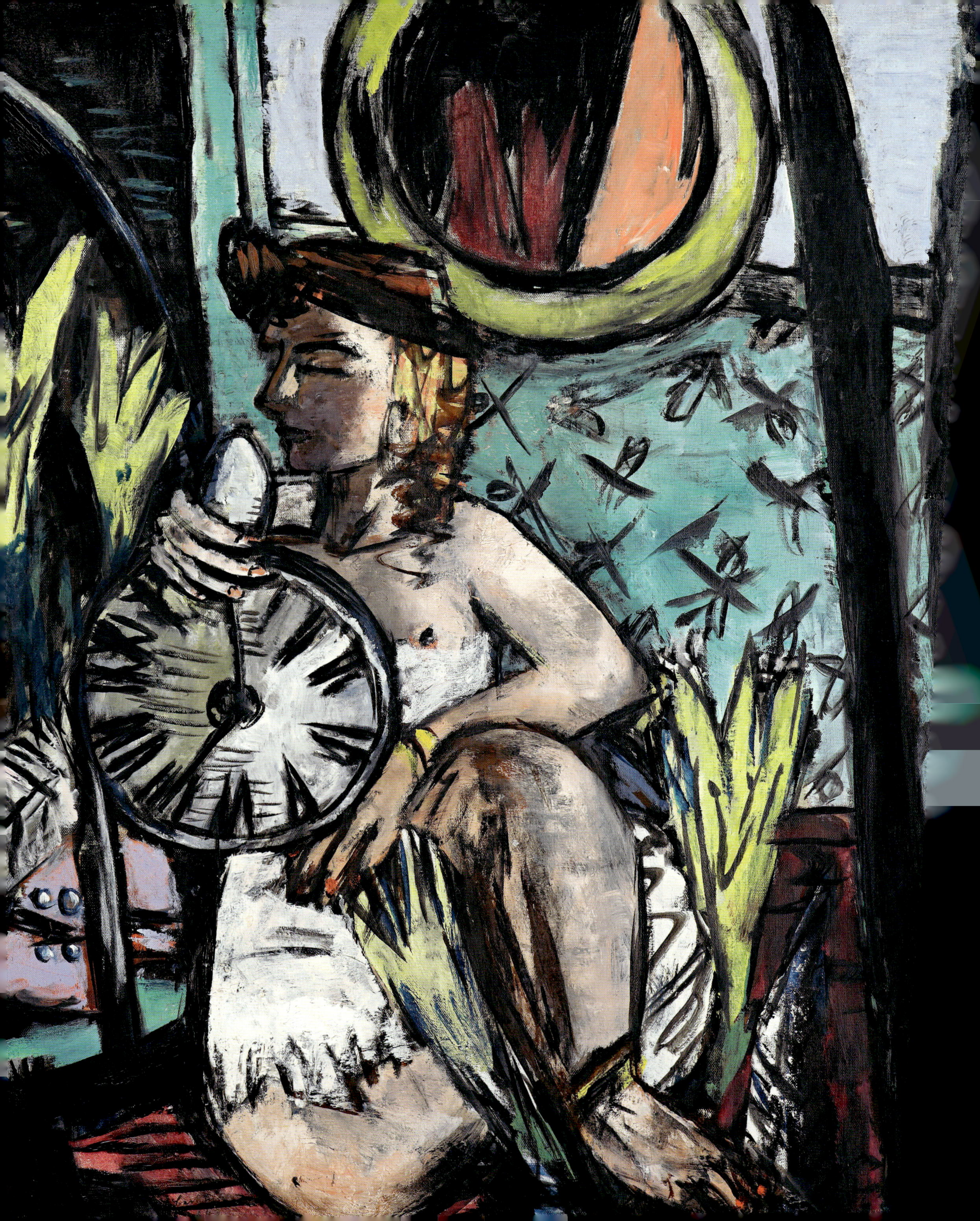

Jean Dubuffet
1901 Le Havre – 1985 Paris

Oil on canvas
Signed and dated upper right:
J. Dubuffet 49
89.5 × 116.5 cm

Inv. no.: P42T
Acquired 2010

31 Jean Dubuffet
Paysage noir avec joueur de fifre
1949

It was not until 1942, at the age of forty-one, that Jean Dubuffet finally gave up his wine business altogether to devote himself entirely to painting. Previous attempts to work exclusively as an artist had failed, particularly since he was not interested in classical painting, an attitude reinforced by the Surrealists with whom he became acquainted in Paris in the 1920s and 1930s. He clearly shared their interest in children's drawings, the art of the mentally ill and in "primitive" art, and had read Hans Prinzhorn's book *Artistry of the Mentally Ill* with great enthusiasm in 1924. In the 1940s, he began collecting outsider art, for which he coined the term Art Brut, literally "raw art". He started painting his first series of pictures, such as *Métro,* in 1943. A year later, Dubuffet made a suite of lithographs titled *Matières et Mémoires* (Materials and Memories), a revealing title that could easily apply to his entire oeuvre.

Paysage noir avec joueur de fifre (Black Landscape with Piper) is one of the *Paysages grotesques* (Grotesque Landscapes), a series of works painted in 1949. The series reflects Dubuffet's experiences during visits to the Algerian oasis El Goléa in 1947, 1948, and 1949. Painted on a coarse canvas, the work pictures a scene of this oasis, one of the most beautiful and exceptionally fertile in the Sahara, known for its palm trees, orchards, and vegetable gardens. Dubuffet scratched the images out of the dark ground of thick but unevenly applied layers of paint—as if the desert wind were blowing through the picture. Orange trees, palm trees, beds of vegetables, buildings, people, and paths look like washed out graffiti. The circles, dots, and many variations of hatching recall Paul Klee's depictions of landscapes and cities. The artist has superimposed his motifs with no regard for perspective. Somewhat childlike, but drawn with great fluidity, the figures cover the entire picture plane like a carpet except for a narrow strip at the top marking the sky above the mountains in the distance.

In an essay published by Gallimard in 1946, Dubuffet wrote that he refused to bow to the constraints of optical perspective because that would curtail the freedom he required to picture all of the objects that he imagined. He elaborated his critique of civilisation in a lecture given in Chicago in 1951: "Western man despises trees and streams. He hates the very thought of being like them. The 'primitive' however loves and admires trees and streams. ... These 'primitive' societies certainly have a greater respect than western man for all the creatures on the earth. They do not see humankind as the lord of other creatures but merely as one of them." This is indeed the mood conveyed in Dubuffet's landscape.

The title alludes to Manet's famous painting *Le fifre* (The Fifer, 1866), rejected in its day for being too simple and modern, but nonetheless admired by Emile Zola. The *Images d'Épinal,* prints of popular subjects sold in France in the nineteenth century, no doubt reverberate in the motif of the flautist. AS

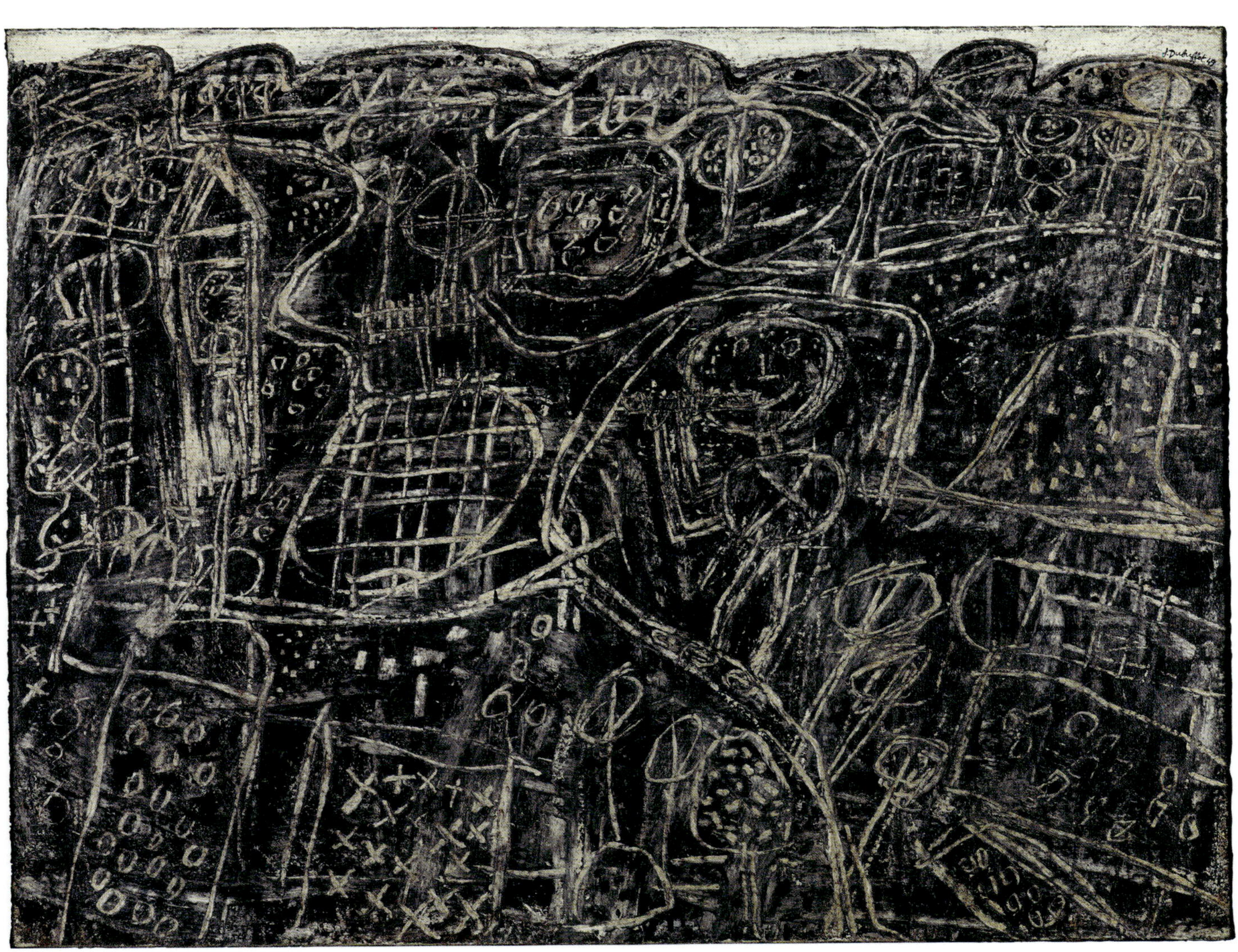

Wols
1913 Berlin – 1951 Paris

Oil on canvas
41 × 33 cm

Inv. no.: P48T
Acquired 2011

32 Wols
La flamme
1946–47

Wols—his real name was Wolfgang Schulze—created some 1800 photographs, 2000 drawings and watercolours, and approximately 80 to 100 paintings. Much of his oeuvre was lost in the brief thirty-eight years of the artist's turbulent life. The first paintings, made shortly after the war in 1946 and 1947, were exhibited in the upscale René Drouin gallery at Place Vendôme in Paris. Drouin also supplied him with oil paints and canvases. The works did not attract much attention at the time, becoming more widely known only later in the wake of art-historical interest in Art Informel and Tachism. They were preceded by fifteen years of personal artistic development with no classical training, although no doubt with a knowledge of Surrealism. Having emigrated from Germany to Paris in 1932, Wols initially worked as a photographer and later concentrated on drawing, watercolours, etching, and finally painting. In addition to his delight in telling and inventing stories, one can detect stylistic similarities between the photographs and watercolours, especially an intense interest in the small and delicate structures of a wide variety of organisms that often remain hidden from the naked eye.

Wols mit der Lupe (Wols with His Magnifying Glass): thus the title of philosopher Bernard Collin's aphorisms in which he conducted an ongoing conversation with the artist. It is through Collin, who was still a student when he probably acquired La flamme from Drouin in 1948, that the work is now held by the Hilti Art Foundation. Wols ordinarily left his work untitled to protect it from premature and facile interpretation. *La flamme,* like the second title *Le bouquet,* presumably stems from Olga Drouin.

The small, unsigned picture shows a shape with a complex inner structure placed against a light-grey ground mixed with white. The shape, basically symmetrical in composition, acquires a slant through the red lines that form a slightly tilting cross. The turbulence in the centre is accentuated by round shapes of different sizes made by the imprint of tubes of paint; they might be interpreted as eddies or drops or eyes. Fragile, partially broken contours delimit strands of paint left and right that Wols structured like the bark of the tree. He used the handle of his paintbrush to make scratches in the bundles of thin, swaying lines, sprouting out of the edges. They resemble magnetic field lines but also evoke a variety of associations: trees, underbrush, a seed, a piece of sliced-open fruit, and, of course, body parts. In his own undated aphorism, the artist wrote, "But Wols honestly loves / the matter that surrounds us."

Wols pencilled CACCA into the top left corner. This is not only an ironic commentary, like the much-quoted words that Wols attributed to his dog Rip, "Your painting is idiotic." More importantly, Collin refers in his aphorisms to Antonin Artaud, whom Wols knew and greatly admired. Collin writes, "Caca, here the cry of Artaud / Is God leaving or staying?" AS

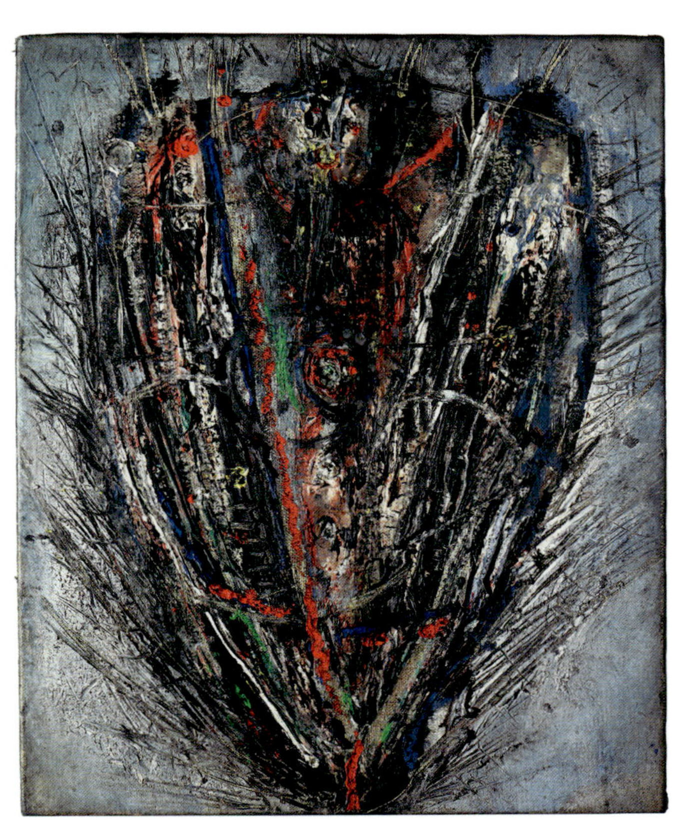

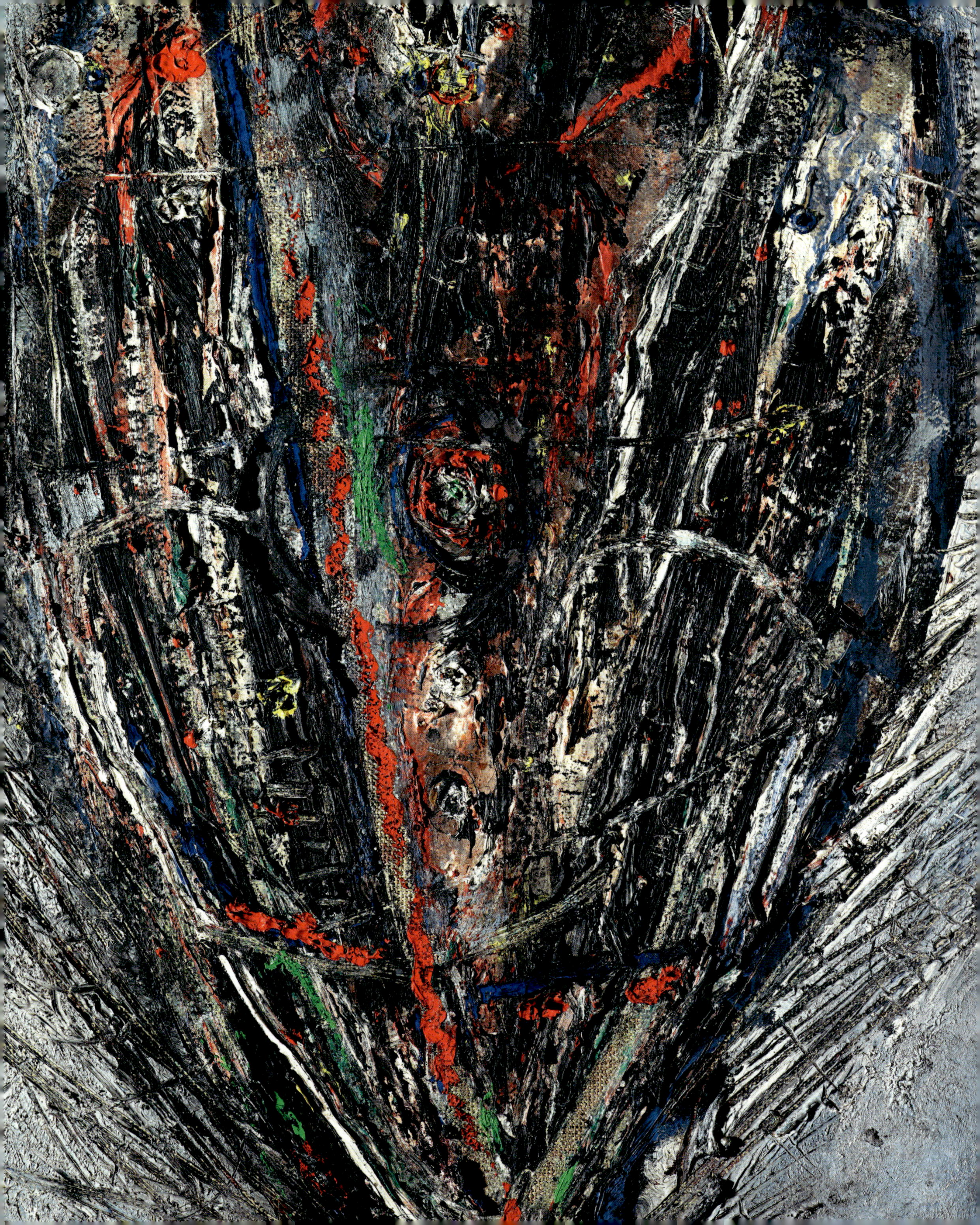

Painted plaster
21 × 16 × 8.2 cm

Inv. no.: S30T
Acquired 2005

33 Alberto Giacometti
Petit buste d'homme
1950–51

When Giacometti left Geneva in September 1945 to return to his Montparnasse studio in Paris, his sculptures were so small that they fit into a matchbox. They had progressively shrunk in size as a consequence of his desire to render the figures as he had seen them in the distance, together with the space around them. However, gradually his sculptures began to grow again, turning into slender, elongated, sometimes even skeleton-like figures, standing uncertainly on their large feet. The heads of his busts, sometimes placed on a pole, evoke skulls and war.

Another change made an appearance in 1949. Giacometti was now working almost exclusively with models, primarily with his brother Diego and his wife Annette. With renewed intensity, he had returned to the old question of what a head actually is and how it might be formed "as an equivalent of life". *Petite buste d'homme* (Small Bust of a Man) cannot be attributed to any of Giacometti's usual models. The torso and, in fact, the entire figure are shown facing the artist head on, as he saw his model sitting opposite him. The jacket and sleeves, looking slightly padded, are clearly distinguishable, despite the glacier-like furrows and gouges in the structure of the plaster. On the long stem of a neck sits a narrow elongated head, resembling a sad clown or a philosopher of antiquity plagued by doubts.

Before coating the entire plaster figure with shellac, Giacometti painted a web of black and red lines onto certain portions with a pointed brush, the currents of energy rising up to the head and converging in the face. Among other things, they mark the large, blank eyes that gaze neither inwards nor outwards but instead appear as if paralyzed, looking at something that remains hidden from us. According to Giacometti, it was reality that had abruptly metamorphosed into the shock of the unknown. Something never before seen, utterly unknown, something wonderful, he later explained in a 1961 interview with Pierre Schneider. AS

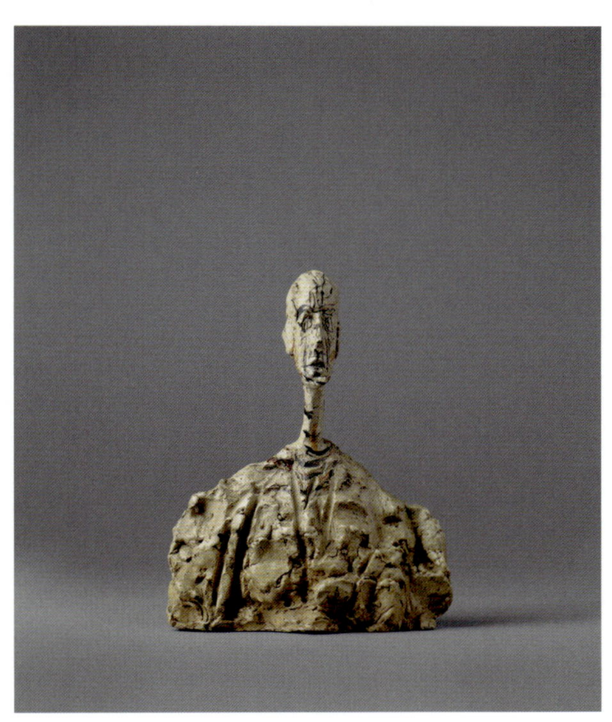

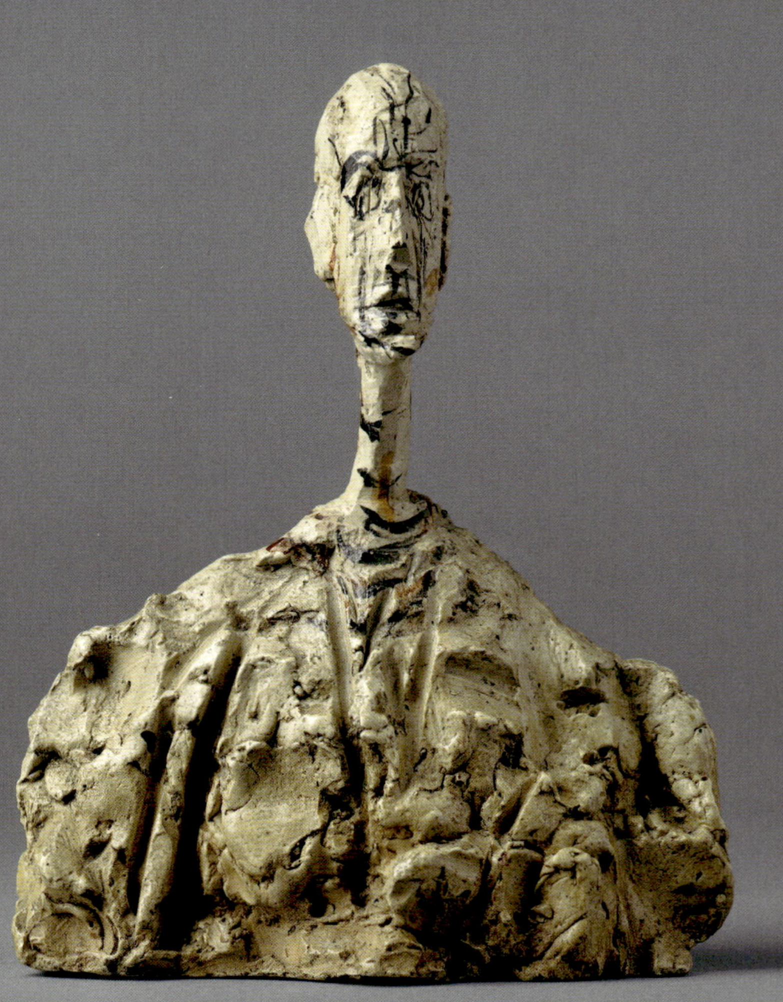

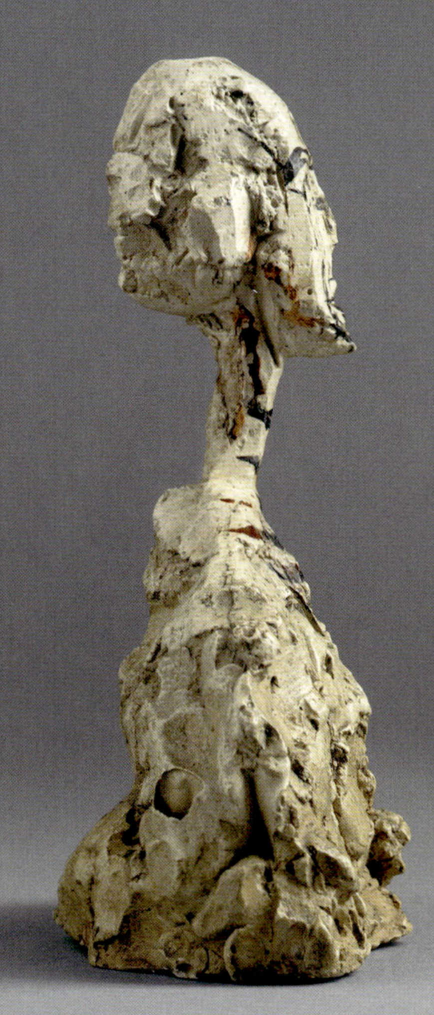

Immanence and Transcendence

Norbert Kricke
1922 Düsseldorf – 1984 Düsseldorf

Painted steel
44 × 52 × 45 cm

Inv. no.: S175M
Acquired 2006

34 Norbert Kricke
Raumplastik (Gelb – Weiss – Schwarz)
1952

In the early 1940s, in the midst of the war, a young Norbert Kricke discovered sculpture as his personal calling, as the "sublime pleasure of creation". He did not carve his human figures out of stone or wood but moulded them out of clay. Professional help furthered his skills, but it was not until after the war that he was able to enjoy a formal education at the University of Fine Arts in Berlin. He continued making figures in natural and classical poses, some of which reflect his admiration of such artists as Rodin and Lehmbruck. The year 1950 was a radical turning point. Kricke abandoned figuration and stopped working in clay, plaster, and bronze, choosing instead to make filigree constructions of wire and steel with architectural leanings. He called them "space sculptures". They explicitly addressed the then contemporary sculptural discourse on material, form, and subject matter. In 1954 Kricke wrote, "My problem is not the mass, it is not the figure, it is space and it is movement—space and time."

In the 1920s, such artists as Naum Gabo, Rodchenko, and Moholy-Nagy had already abandoned figure and mass, the fundamental properties of conventional sculpture. That same decade Picasso and Calder experimented with works made of wire, although in a more playful and anthropomorphic mode than the constructivist, architectural approach cultivated by the artists from Eastern Europe. Kricke's *Raumplastik Gelb – Weiss – Schwarz* (Space Sculpture Yellow – White – Black, 1952) is a prime example of his wish to visualize space and movement instead of rendering figure and mass. It consists of a straight steel wire that he has bent ten times at variously sharp and rounded angles, following a course that takes several intersecting directions until finally returning to its starting point. The artist has thus created a shape with neither plane nor volume through the exclusive use of line and contour. Although the stand suggests four privileged vantage points, it is only by walking around it that one can fully appreciate the asymmetrical, intricately balanced views. These testify to the unerring sense of scale and proportion that Kricke acquired in the course of studying the human figure. The sculpture is actually small enough to be taken in at a single glance, but viewers cannot fully appreciate the rhythm, the dynamic, and the sensuality that characterize the line without visually following the succession from yellow to white to black, for only then will they experience the sculpture's movement in space and through time.

The "space sculptures" occupy a singular place in the history of art in the second half of the twentieth century and have met with international acclaim. They underwent countless metamorphoses for the remainder of Kricke's life. He multiplied, stretched, bundled, knotted, and bent his linear constructions until they became positively chaotic only to morph back into the clarity of playfully light "curves", gliding, as if utterly aimless, through space and time. The works demonstrate what Kricke meant when he wrote, "Away from measurable reality—it is a stiff corpse in our space—and toward imagined, transformed reality—then we will be saved." UW

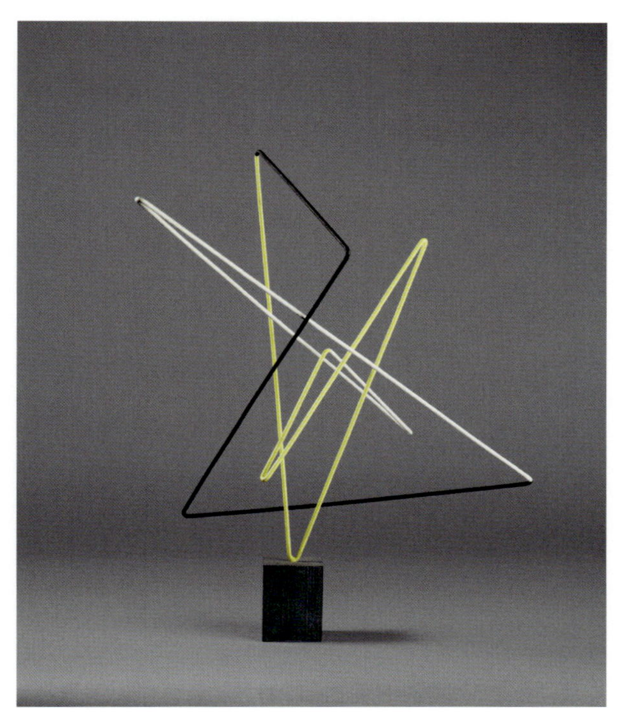

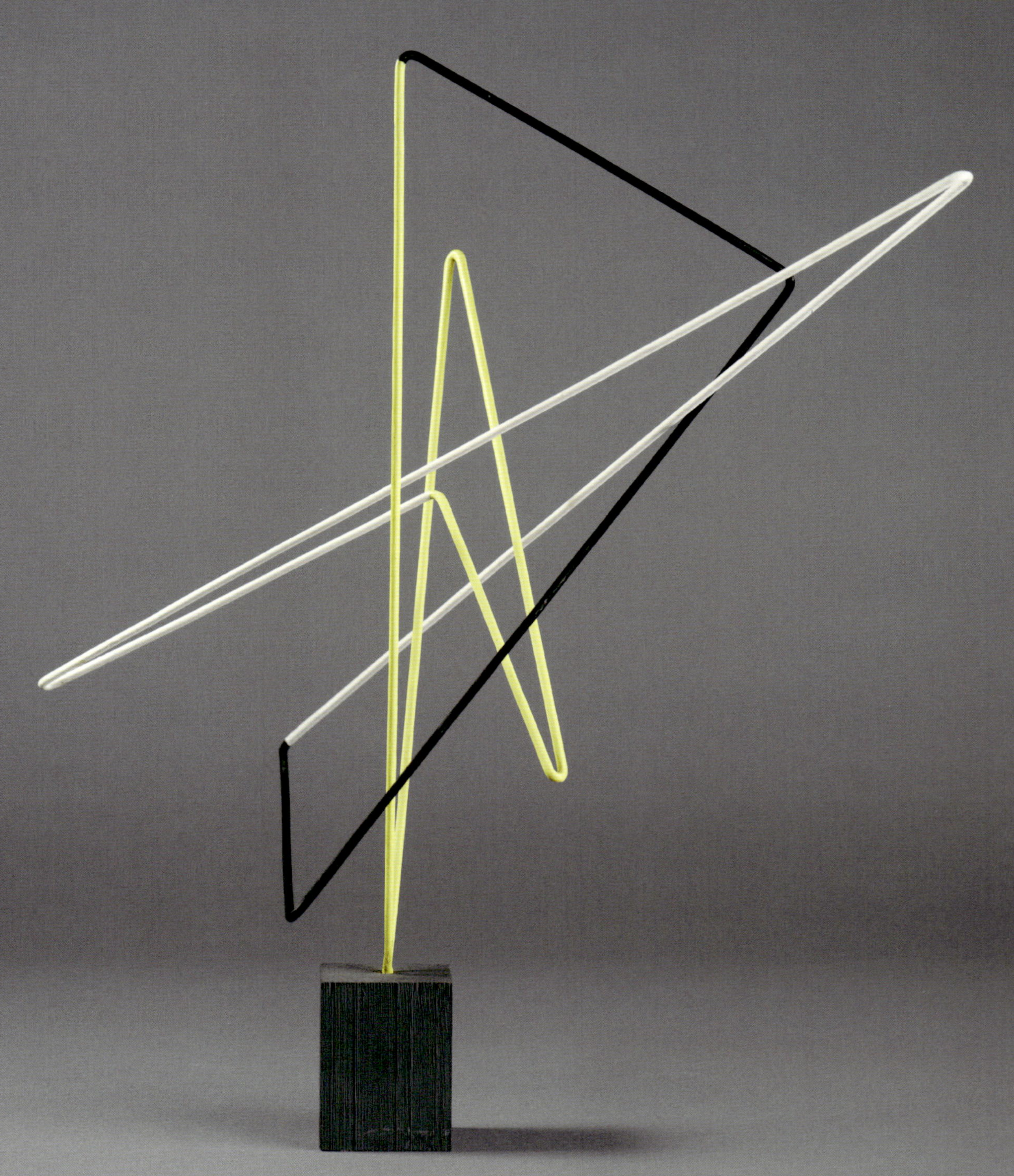

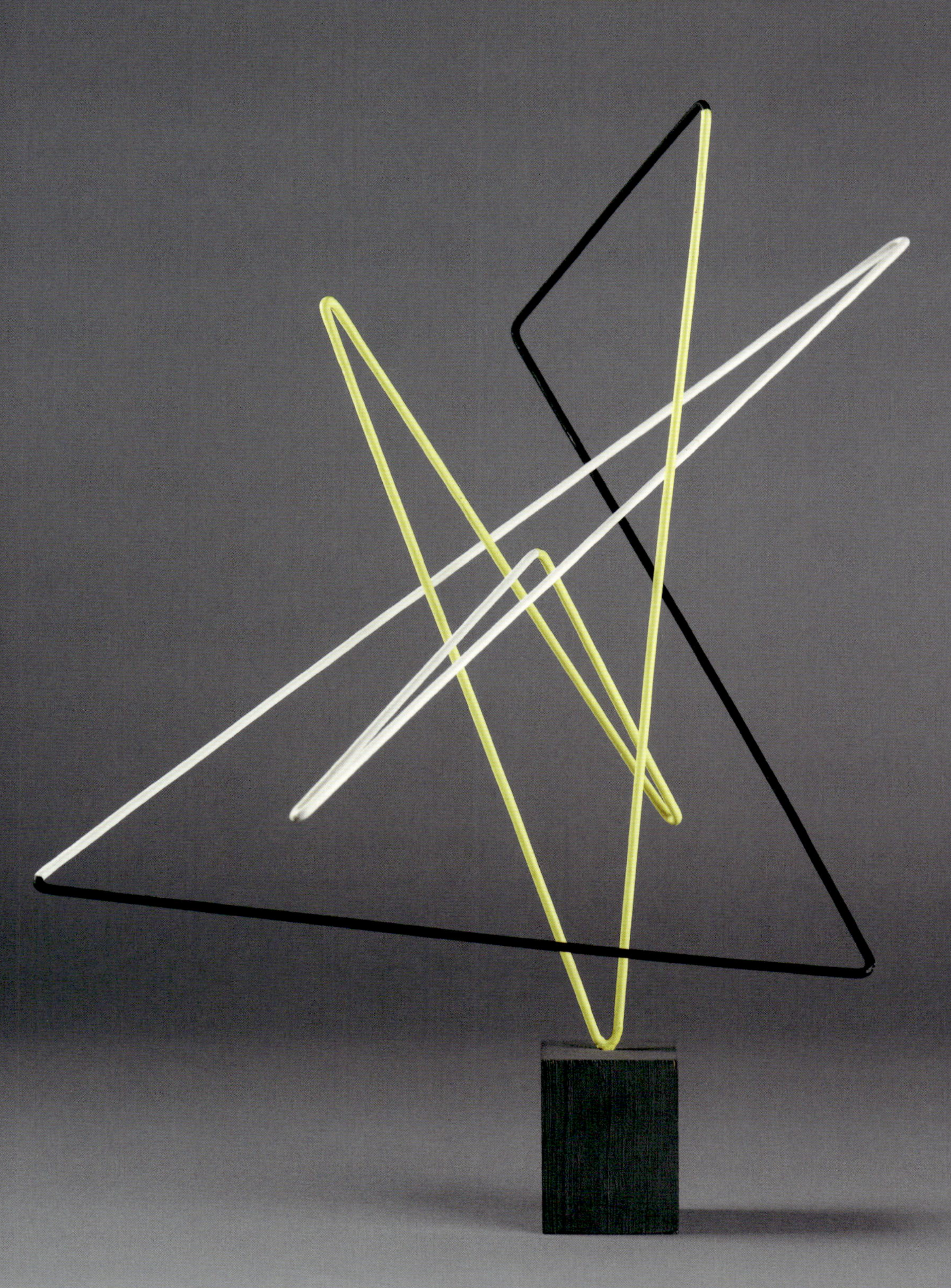

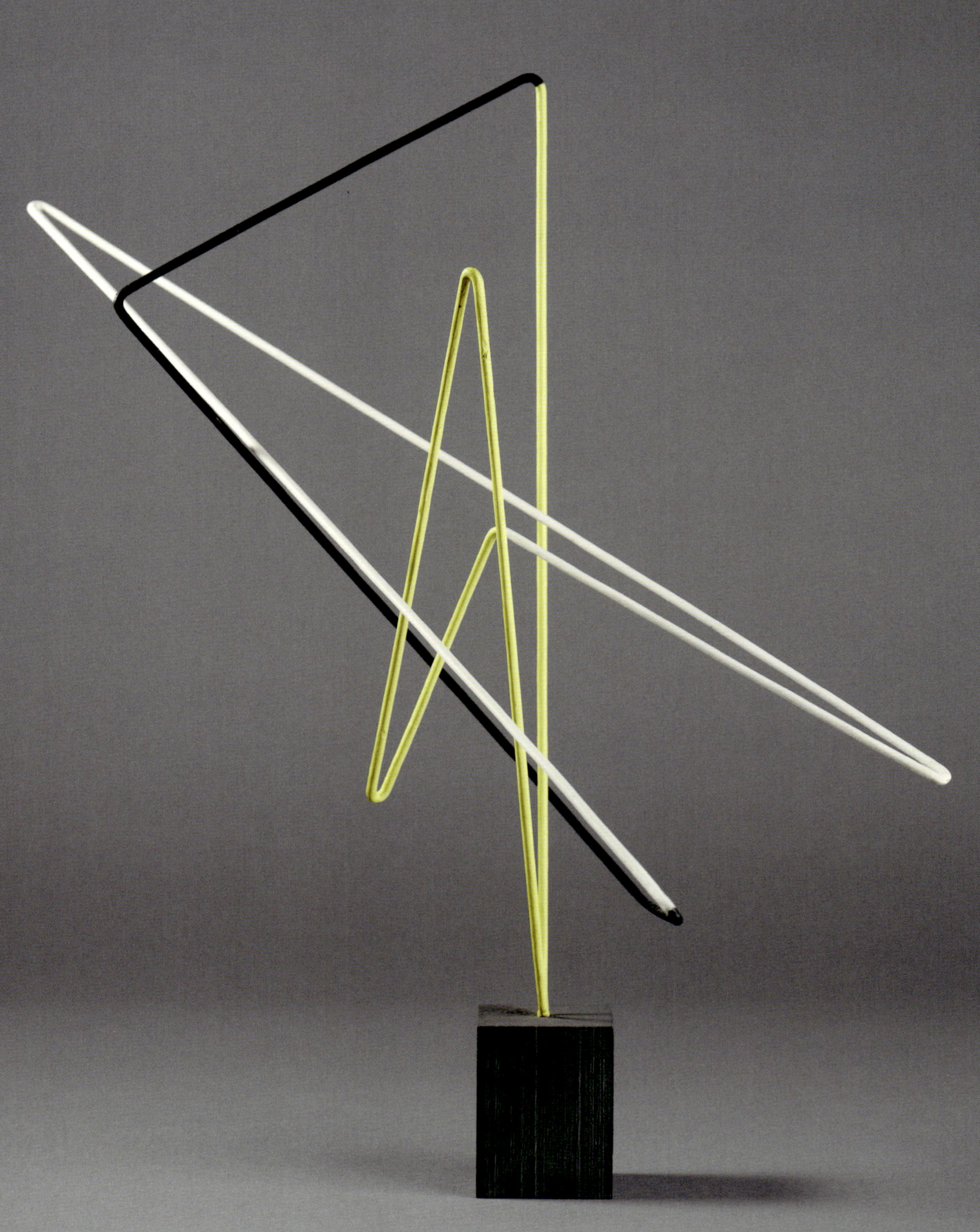

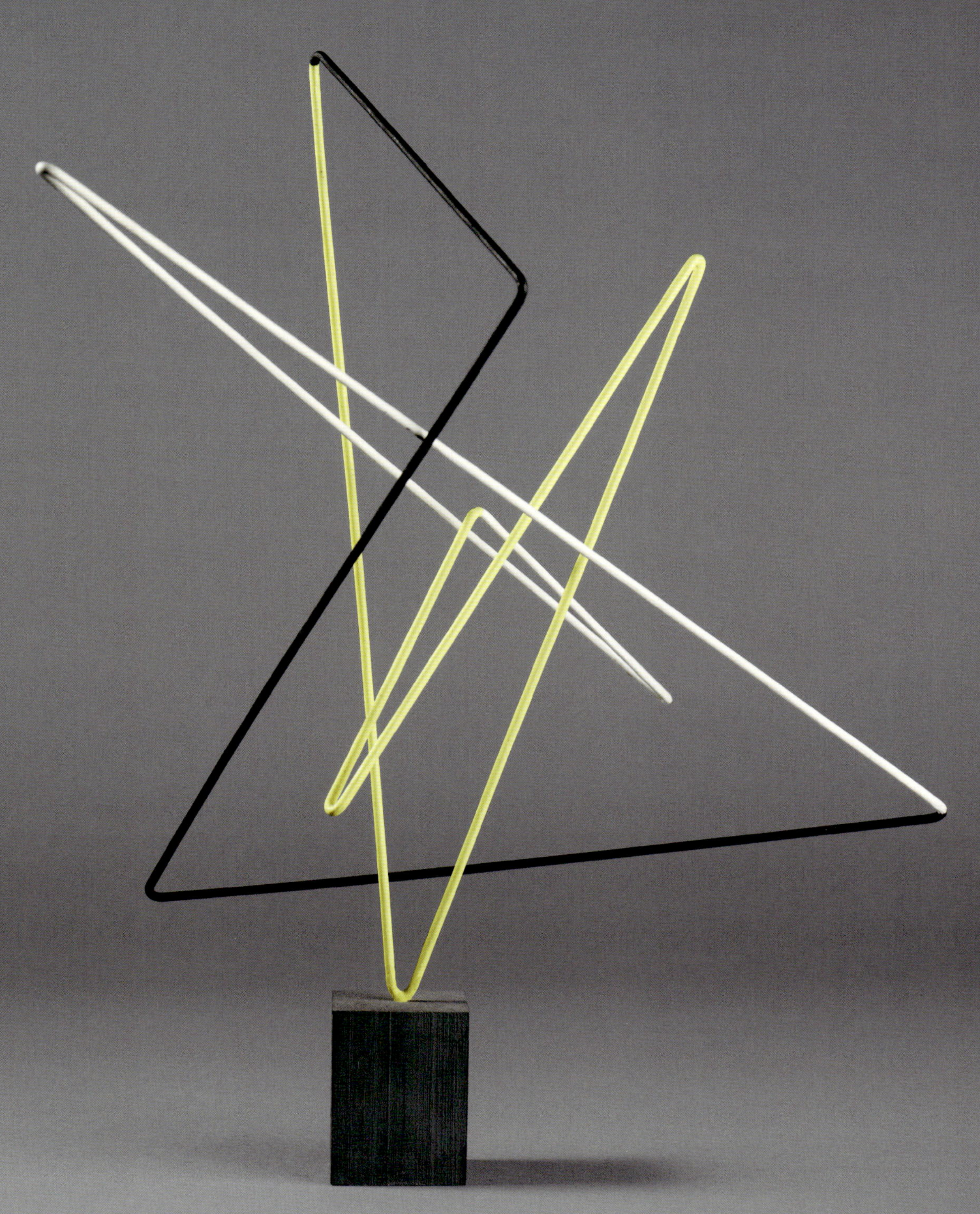

Josef Albers
1888 Bottrop – 1976 New Haven, Connecticut

Oil on Masonite
Signed and dated lower right: A59
121.5 x 121.5 cm
(123.4 x 123.4 cm with frame)

Inv. no.: P205M
Acquired 2009

35 Josef Albers
Homage to the Square
1959

The title of the painting could well suggest that Josef Albers was paying tribute to a geometric shape that has left an indelible mark on the history of art ever since Malevich painted a black square on a white ground (1914–15). However, Albers, who enjoyed a long, successful career as a teacher at the Bauhaus in Weimar and Dessau and later at Black Mountain College and Yale University in the United States, was more interested in colour than in form. To show how "deceptive" colour can be, he created *Homage to the Square,* a series begun in 1950 and exemplary of his entire oeuvre. In this series he drew attention to the discrepancy between physical/objective reality and sensual/subjective appearance, the latter inescapably influenced by context, specifically by the juxtaposition of different colours. In this way, Albers wanted to hone our perception of colour and, by proxy, of the phenomena of the visible world in general.

The discovery of pre-Columbian art and architecture acquired in the course of numerous trips to Mexico in the 1940s not only heightened the artist's sense of colour. Having already taken the step from figuration to abstraction, Albers started making architectural compositions reduced to three or four superimposed squares. The pattern of squares, although variable in size and scale, remained consistent from 1950 onwards. Deliberately restricting himself to this simple geometric shape in order to focus on colour, he squeezed his oil-based paint directly from the tube and applied it directly to the canvas with a palette knife, invariably leaving a narrow margin unpainted along the edges, thereby clearly defining the picture as a plane. Albers described what happens on the picture plane as the "interaction of colour". This interaction is a given since we do not ordinarily see colours in isolation; they are always interacting, generating tension, vibrating, and even creating an illusion of depth despite the flatness of the picture plane. Dark colours, for instance, are perceived as being closer to the front than light ones—a fact that already played a role in Mondrian's work (see cat. 22). Above all, however, even if the paint has come from the same tube, the appearance of the colour changes depending on its neighbours.

Albers's paintings are concrete, matter-of-fact, and of a contemplative serenity. They do not represent personal expression of any kind; instead, they are a means of presenting a sensual and inevitably relative phenomenon, accessible only through visual perception. Regardless of how he combined his colours, Albers did not show any preference for a particular chromatic harmony. Everything was possible, as in the real world. Through his investigation of colour, he came to the conclusion that "colour in my opinion behaves like man ... First in self-realization and then in the realization of relationships with others. ... We must combine both being an individual and being a member of society. ... You may conclude that I consider ethics and aesthetics as one." UW

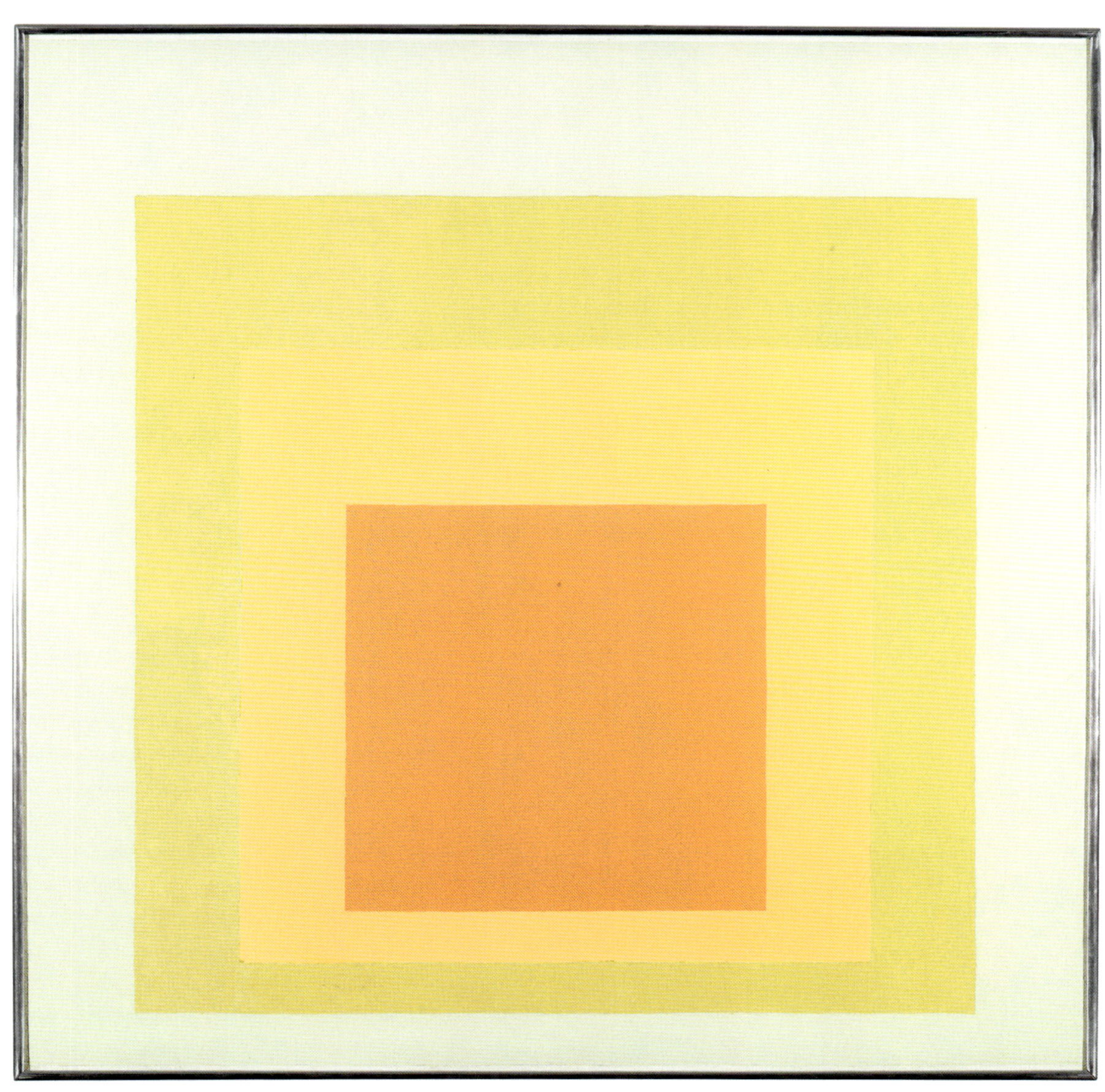

Gianni Colombo
1937 Milan – 1993 Melzo, Milan

Steel, nylon, two engines
c. 82 × 82 × 100 cm

Inv. no.: S196M
Acquired 2008

36 Gianni Colombo

Spazio elastico

1968

By the end of the 1950s, Gianni Colombo was already experimenting with both visual and haptic phenomena. He started out working in ceramics and then expanded, incorporating felt, cotton, rubber, polystyrene, cardboard, wood, metal, and other materials into his work. He not only gave viewers the opportunity to look and touch; he also devised mechanical devices so that they could actually initiate change. Colombo placed great emphasis on works characterized by openness, variability, and interaction.

In the context of artists' groups like Gruppo T, which he cofounded in Milan in 1959, or Nouvelle Tendance, Colombo concentrated on kinetic works in the 1960s, using engines in some cases and reaching out into architectural space. In 1967, he created a suite of works, which he called *Spazio elastico* (Elastic Space)—dark rooms, cubic in shape, their stereometry made visible in the form of fluorescent elastic strings. By stretching, contracting, and twisting the strings, the artist created optical effects in space that disorient viewers.

The *Spazio elastico* (1968) in the collection of the Hilti Art Foundation is related to these environments. Steel rods are suspended from the ceiling, forming eight successively smaller open squares, lined up one behind the other. The squares are tied with nylon thread to a metal frame mounted above them, where two engines slowly and seamlessly transform the squares into parallelograms running in opposite directions, thus generating the impression of a curving space in constant motion.

Gianni Colombo's oeuvre challenges sensual perception. The conventional parameters of daily life no longer prevail, undermining the supposed reliability of assumptions and expectations. The artist's inquiry into the psychology of perception is buoyed by a playful treatment of material and a poetry of form that lend these works the status of art. UW

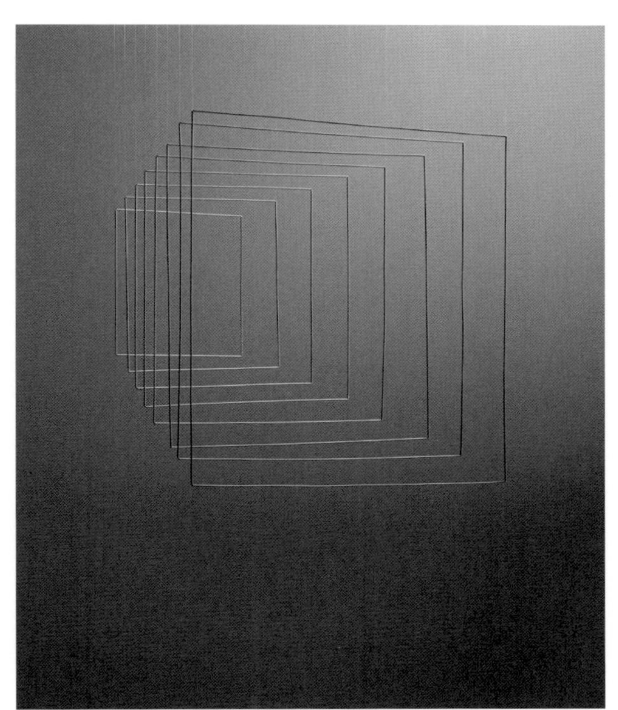

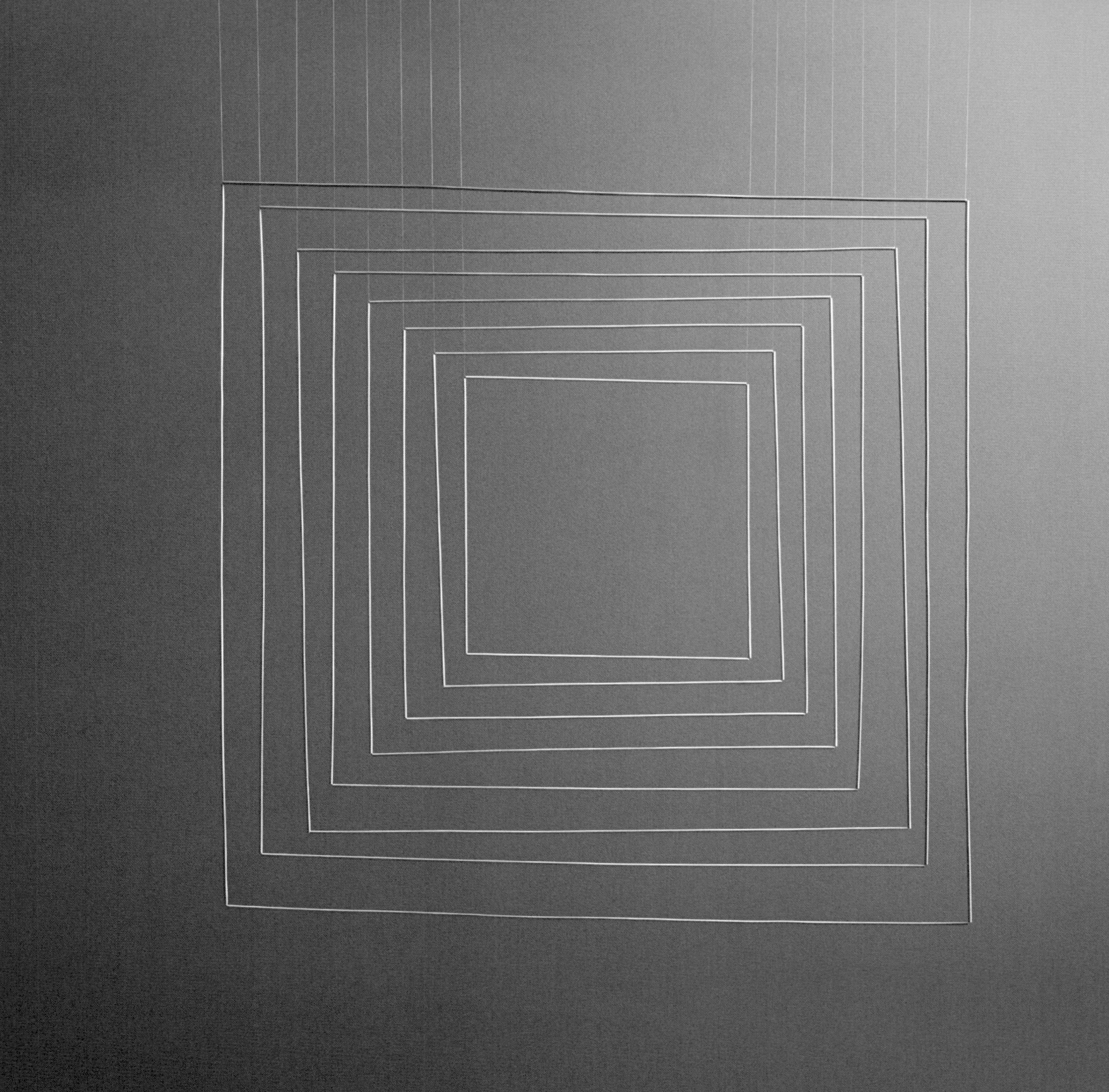

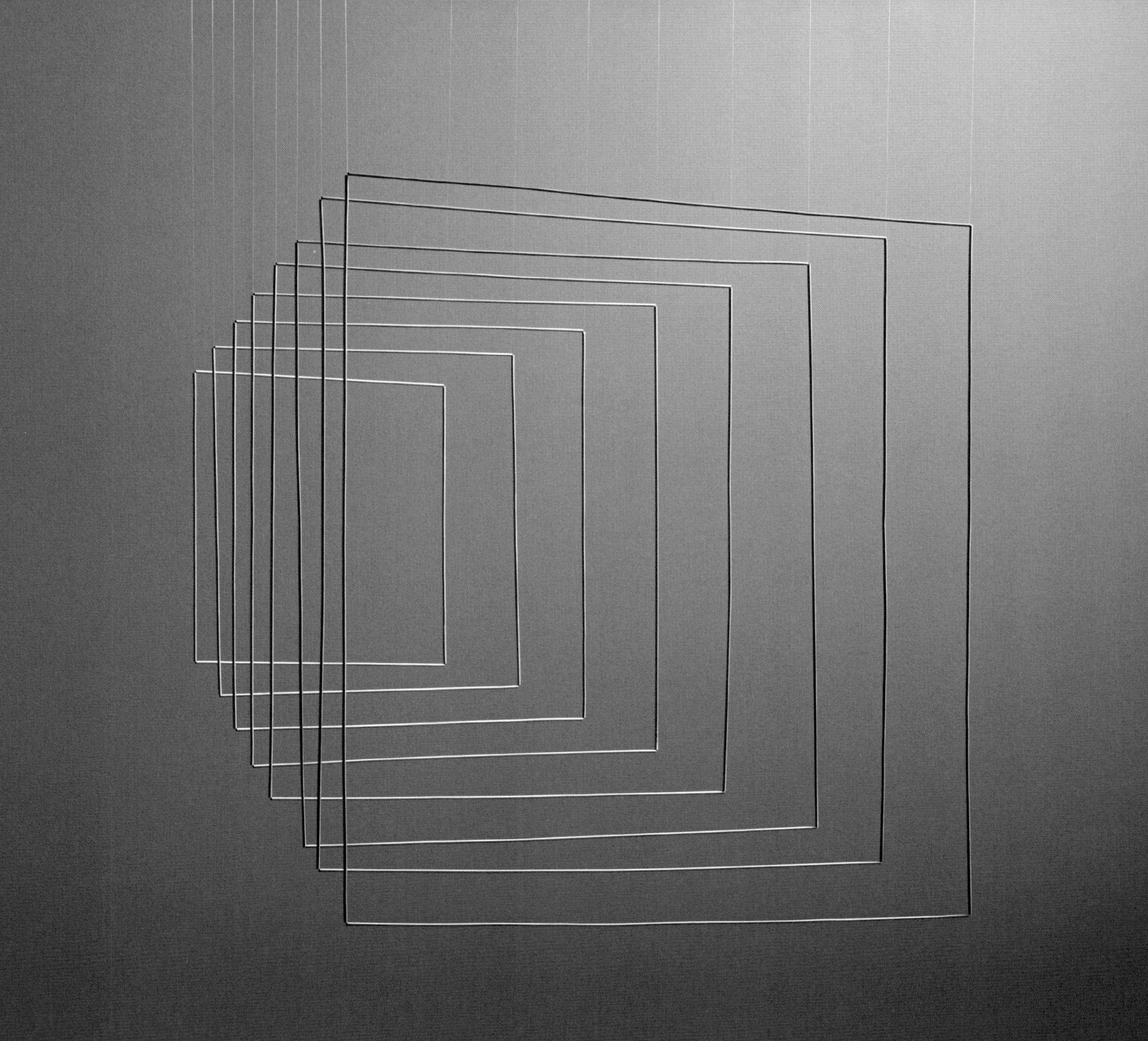

Lucio Fontana
1899 Rosario de Santa Fé – 1968 Comabbio, Varese

Watercolour on canvas
Signed on verso: "L Fontana / ATTESA / Concetto Spaziale / Quante fesserie sento nella giornata"
55.6 × 46.2 cm

Inv. no.: P159M
Acquired 2005

37 Lucio Fontana
Concetto spaziale – Attese
1966

In 1958 Lucio Fontana took a knife and slashed the white plane of a canvas, an act of destruction as symbolic as it was real and targeting a medium that artists have used for centuries as a surface on which to project their will to represent and express their ideas. Fontana had already taken a step in this direction nine years earlier when he perforated his paintings with pointed tools. "Iconoclastic" gestures of this kind subvert the secondary function of a canvas as a picture support, drawing attention to its physical reality as an object in and of itself. Slits and holes are, of course, not merely destructive; they are an artistic means of revealing the space behind the canvas and incorporating it into the work of art. Devoted to the realities of surface and plane, this group of works is tellingly entitled *Concetto spaziale* (spatial concept). Fontana's *Manifesto blanco* of 1946 calls for "an art which is free of all aesthetic artifice" and is instead devoted to matter, time, and space as the "primary values of existence", in other words, to all that is "true and natural in man". Heinz Mack, who dedicated his *Lichtmaschinen* (Light Machines) to his thirty-year-older colleague, astutely remarked that Fontana's "iconoclastic" gesture "did not kill the picture" but rather became a picture in its own right, a picture with one, five or seven slashes on a white, gold, or red ground. No matter how much Fontana's slashed canvas has acquired the nature of a trademark, it cannot eclipse the original radicalism of his act and its profound impact on art in the 1960s, specifically on ZERO and Arte Povera. UW

Yves Klein
1928 Nice – 1962 Paris

Pigment in Rhodopas on canvas
Signed in pencil on verso: Yves
65 × 54.5 cm

Inv. no.: P18M
Acquired 1995

38 Yves Klein
Monochrome (IKB 180)
1958

IKB stands for International Klein Blue, a radiant ultramarine blue. In *Mon Livre* Yves Klein wrote in 1960, "Blue has no dimensions, it is beyond dimensions, whereas the other colours are not." For Klein, blue is the incarnation of cosmic feelings and, like all other pure colours, of unadulterated freedom. At the age of eighteen, he "signed" his first blue painting, the expanse of the southern skies, lying on his back on the beach in Nice. Years later, he would recall how he hated the birds for flying back and forth and "trying to make holes" in his greatest work.

Klein conducted his earliest experiments, designed to give substance to these poetic sensations of space, while working in London in 1949–50 for the framemaker and gilder Robert Savage. Fascinated by the magical luminosity of pure powdered pigments, Klein created his first *Monochromes*. However, as soon as he added a binder to the powders, they lost their luminosity, and without a binder, they did not adhere to the canvas. In 1955, Klein found a working solution with the help of the Parisian chemist Edouard Adam. Instead of using conventional binders, they suspended the dry pigment in diluted Rhodopas, a petroleum extract ordinarily used to fix paintings. The combination of dry pigment and Rhodopas M60A produced a quick drying but poisonous paint that Klein applied with a roller, deliberately precluding the possibility of an individual signature. Since the pigment now adhered to the canvas without losing its luminosity, the picture had come to life, thereby embodying an adequate materialization of the cosmic sense of space. Klein generally spoke of the "cosmic sensibility" or at times of the "pure" or "poetic" energy of these works. Their impact and significance are not, however, permanently fixed and rigid, for they depend on the viewer's disposition. AS

Piero Manzoni
1933 Soncino, Milan – 1963 Milan

Kaolin, cotton
57.6 x 73 cm

Inv. no.: P82M
Acquired 2001

39 Piero Manzoni
Achrome
1959–60

Piero Manzoni ranks among the most complex and radical artists in Italy after the Second World War. His early oeuvre, indebted to Art Informel, later gave way to an approach between the "Informel gesture and a new bodily concept of reality" (Martin Engler). In only five years, from 1957 until his premature death in February 1963, Manzoni produced a body of work that reduced painting, sculpture, happening, and action to absurdity; he robbed these categories of their traditional foundations and redefined them. His provocative thrust, intended to abolish art altogether, proved to do quite the opposite, expanding it and even adding a heroic touch. When he breathed his "spirit" into balloons in *Fiato d'artista* (Artist's Breath, 1959–60) or signed his living sculptures, usually naked women, or produced his now notorious cans of artist's shit, *Merda d'artista* (1961), these were not simply carnivalesque events, but rather a profound redefinition of art. In *Merda d'artista,* Manzoni filled cans with thirty grams of his excrement and sealed them off, elevating what the artist excretes to the status of art, quite apart from what it actually is. We understand the process of production, the artistic gesture, and the product even though they remain invisible. The contents of the can elude simple, ordinary verification. When a can was opened almost thirty years later, in 1989, by the French artist Bernard Bazile as part of an artistic action, it was no longer possible to determine whether the contents were brown sienna soil or excrement.

At first sight Manzoni's white paintings—he called them *Achromes* (Colourless), coining a word in French—appear to be unrelated to the above-described actions. First made in 1957, these works also link the physical gesture—the folding of the cotton and pouring kaolin on it—with the visual object. On pulling the cotton taut on the stretcher, Manzoni created a picture plane covered with smaller and larger folds. They express the artist's extraordinary tension and yet look relatively neutral, an impression reinforced by the kaolin that he poured on the cotton. Kaolin is extremely fine white clay used primarily in the production of porcelain and paper; it is also a basic ingredient of powder. Its creamy smoothness enhances the quality of the picture as an object, whose solidified surface establishes a mobile and differentiated space of its own.

The *Achromes* vary in structure and material. In the early 1960s, Manzoni used cotton, rabbit skin, bread rolls dipped in kaolin, and synthetic fibres, all of which were basically white. As emphasized in the secondary literature, this white does not stand for infinity and purity, as it did for the Suprematists, but for the absence of colour. Despite their neutrality and detachment, Manzoni's *Achromes* still evoke associations. The surface structure of the early works of fabric pulled taut remind the writer and psychoanalyst D. Laporte of clinical bandaging. They also look like bed sheets. Bandaging and linens in turn refer to the fragility of our existence between birth and death. AS

Gerhard von Graevenitz
1934 Schilde, Mark Brandenburg – 1983 Traubachtal

Wood, paint
Height: 103.5 cm, Diameter: 3.6 cm

Inv. no.: S258M
Acquired 2014

40 Gerhard von Graevenitz
weisse struktur, rundstab mit homogener verteilung
1959

Gerhard von Graevenitz is frequently associated with the ZERO artists' group. He was only slightly younger than its representatives and, with the exception of a few early works, he too concentrated on white paintings and white kinetic objects. However, there are significant differences. Von Graevenitz was primarily interested in systematic, scientific inquiry into visual imagery, which he specified in June 1961 in the form of an aphorism: "i go on the assumption that words / light / dots / motion / chance / orders / series / say something about my pictures. each of them designates an essential element of / my painting." Referring to the philosopher Ludwig Wittgenstein, he continues: "so i can say / my pictures are / dot-pictures and / dot-light-pictures and / serial-dot-light-pictures and / moving-seria-dot-light-pictures and /..."

The slender, elegant rod is a neutral object. Unlike Uecker's *Säule* (Column, 1959) with nails hammered into it, it is not charged with meaning. It is more in the nature of a tool; it could, for instance, be an experimental device to form bubbles. It was also made in 1959, when Von Graevenitz was officially still a student at the Munich Academy of the Fine Arts, where he complemented his studies by experimenting with materials. Protruding from the rod, which has been covered with a white primer, are over 1000 evenly spaced white knobs, all of the same size. This allover structure is based on theoretical study of Jackson Pollock's work and eschews a hierarchical order. Speaking about the summer semester of 1960, Graevenitz wrote, "for some time now, i have been working exclusively with dots. the dot is the simplest and purest sign, rest and movement at once."

The movement is generated by light. Depending on its incidence angle, the knobs are perceived as protruding bumps or as dimples in shadow. The viewer attempts to trace the course taken by the little white bumps, trying to fix them in place and assess their intervals. In the process, the whole eludes vision before consolidating into a single form again. Although—as stated in the title—it is a homogeneously distributed white structure, it appears noticeably differentiated, slightly diffuse, and individually detailed when seen from a distance. Graevenitz's desire to counteract a personal signature is even more explicit in another *weisse struktur* (white structure, 1960), a cylinder with negative and positive dots. He wanted to liberate art from its cultic context by refusing to prescribe either content or composition. The viewer's appreciation of the artwork was meant to lead to "a state of freedom". AS

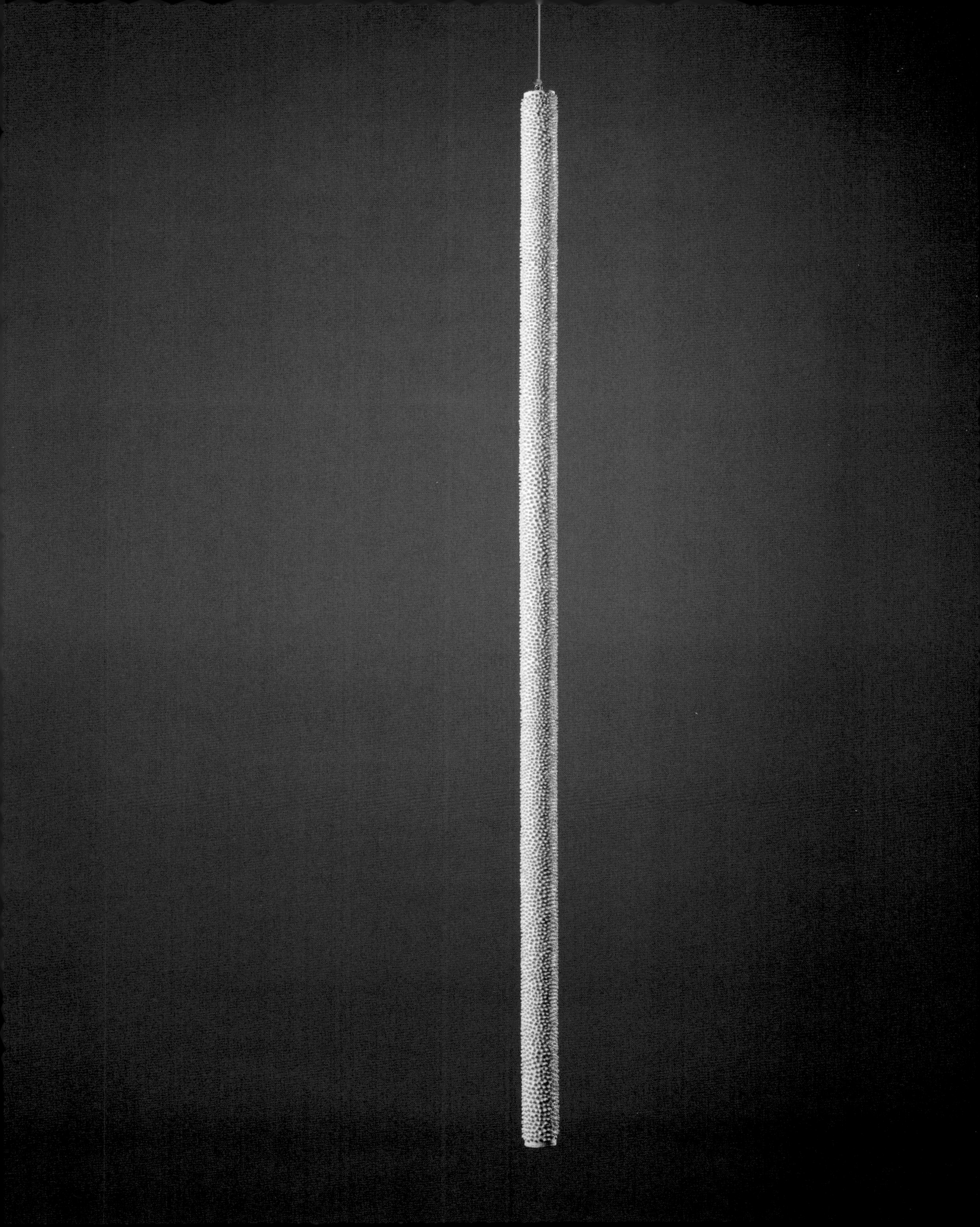

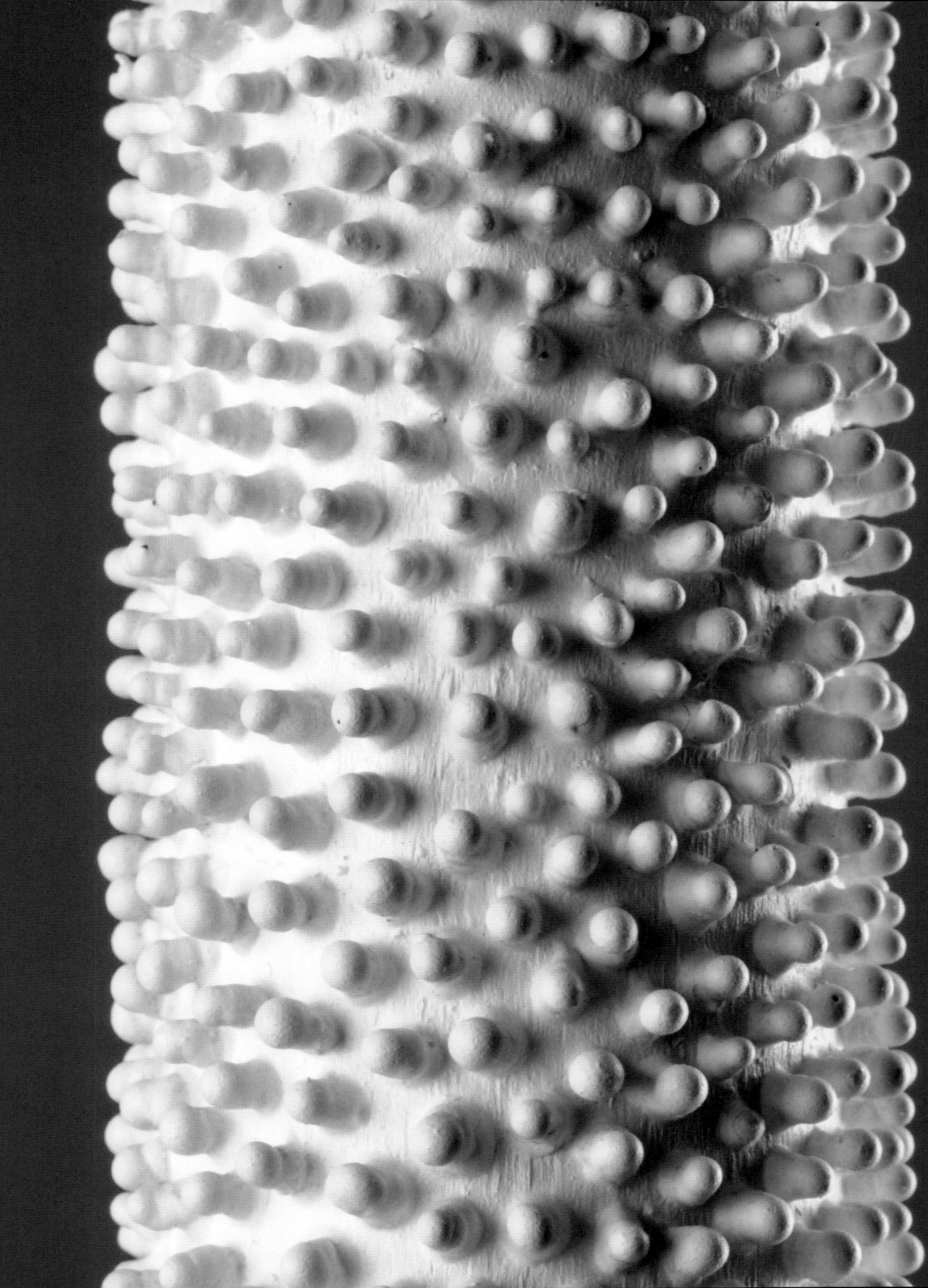

Klaus Staudt
1932 Otterndorf, Niederelbe – lives and works in Frankfurt am Main

Wood, emulsion paint
Titled, signed, and dated on verso:
Kreisformation II / Klaus Staudt 1965
Diameter: 60 cm

Inv. Nr. P242M
Acquired 2013

41 Klaus Staudt
Kreisformation II
1965

Klaus Staudt's *Kreisformation* (Circular Formation) looks at first sight as if countless circular yellow cylinders had been randomly scattered on a round, white picture plane. This impression leads to a lively, almost cheerful sensation that prevails even on closer, systematic study of the work. The latter reveals that the cylinders, all cut off at an angle, consist of four different sizes and diameters. The cadmium yellow also shows four different levels of brightness. In addition, equidistant, concentric circles determine the arrangement of the cylinders. However, this pattern is not easily legible since the distribution of the cylinders on the picture plane—their size, their mutual intervals, and the direction of their slanted ends—is governed not by objective, mathematical laws but by subjective, sensual decisions, which precludes formal rigidity.

The density of the yellow cylinders in *Kreisformation II* varies, leading to site-dependent variations in light and shadow—two phenomena of great significance for Staudt, despite his love of Constructivist sculptural design. He combines material and immateriality just as he does objectivity and subjectivity or regularity and irregularity. Light and shadow, subtly modulated by form and colour, in particular white and shades of yellow, dematerialize the tangible composition and transcend the immanent.

Klaus Staudt, whose oeuvre as a whole is indebted to the inspiration of the classic Modernist movement Constructivism, above all to Piet Mondrian, as well as Albers, Vasarely, and Nicholson, has always shown a preference for the relief, that Janus-headed genre between plane and space, between picture and sculpture. This enables him to "confess" that he also paints "with sculptural structures that capture light." But no matter how Staudt chooses to work with light and shadow, plane and space, form and colour, in other words with elementary visual parameters, he never does so for their sake alone but above all as a challenge to hone our perception. Indeed, highly focused visual study and thought are indispensable to understanding Klaus Staudt's art. Only then can these works function as instruments of insight; only then are they a genesis and not a product. And, for Staudt, this applies to art in general.
UW

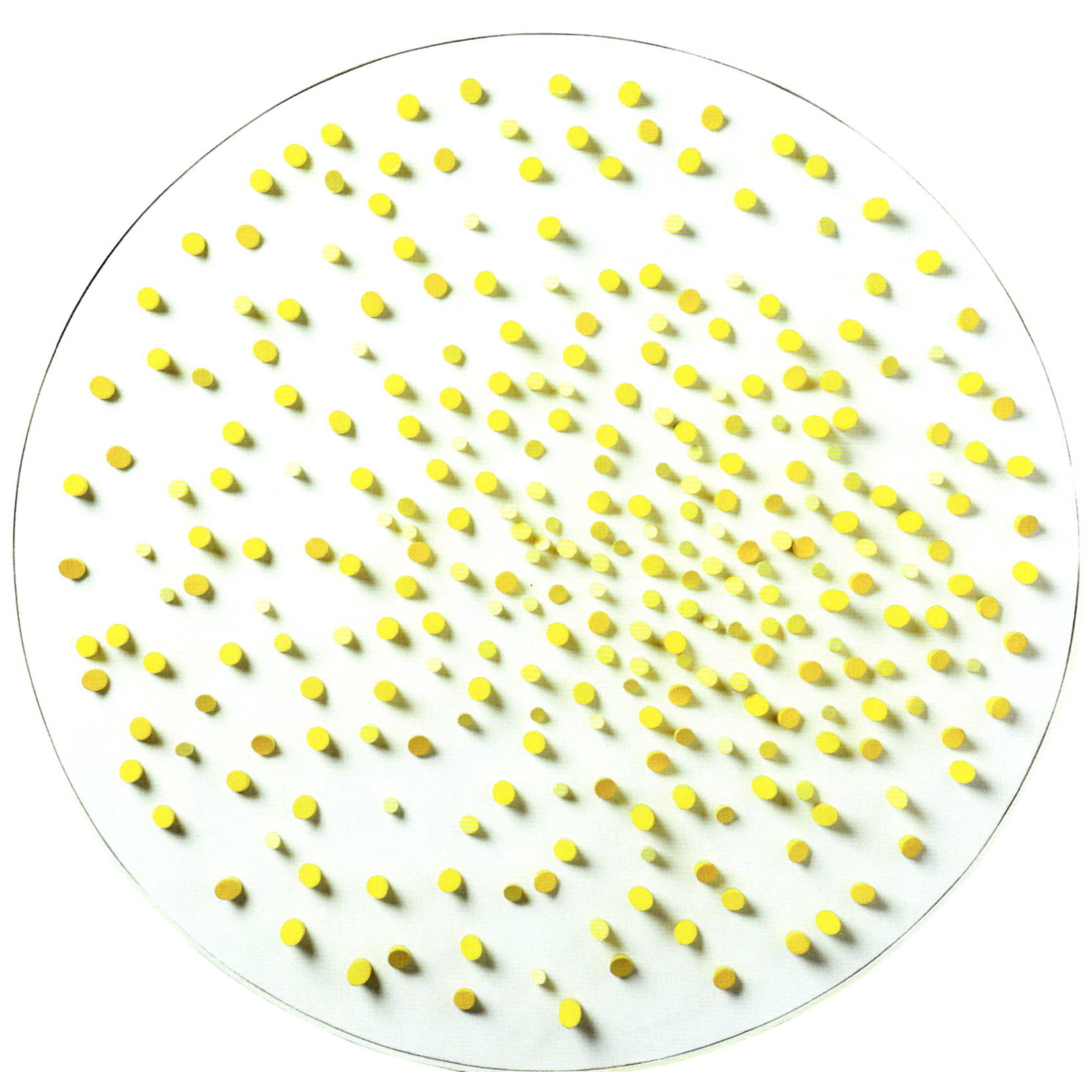

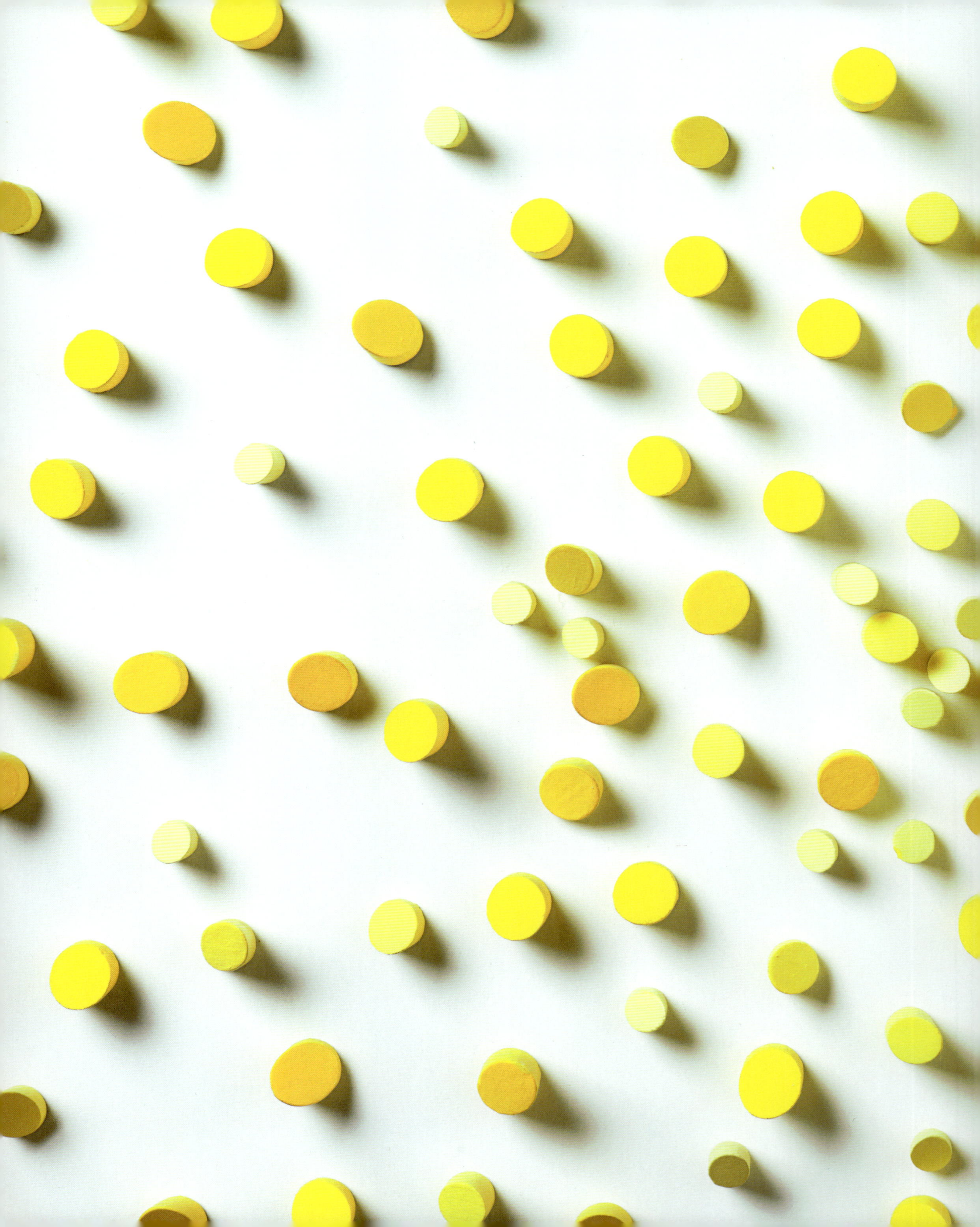

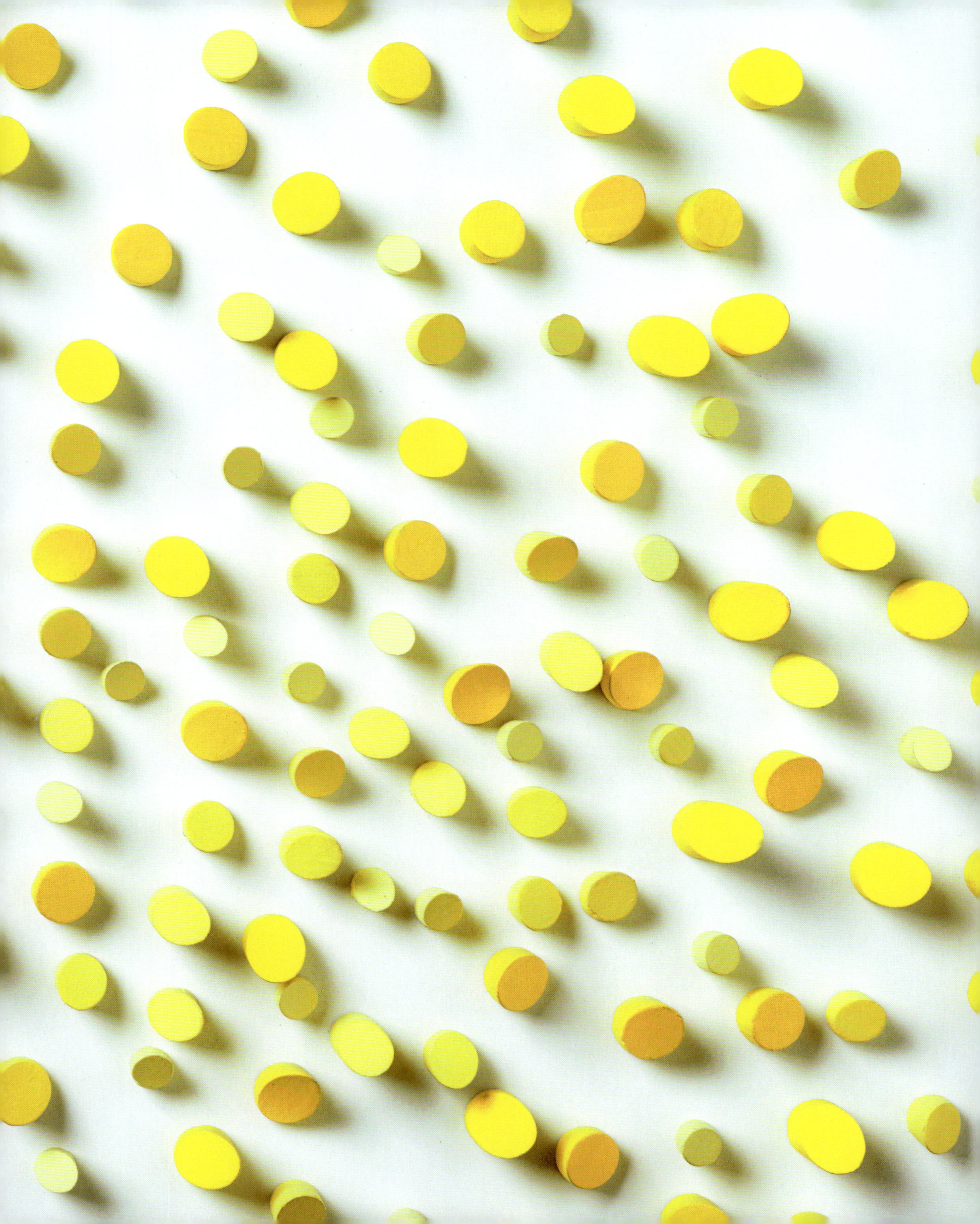

Günther Uecker
1930 Wendorf, Mecklenburg – lives and works in Düsseldorf

Nails, paint, canvas on plywood
Signed, dated, and titled on verso:
Uecker 67 / Großes Feld
175.2 × 175.2 cm

Inv. no.: P154M
Acquired 2004

42 Günther Uecker
Grosses Feld
1967

Uecker made his first nail picture in 1957. Since then reception of his oeuvre has often shown a one-sided bias for interpreting his work in terms of this per se non-artistic item of the ordinary working world. However, the implications of Uecker's oeuvre are wider, for he is among those who experienced the catastrophes of the Second World War as a teenager. He wanted to find a fundamentally new beginning for art beyond Art Informel and Realism, beyond self-perception, incitement, and propaganda. On moving from East Berlin to Düsseldorf in 1955, he met two like-minded spirits, Otto Piene and Heinz Mack, or as Piene wrote, "artists with similar ideas". Calling themselves ZERO, the group promulgated an open and free concept of art not only in Germany but all over Europe (Dieter Honisch). For them, ZERO was an "incommensurable zone in which the old state turns into the new".

Although Uecker did not officially join the group until 1961, his works from the early ZERO years 1957–58 categorically eschewed all forms of traditional painting. As a rule, the works consisted of canvases, painted white and mounted on wood, into which the artist hammered nails, resulting in structures that range from impulsive, uncontrolled orders to geometric ones. The act of aggression (hammering) reveals the processual nature involved in making the work and the consequent violation of the canvas. This form of action is crucial to Uecker's art. He made repeated incursions into real life by hammering nails into tables, chairs, a piano, and a television set. He would attack what he called the "cultural fetishes" of life until they looked as if their hair were standing on end, thereby putting them up for debate and undermining them as items of consumption.

Uecker made *Grosses Feld* (Large Field, 1967) the year after ZERO mounted their last exhibition in October 1966. It is a classical work heralding the end of ZERO. Hundreds of irregularly spaced white nails, hammered into the surface, form gentle undulations. They are, as Uecker once said, "the extension of a point in space". Depending on vantage point and lighting, they cast different and delicate shadows, lending the whole a silent poetry. Their arrangement on the picture plane generates an impression of potential mobility. The structure looks like magnetic field lines but it might also be compared to a field of stubble or of sprouting seeds. To quote Piene again, the ZERO artists aimed "to reharmonise the relationship between man and nature … for the artist is not a fugitive from the 'modern world', not at all, but instead makes use of new technical means as well as the forces of nature." AS

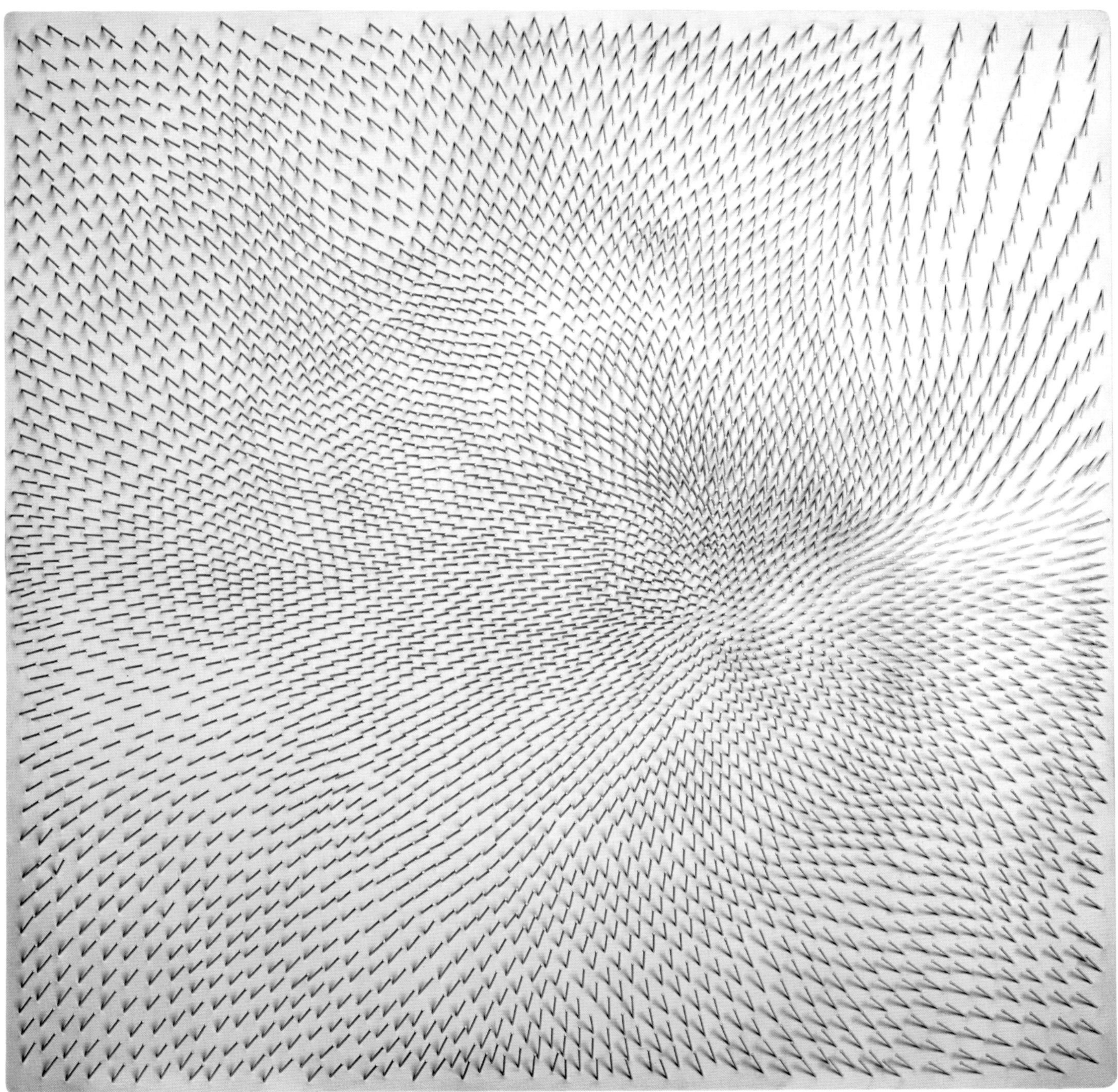

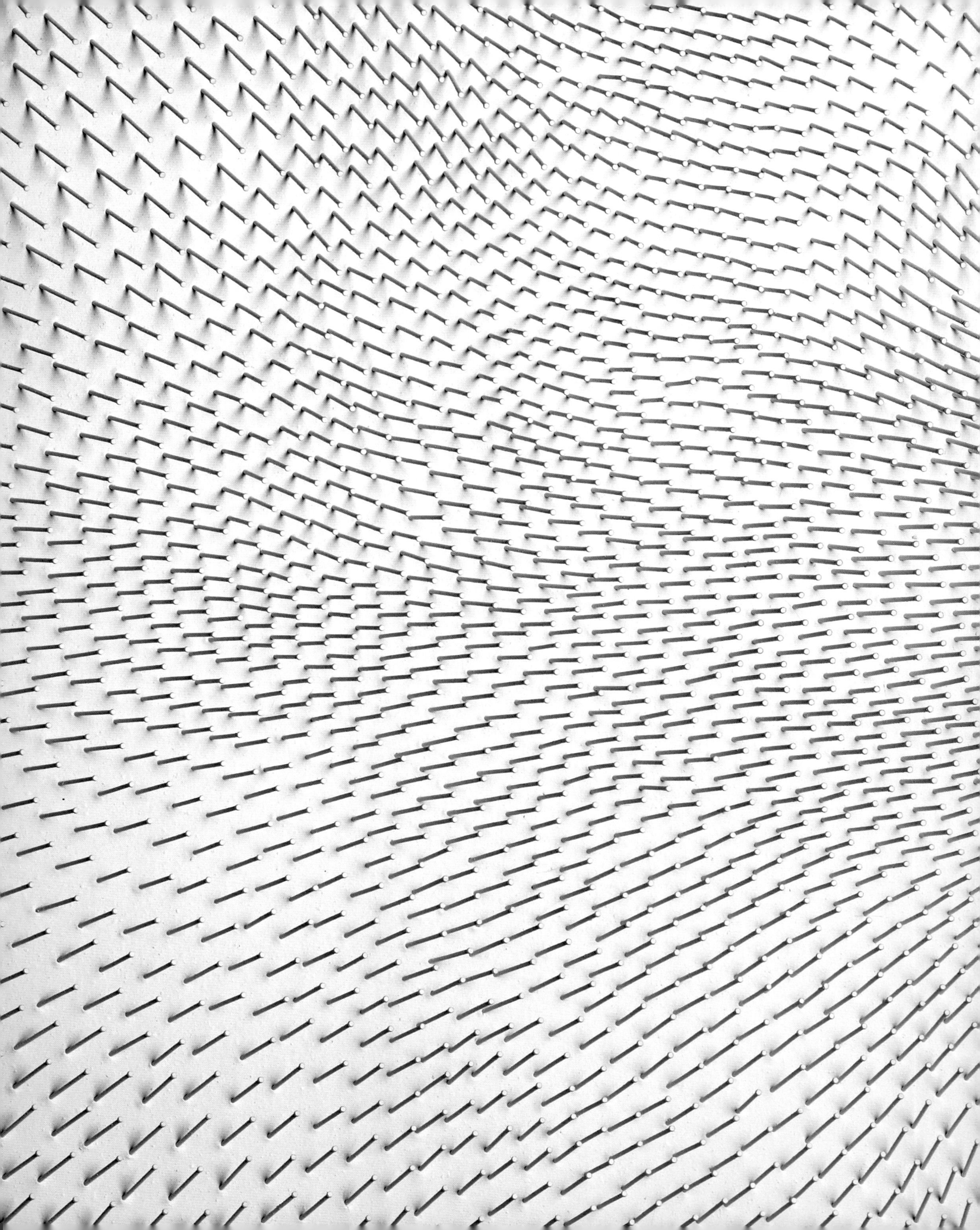

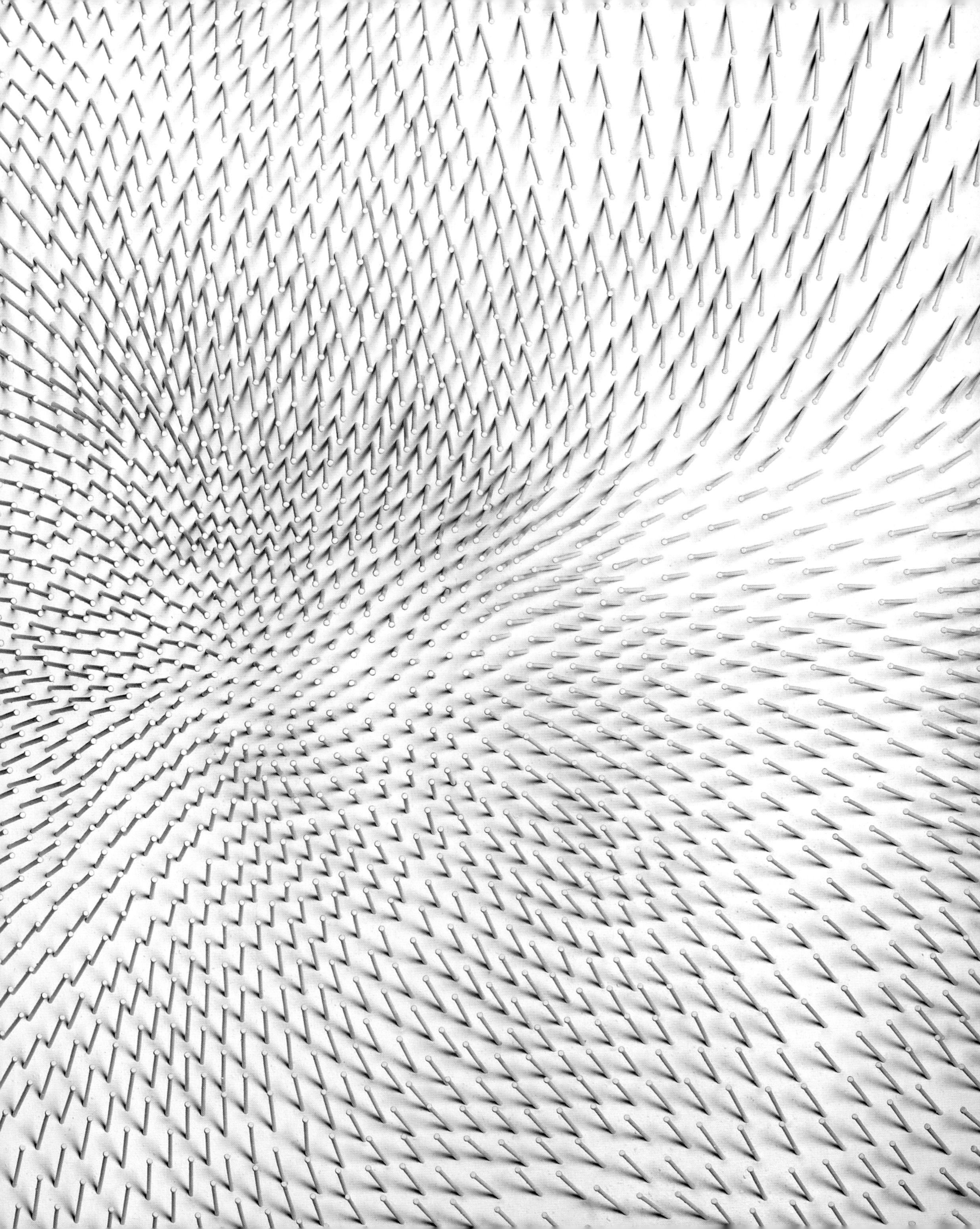

Gotthard Graubner
1930 Erlbach – 2013 Neuss

Foam cushion on canvas,
covered with Perlon and painted
Signed, dated, and numbered on verso:
Gotth. Graubner / 68 / "lichter körper"
100 × 100 cm

Inv. no.: P191M
Acquired 2008

43 Gotthard Graubner
Lichter Körper
1968

Gotthard Graubner's artistic interests were focused primarily on organic life processes. When he did take note of subject matter, for instance, of a tree or a human figure, his attention was not directed primarily toward contour or shape but rather toward the sense of movement and space that emanates from within the organism. This is verified by his own statements, for instance, that we cannot apprehend a tree unless we begin with the roots; or, it is not the shape of a tree but rather its growth that is of significance. Growth as such is, of course, invisible and therefore beyond representation. Nonetheless, it does find a correspondence in the artistic process where it can be traced sensually and conceptually in each and every work. Graubner's remarks and emphasis on becoming rather than being reflect the genetic nature of his perception or, to put it differently, he is motivated by an interest in probing the origins of organic life from inside out.

Graubner's choice of materials such as paper and cardboard, taffeta and nylon, sponge and cotton, fleece and canvas, pigment and binder reveals the perception of the organic life that he sought to render in his art. His investigations led to watercolours and gouaches, to his "cushion paintings" and "paint bodies" as well as the "colour-space bodies" that he made from the early 1970s until his death, giving physically tangible, visual shape, through abstraction and reduction, to his understanding of organic nature and especially the human body.

Lichter Körper (Luminous Body), a tenuously physical visual object that might be described as a cell, visible under a protective membrane, is seen against the background of the barely visible bipolar aura that it has itself generated as if to indicate the division of a still compact "cell body" and, hence, of growth. Light, which might be said to be the primary cause of this growth, weaves in and out of the membrane which is as vulnerable as it is protective, producing on and beyond its surface gradations of white so fragile and delicate that they fade into immateriality.
UW

Imi Knoebel
1940 Dessau – lives and works in Düsseldorf

Dispersion on linen on fibreboard
Signed, titled, and dated on verso:
IMI W KNOEBEL / FIG. 11 / 29 JUNI 68
160.2 × 130.2 cm

Inv. no.: P231M
Acquired 2011

44 Imi Knoebel
Untitled (119 Linien / 11 mm Abstand)
1968

From 1966 to 1968, even before completing his studies at the Düsseldorf Academy with Joseph Beuys, Imi Knoebel produced a series of ninety *Linienbilder* (Line Paintings), initiating an oeuvre that would prove to be entirely different from that of his teacher. The series includes eleven portrait-format white paintings with vertical black lines at intervals ranging from twenty to ten millimetres. Knoebel used a ruling pen, drawing the lines with great precision on white primed linen mounted on fibreboard. The number of lines increases at uneven intervals from 65 to 130. Nine other paintings are related to this suite: not only do they show a steady, similarly irregular increase in the number of lines but also an increase in width, from 0.2 to 1.0 centimetres. This means that the paintings become darker and darker until they appear to be black paintings with white lines. Only in their totality can we perceive the serial logic of these twenty almost equally sized *Linienbilder*.

However, even individually, they reveal the central issue that has motivated Knoebel from the beginning of his artistic career: the validity of elementary forms of composition in relation to geometry. Knoebel also shared the larger visual concerns that propelled artistic discourse in the 1960s: inquiry into the function and content of pictures in general. It seemed as if Kazimir Malevich had already found the absolute answer in 1915 when he painted his black square on a white ground, a work that seminally influenced Knoebel. Liberated from any reference to nature, it offered the experience of pure nonobjectivity. This icon of Modernism was a cornerstone of geometric abstraction in the fine arts—and of Imi Knoebel's oeuvre as well. But the purity and rigour of his black and white *Linienbilder* did not share the pathos of the philosophy championed by the pioneers of classic Modernism; they were rather a means of seeking a possible beginning. And indeed, this beginning, that is, the meticulous, handcrafted drawing of lines on the surface of a traditional rectangular painting, proved to be viable.

A look at Knoebel's entire oeuvre up to the present day clearly indicates that he exploited the universal vocabulary of geometry. However, in contrast to Malevich and Mondrian, the trailblazers of geometric abstraction, Knoebel's works oscillate between analysis and synthesis, between gravity and irony, between production and playfulness, so much so that it is not only impossible to contain them within a formal dogmatic; they go still further by allowing for open-ended inquiry into the aesthetic and substantial meaning of a picture as picture and therefore also of art as art. UW

Jan Schoonhoven
1914 Delft – 1994 Delft

Wood, pasteboard, paper, latex
Signed, dated, and inscribed on verso:
Jan Schoonhoven / 23 VII ,72 /
Delft. / "R72-25"
156 × 156 cm

Inv. no.: P202M
Acquired 2008

45 Jan Schoonhoven
R 72–25
1972

Schoonhoven's white reliefs first attracted international attention about the same time that he founded NUL (the Dutch counterpart to ZERO) with Armando, Jan Hendrikse, and Henk Peters in 1960. Schoonhoven, who worked for the Dutch post office from 1946 until he retired in 1979, was forty-six years old at the time. After studying at the Royal Academy of Fine Arts in The Hague from 1930 to 1934, he devoted himself almost exclusively to the medium of drawing, creating a sophisticated and subtle body of work. Influenced, among other things, by studying the structural aspects of Paul Klee's art, it would form the basis of his serial reliefs. Geometric structures as well as sequences and the repetition of identical but modified forms would become a crucial feature of Schoonhoven's drawings and reliefs.

R 72-25 (1972) belongs to the artist's mature work, created between 1960 and 1979, a phase characterized by a compelling harmony, balance and traction of verticals and horizontals, of single forms and overall composition. Like many of the other works that he made at this time, *R 72-25* is a relatively large square, measuring 156 by 156 centimetres. A precisely calculated order of 10 by 10 smaller units, each a tenth of the whole, that is 15.6 by 15.6 centimetres, yields a perfectly symmetrical composition. Each of these units is, in turn, subdivided, the "flaps" alternately leaning in opposite directions. Despite the clarity of structure, a labyrinthine impression results, which disrupts the harmony of the whole.

As in most of his work, Schoonhoven used pasteboard (or papier-mâché), which he covered with paper and painted white. Pasteboard is an ordinary, unspectacular material that ensures neutrality. Slight imperfections in the application of the paint and minimal inaccuracies at the seams testify to the artist's personal "signature". As Schoonhoven explains in an interview of 1985, "when I have a rectangle and paste it like that and make a relief out of it, then it should be a little poetic—I think. So that it comes to life. Otherwise I could have a factory make the work." The white plane, broken by the movement of the flaps, provides an ideal space for the reflection of light and the sensitive shadows that sometimes seem to sink into the darkness. Despite the unsettling effect of the overall composition, the impression that the elements are the same dominates. As art historian Beat Wismer observed in 1995, "The serial order of identical, but individually made units undoubtedly corresponds to an ethical and political conviction that sameness is the ultimate, existential requisite of individual freedom and individuality."
AS

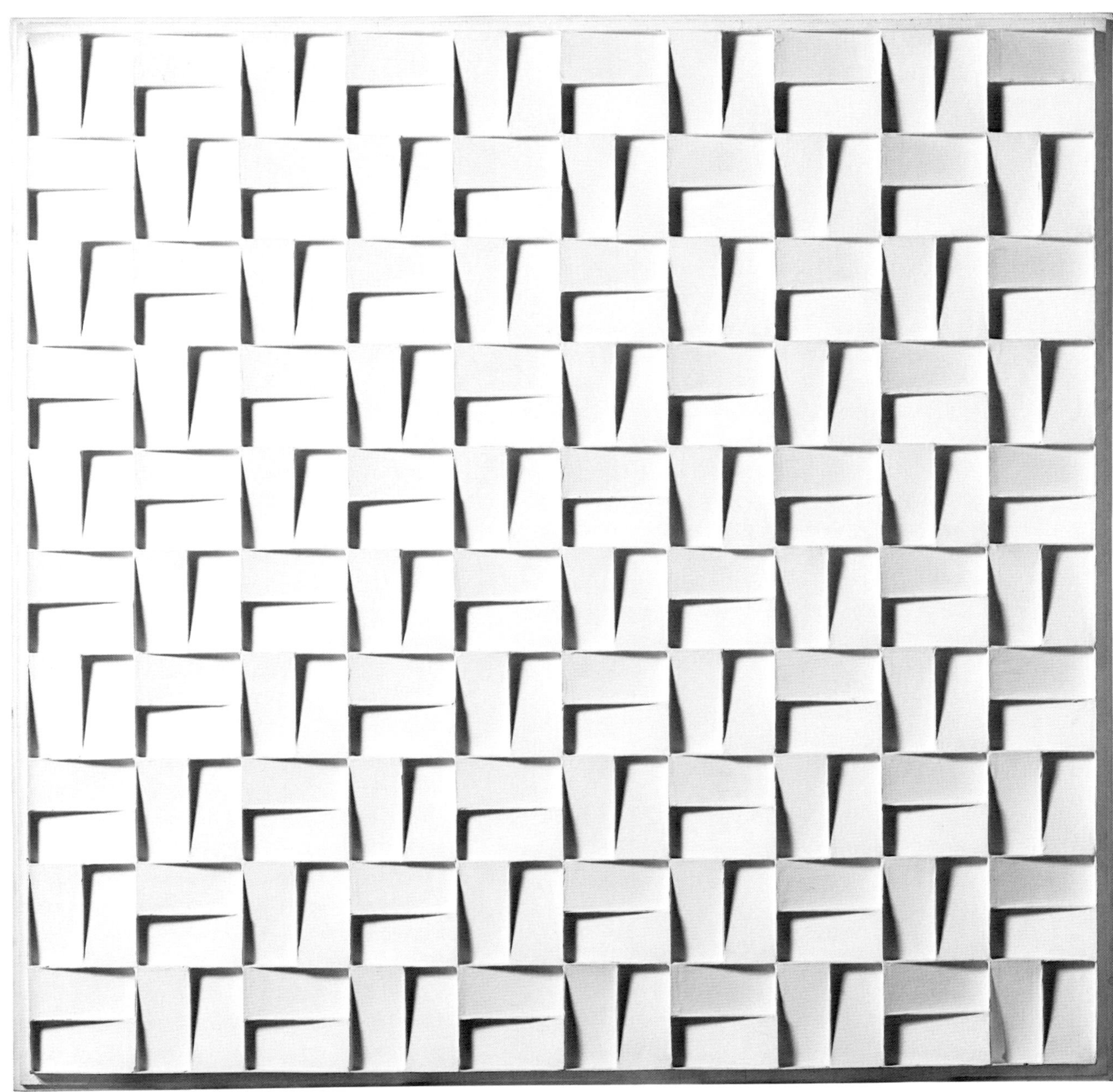

Günter Fruhtrunk
1923 Munich – 1982 Munich

Acrylic on canvas
Signed and initialled on verso:
FRUHTRUNK / PARIS, (monogram)
140 × 148.5 cm

Inv. no.: P190M
Acquired 2008

46 Günter Fruhtrunk
Diagonale Progression Schwarz–Weiss (Studie II)
c. 1970

With the exception of a few late works, Fruhtrunk's paintings feature great constructive clarity and vitality. They reveal the artist's admiration of Kazimir Malevich, to whom he paid homage by dedicating a painting to him in 1954, and of Fernand Léger, in whose studio he worked in 1952. In contrast to the then dominant movement of Tachism with its "ego outpourings", Fruhtrunk remarked how gratifying it was to note that his long-term friend Hans Arp and Léger both subordinate the ego to the task at hand namely, a reason-oriented emphasis on making a good piece of art. These were the underpinnings of the oeuvre that emerged thanks to grants from Baden-Württemberg and the French government, which enabled Fruhtrunk to go to Paris.

By 1963, the self-imposed formal and tectonic parameters of Fruhtrunk's painting, which the artist had already detailed in a letter to Max Bill in 1958, had become closely associated with the desire to lend increasingly dense rhythm to his compositions exclusively by painting vertical, horizontal, and diagonal bands of colour. Irregular modifications of rhythm, direction, length, and width of these bands as well as shifts or "cuts" governed only by visual and not by mathematical considerations, which challenge viewers' sensual perception and interpretive thoughts—a process clearly illustrated in the painting *Diagonale Progression Schwarz-Weiss* (Diagonal Progression Black-White). The dynamics of the diagonal structure in black and white do not come to rest within the framework of a square but acquire an additional thrust through the slight horizontal elongation of the format. The up-and-down of the diagonals prevent the gaze from coming to rest and do not gratify the attempt to distinguish between figure and ground. The intensity of the contrast between black and white is moreover disconcertingly heightened by the narrow marginal strips of blue and violet. However, this is not about the superficial stimulus of the retina in the sense of Op Art of the 1950s and 1960s, nor about the uncommitted playfulness of non-objective forms in Concrete Art, which dates back to the 1930s. Instead, Fruhtrunk wanted to find means of intensifying visual experience and, with it, the experience of human existence. As he saw it, painting was an indispensable means of counteracting increasing mechanization of thoughts and feelings. UW

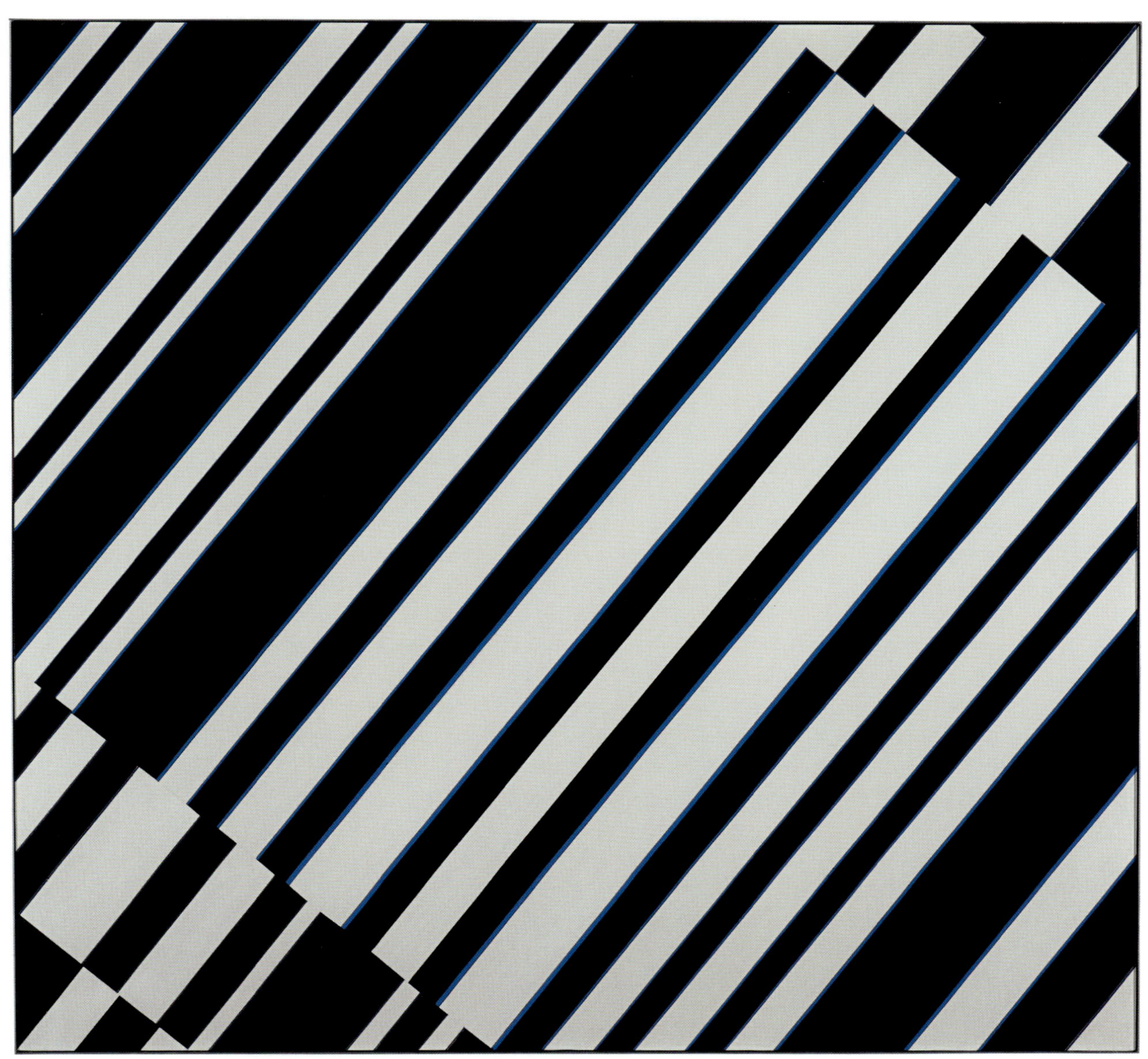

Gottfried Honegger
1917 Zurich – lives and works in Zurich

Oil, acrylic, board on canvas
Signed and dated on verso:
HONEGGER 1979 / Z.825.1
200 × 250 cm

Inv. no.: P211M
Acquired 2009

47 Gottfried Honegger
Tableau-Relief
1979

Honegger's *Tableaux Reliefs* are prefigured in the small-format, lyrical works that he painted prior to 1957—abstract patterns of folds and cells that are still derived from natural shapes and that seem to be tangibly set off from the ground of the painting. Honegger translated them into rectangular or square modules of cardboard, which he applied to the canvas, thereby taking a step from illusion to reality, from abstract to concrete nonfiguration. His "concrete" work, like that of his Zurich friends Max Bill, Richard Paul Lohse and Camille Graeser is not without precedent; it is indebted to Kazimir Malevich, Piet Mondrian, and above all Theo van Doesburg, who introduced the term "concrete art" back in 1930. Max Bill later elaborated on the concept of concrete art, defining it as "those works of art that have been made on the basis of their own intrinsic means and laws without any external reference to natural appearances, in other words, not through abstraction."

Honegger spent two years in New York from 1958 to 1960, during which time he consolidated the path he had chosen to take. A successful exhibition at Martha Jackson Gallery, where he showed only red *Reliefs,* led him to give up his livelihood as a commercial artist and devote himself exclusively to fine art. Upon his return to Europe, he took inspiration from the burgeoning American art scene and painted monochrome works in medium, large, and even outsized formats, which resulted in his long-term series of *Tableaux Reliefs*.

As in all the works of this type, the strict grid of almost square cardboard modules in *Tableau Relief* (Z.825.1) shows slight irregularities and a haptic sensual quality because of the blurred relief of the adjoining edges. These accidental characteristics, generated by the properties of the material and their manual processing, are extremely welcome to the artist because purely "geometrically determined art" as practiced by the concrete artists from Zurich is, as he says, ultimately alien to his soul. But what really and essentially distinguishes Honegger's oeuvre from a rigid geometry based on scale and number is the monochrome painting, the appreciation of every single colour as colour—whether it is a warm yellow that embraces the entire picture plane or any other colour–presented as a sensual phenomenon and for its own sake alone. UW

Verena Loewensberg
1912 Zurich – 1986 Zurich

Oil on canvas
Signed and dated on verso, on stretcher and on canvas: Loewensberg 84/85
100 × 100 cm

Inv. no.: P248M
Acquired 2013

48 Verena Loewensberg
Untitled
1984–85

From the beginning, Verena Loewensberg always felt especially at ease with what she called the language of geometry. Commuting between Zurich and Paris, she made the acquaintance of Max Bill and Georges Vantongerloo, who were an important force in her career. Although she was later linked to the circle of so-called Zurich Concrete artists, including Max Bill as well as Camille Graeser, Richard Paul Lohse, and others, Loewensberg felt that the term "concrete" as defined by Theo van Doesburg in 1930, did not really apply to her work; she preferred the term "constructive". Even then, the constructive idiom, in her case, always led to a geometry inspired by mood, which was accordingly informed with an emotional accent.

The *Zweifarbigen Bilder* (Paintings in Two Colours), a series of twenty-six paintings created between 1983 and 1986, in other words at the end of her life, may well be considered her artistic legacy. The series not only links two distinct visual ideas, defined at an early stage—the staggered rectangle and the dialogue between two colours—but also shows a clarity, an almost floating serenity of form and an exceptional subtlety in the choice of colour, testifying to years of artistic endeavour and experience.

The twenty-six works, all measuring 100 by 100 centimetres, consist of a monochrome shape set off against a monochrome ground in a different colour. Their almost square shape has multiple right-angled edges. The artist always made a small-format study on graph paper, which she then transferred to scale on a primed canvas. Without the help of tape, she then painted the shape and ground with great precision, colour by colour, layer by layer, until she had achieved a homogeneous picture plane, whose quality and texture are indebted as much to the painting technique as they are to the oil binder. None of the shapes in the twenty-six pictures is identical; they are marked by subtle variations in outline through the number, position, and depth of the angles, while the dialogue between the colours is based on combinations that range from clearly contrasting to subtly differentiated. Their selection is not a product of theory but inspired exclusively by sensual perception, a factor that enhances the great appeal and value of the series even more.

Whether studied singly or as a whole, appreciation of the works is a matter of great concentration, ultimately becoming a question of meditation. Crossing boundaries is conceivable—from the immanent world of concrete shape and colour to a transcendental place of sublime weightlessness. UW

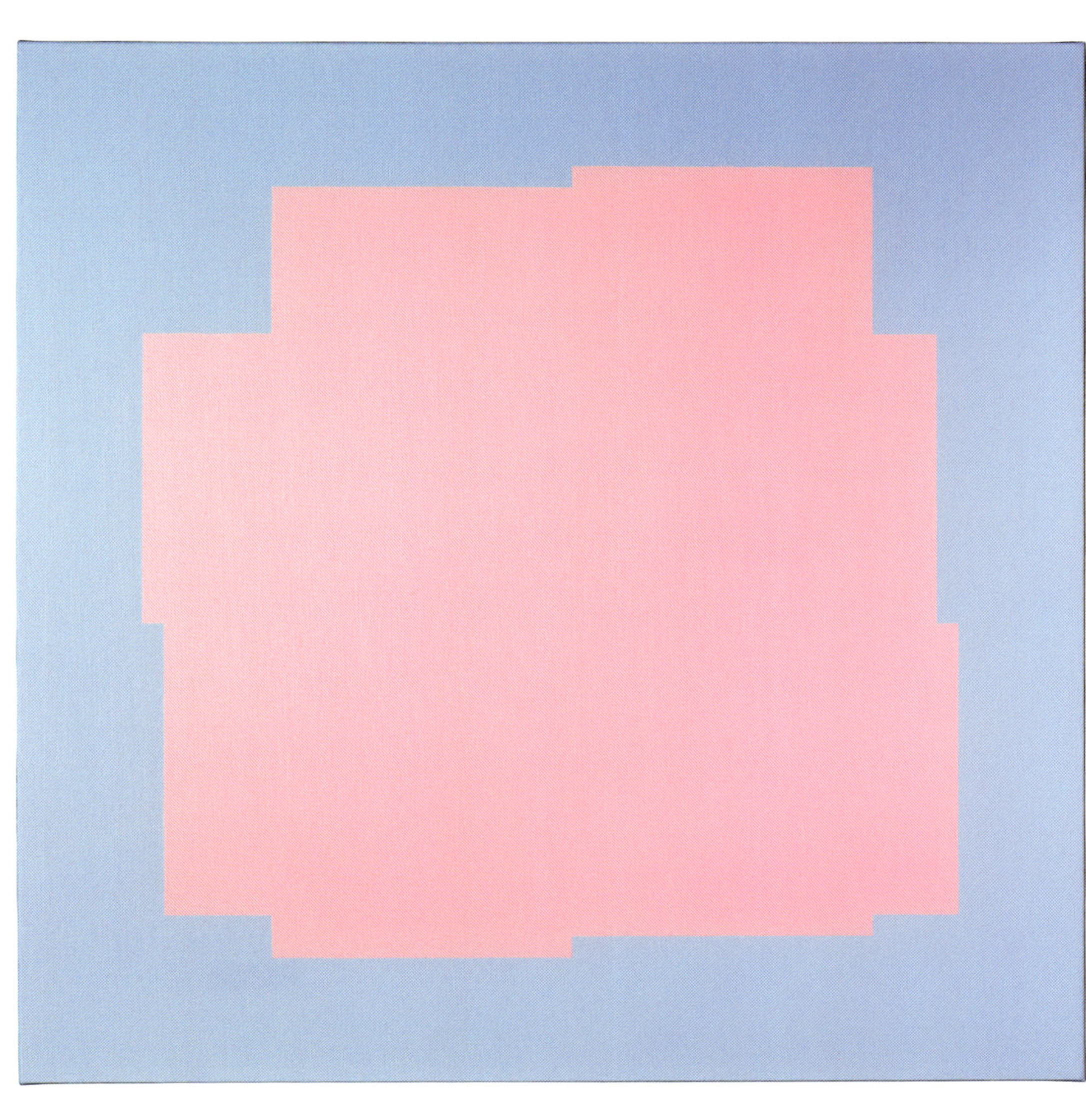

Verena Loewensberg
1912 Zurich – 1986 Zurich

Oil on canvas
100 × 100 cm

Inv. no.: P249M
Acquired 2013

49 Verena Loewensberg
Untitled
1985

This painting, listed in Elisabeth Grossmann's catalogue raisonné as number 632, is the last work Verena Loewensberg made before she died. Like all of her works, it is untitled since she wanted to ensure viewers a maximum freedom of perception and thought. UW

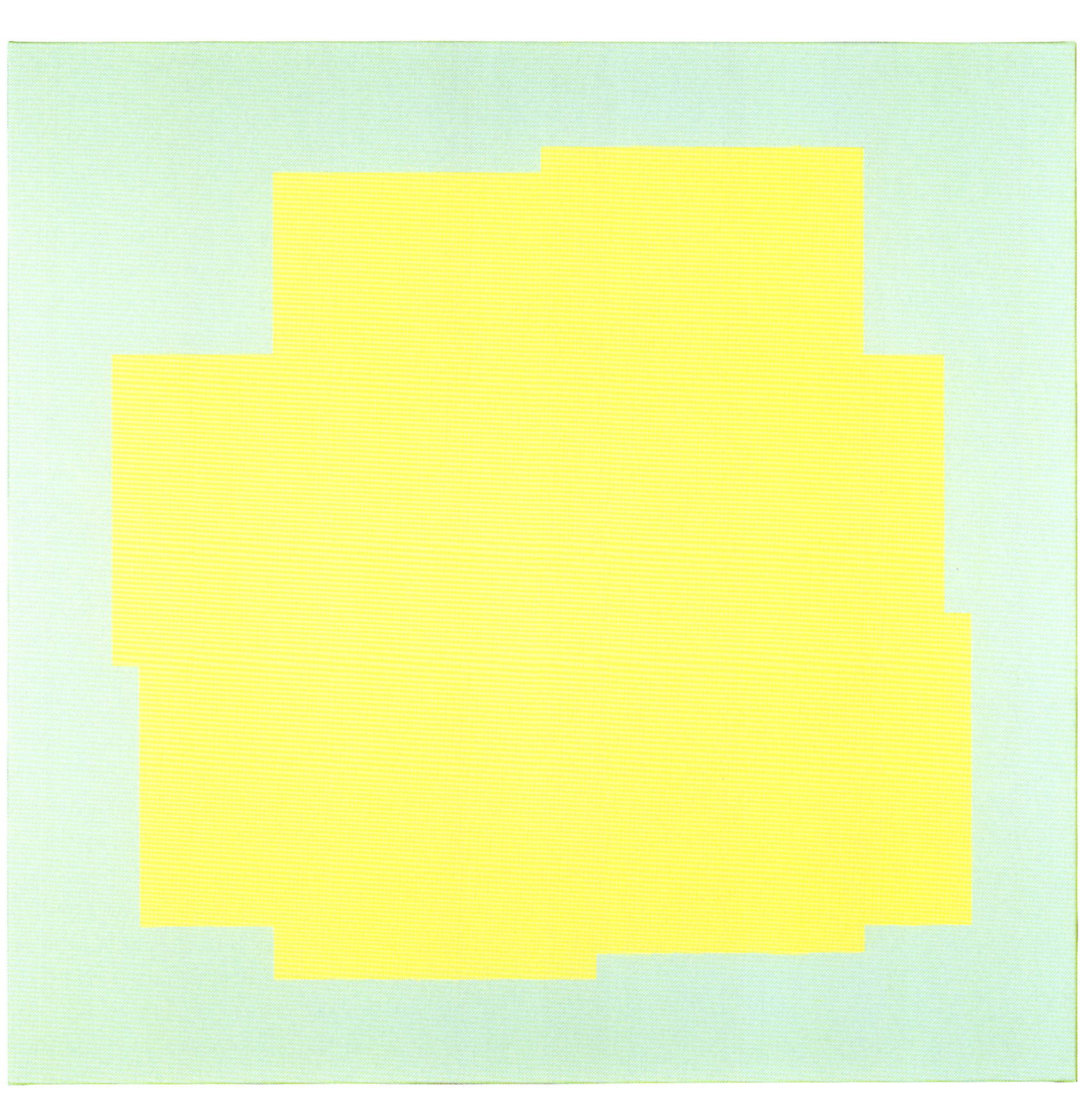

Imi Knoebel
1940 Dessau – lives and works in Düsseldorf

Lacquer on fibreboard
Signed and dated: IMI 90
209.5 × 150 cm

Inv. no.: P229M
Acquired 2011

50 Imi Knoebel
Untitled (Schwarzes Bild no. 9 [von 24], Schlachtenbild)
1990

Although deeply valuing the visual idiom of Malevich and Mondrian, Knoebel has consistently reacted to the geometric rigour of substance and form advanced by the two great representatives of classic Modernism with an undogmatic, playfully creative attitude. At times, he jettisons the geometric syntax altogether, subjecting his paintings to intense gestural treatment not only with paintbrush and paint but also with a variety of tools that violate the picture plane. This clearly applies to the *Schwarze Bilder* (*Schlachtenbilder*) [Black Paintings (Battle Paintings)] but is already prefigured in earlier works such as the *Drachenzeichnungen* (Kite Drawings, 1980–81) and the series *Im Sommer 84* (In Summer 84, 1984). The latter emerged under the influence of extremely rainy weather in France, in other words, under the impression of an elemental experience of nature, transferred by analogy to the picture plane, with the fibreboard not only showing the gestural treatment of paint but already sculpturally scratched and perforated.

In the *Schwarze Bilder* (1990–91), this violent and violating gesture is, as Johannes Stüttgen writes, "dramatically heightened, acquiring a shape of its own". Knoebel gouged, scratched, or cut linear traces of varying width into the picture plane, covering almost the entire surface and even perforating it completely in several places. But the black lacquer with which the artist has coated the panel endows it with great aesthetic nobility despite the coarseness of the damage. Depending on the angle of incidence of the light, the dark surface radiates a lustrous splendour, with flashes of light sparkling in the furrows, grooves, and incisions that occasionally reveal the reddish-brown of the fibreboard.

What appears to be a battle on the picture plane, metaphorically speaking, could also be interpreted as a sensual impression that has erupted on the surface, as in the *Im Sommer 84* series. However, here it seems that the work does not visually render a personal experience, but is rather a gestural event deliberately intended to lend visibility to material, surface, space, and paint per se. Lucio Fontana (cf. cat. 37) already pierced or slashed his canvases in a radical gesture that draws unfiltered attention to the actual components of a painting—its material, surface, and volume. Knoebel's *Schlachtenbilder* do not share the serene elegance of a precisely placed hole or slash; in fact, the vibrancy and energy of his chaotic confusion of lines may be understood as resolute artistic opposition to any kind of formalism.
UW

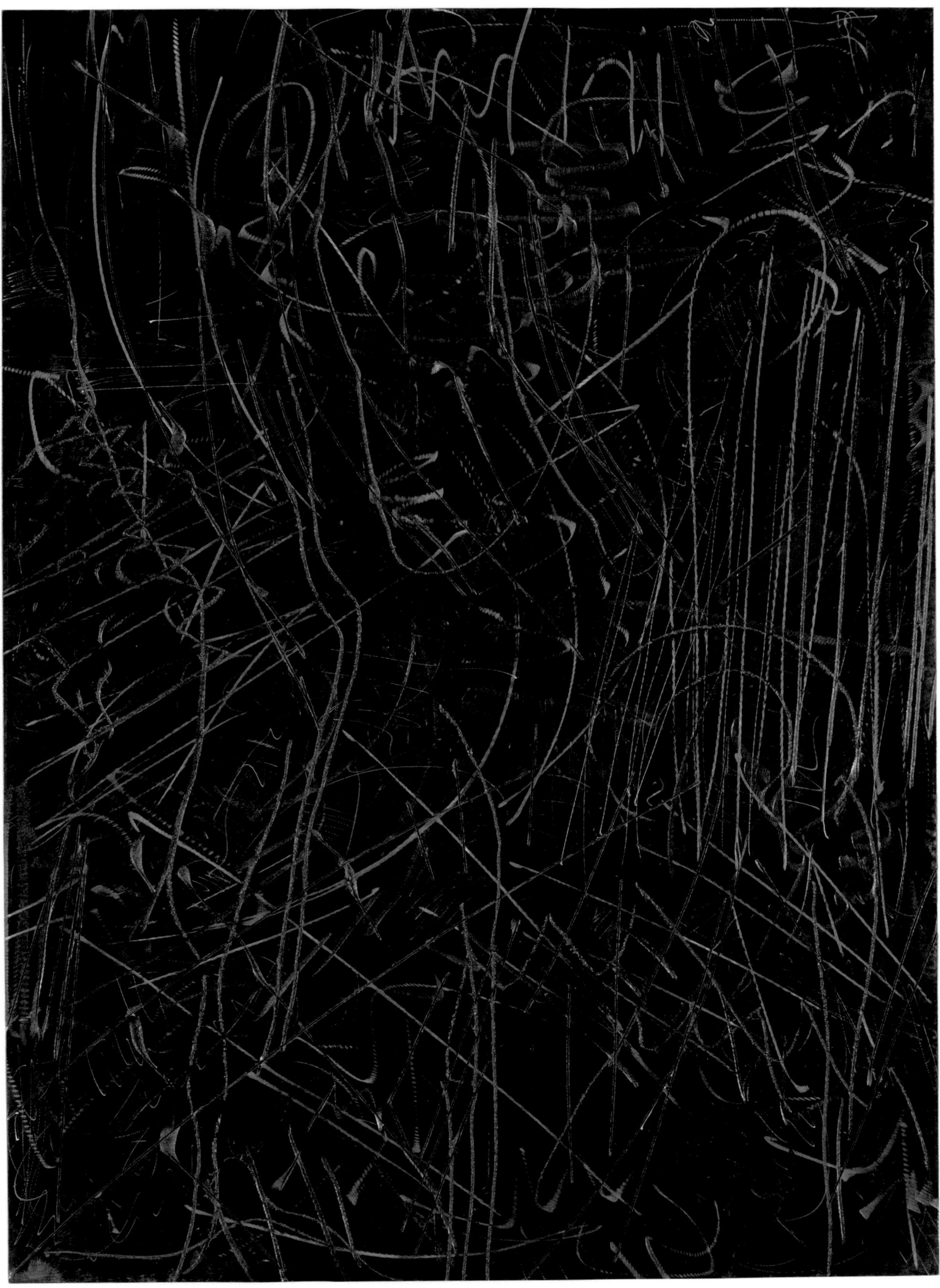

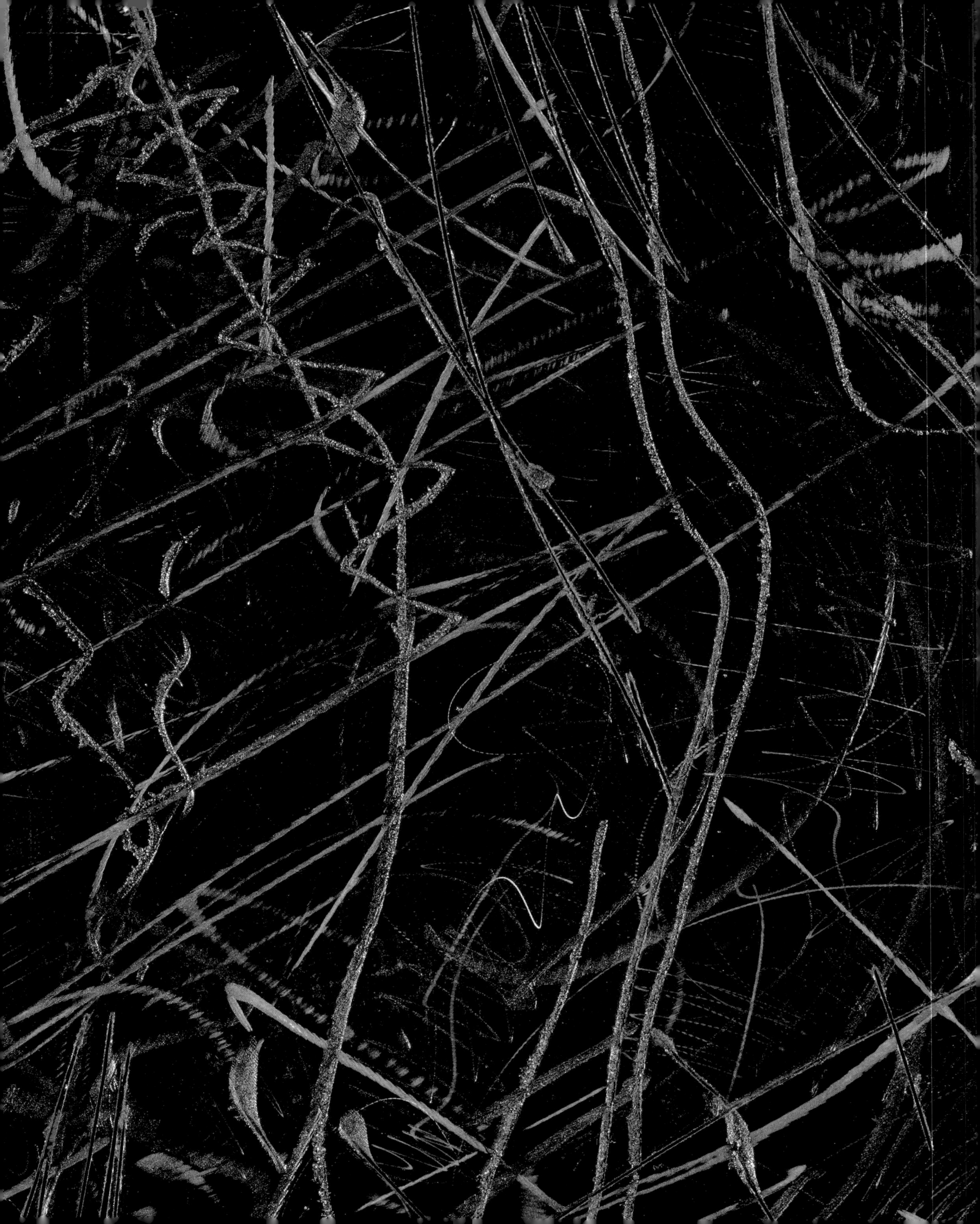

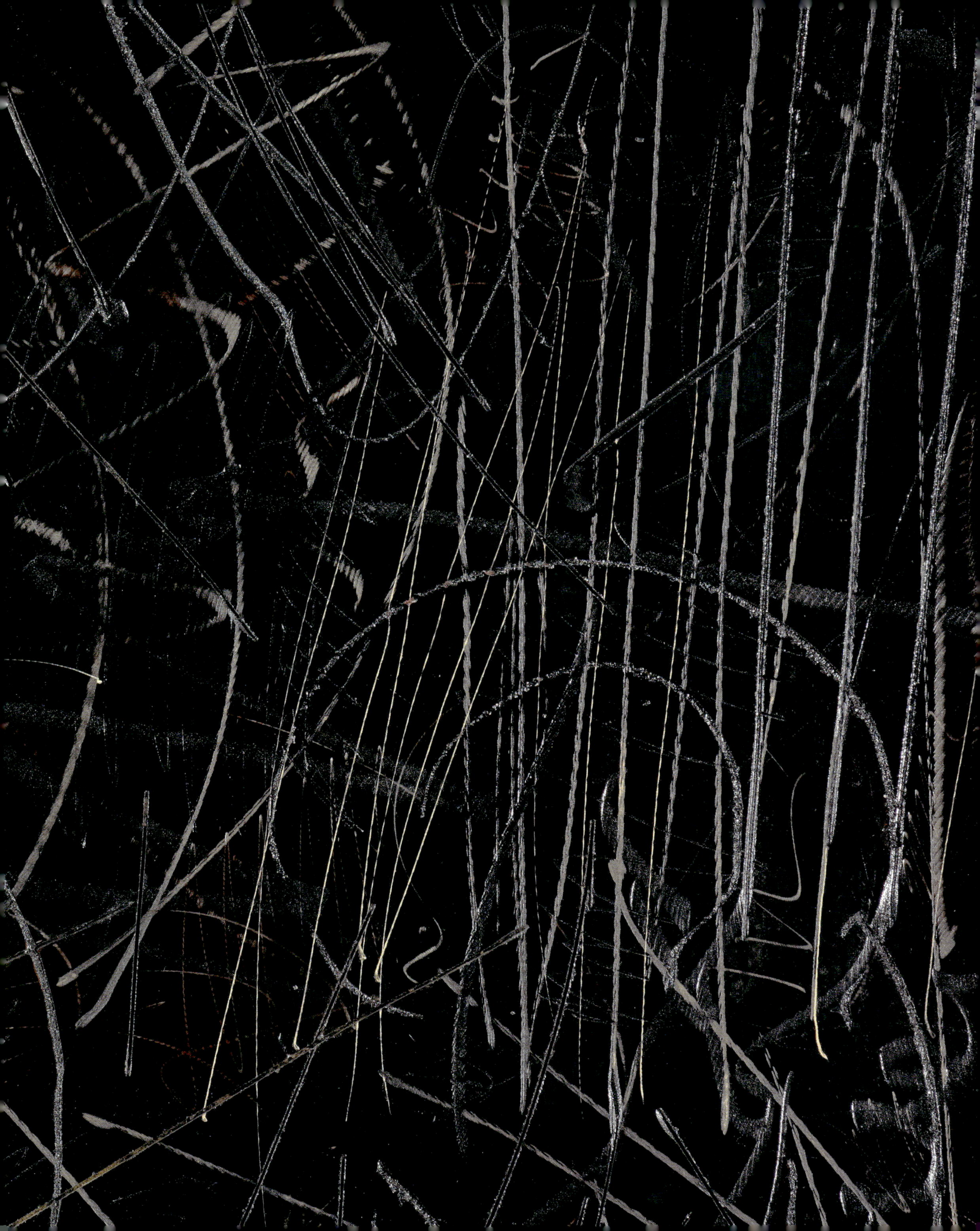

Provenance
Exhibitions
Literature

1

Wilhelm Lehmbruck

Torso der Grossen Stehenden

1910

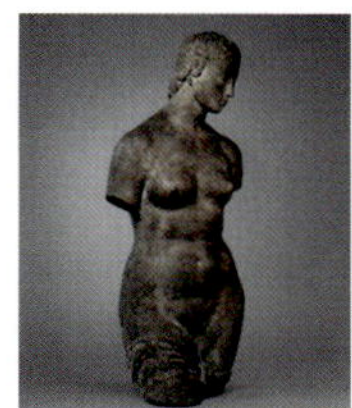

Provenance

Leopold Badt
Kurt Badt and heirs
Christie's, London, 25 June 2001, lot 25
Private collection, Switzerland

Literature

Badt 1920, pp. 169 (fig.), 172
Schubert 2001, p. 57
Schubert 2012, no. 7

2

Ferdinand Hodler

Bildnis Valentine Godé-Darel (La Parisienne I)

1909

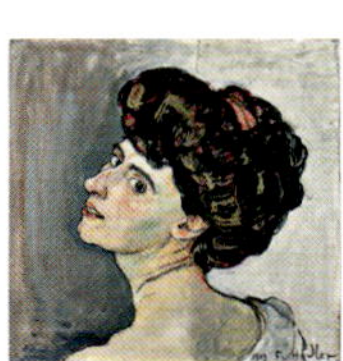

Provenance

Galerie Moos, Geneva
Private collection, Switzerland
Galerie Kornfeld, Bern, 15 June 2012, lot 59

Exhibitions

1910 Interlaken, *II. Internationale Kunst-Ausstellung in Interlaken (Kursaal),* no. 34 (Frauenbildnis)
1918 Geneva, Galerie Moos, *Exposition suisse des beaux-arts,* no. 183
1918 Geneva, Galerie Moos, *Exposition Ferdinand Hodler,* no. 84 (La Parisienne)
1918 Geneva, Galerie Moos, *Salon d'été,* no. 46
1918 Geneva, Galerie Moos, *Expositions. Peinture anglaise moderne. Hodler – Pierre Bertrand et A. Regnier,* no. 164
1919 Geneva, Galerie Moos, *Exposition Pietro Chiesa,* no. 143
1919 Basel, Kunsthalle, *Gedächtnis-ausstellung Ferdinand Hodler,* no. 56
1919 Geneva, Galerie Moos, *Salon d'été. Exposition particulière Alexandre Soldenhoff,* no. 61
1919 Bern, Kunsthalle, *Ferd. Hodler. E. de Fiori. W. Lehmbruck. Herm. Haller. H. Hubacher. E. Morgenthaler,* no. 26
1997 Trubschachen, *15. Gemäldeausstellung Trubschachen. Schweizer Maler von A. Anker bis heute,* Kulturverein, no. 10

Literature

Bloesch 1910, p. 31
Loosli 1919/20, no. 109
Loosli 1921–24, no. 1660
Loosli 1921–24, vol. 3, p. 119
Mühlestein/Schmidt 1942, p. 430
Fischer 1961, p. 9
Vignau-Wilberg 1973, p. 174
Kraft 1984, pp. 308–09
Affentranger-Kirchrath 1994, p. 301
Bätschmann/Brunner/Walter 2012, p. 217, no. 831

3

Raymond Duchamp-Villon

Baudelaire

1911

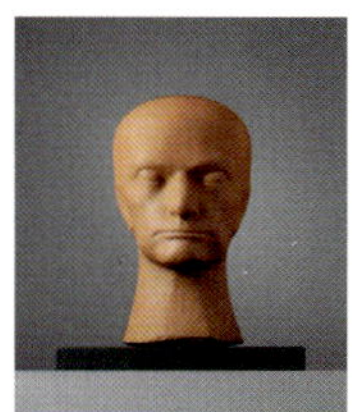

Provenance

Francis Picabia, acquired from the artist c. 1912
Gabriella Buffet-Picabia
Drouot-Richelieu, Paris, 22 November 1996, lot 151b
Private collection, France

Literature

Cabanne 1997
Grandy-Pradel 1998, p. 145

4

Umberto Boccioni

Forme uniche della continuità nello spazio

1913

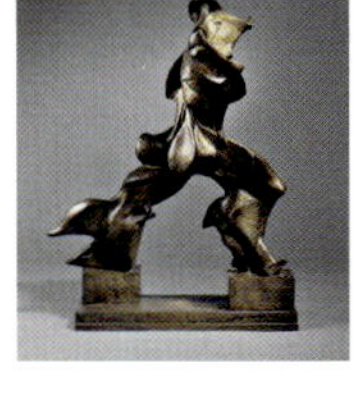

Provenance

Private collection, Italy
Private collection, Switzerland

Exhibitions

2005 Vaduz, Kunstmuseum Liechtenstein, *Werke aus der Hilti Art Foundation. Von Paul Gauguin bis Imi Knoebel,* p. 40, no. 13

Literature

Alley 1981, pp. 60–61
Calvesi and Coen 1983, pp. 466–72
Coen 1988, pp. 216–18
Schneede 1994, pp. 142–51
Wieczorek 2005, p. 40, no. 13

5

Pablo Picasso

Femme dans un fauteuil

1932

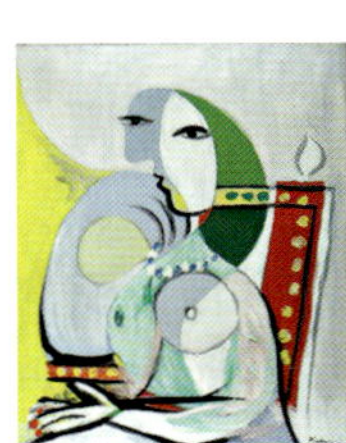

Provenance

Valentine Dudensing, New York
Ernst Zeisler, Chicago
Richard L. Feigen & Co.
Charles Yalem, St. Louis, 1963
Richard L. Feigen & Co., 1966
Robert L. Livingston, New York, 1967
Mollie Parnis Livingston
Collection of the Phoenix Assurance Company
Christie's, London, 3 February 2003, lot 72
Galerie Beyeler

Exhibitions

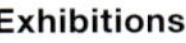

1967 Dallas, *Museum of Fine Arts, Picasso – Two Concurrent Retrospective Exhibitions*
2002 Tel Aviv, Museum of Art, Picasso, p. 25
2005 Vaduz, *Kunstmuseum Liechtenstein, Werke aus der Hilti Art Foundation. Von Paul Gauguin bis Imi Knoebel,* p. 60, no. 22
2006 Riehen/Basel, Fondation Beyeler, *Eros. Rodin und Picasso*
2007 Vienna, BA-CA Kunstforum, *Eros,* pp. 113, 195

Literature
Zervos 1957, vol. VIII, no. 154
Picasso Project, *Picasso's Paintings, Watercolours, Drawings and Sculpture – Surrealism 1930–1936,* San Francisco 1997, p. 128, nos. 32–104
Schneider 2005, p. 60, no. 22

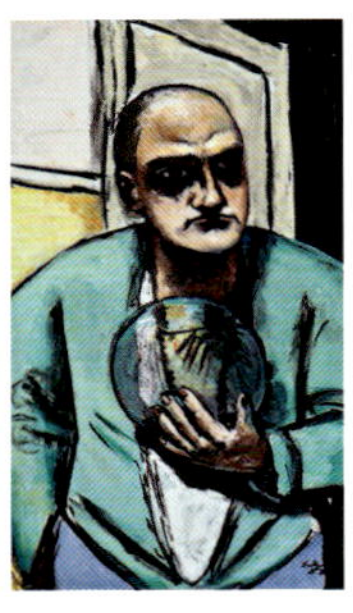

6
Max Beckmann
Selbstbildnis mit Glaskugel
1936

Provenance
Max Beckmann studio
Rudolf Freiherr von Simolin, Berlin, later Seeseiten
Private collection (bequeathed within the family until 2005)
Sotheby's, New York, 3 May 2005, Impressionist & Modern Art, Part One, lot 27
Private collection

Exhibitions
1951 Munich, Haus der Kunst/Berlin, Schloss Charlottenburg, *Max Beckmann zum Gedächtnis 1884–1950,* no. 103
1951–52 Amsterdam, Stedelijk Museum, *Max Beckmann,* no. 36
1953–54 Braunschweig, Kunstverein Städtisches Museum und Haus Salve Hospes/Bremen, Kunsthalle, *Max Beckmann,* no. 51
1955-56 Zurich, Kunsthaus, *Max Beckmann 1884–1950,* no. 74
1956 Basel, Kunsthalle, *Max Beckmann,* no. 64
1956 Den Haag, Gemeentemuseum, *Max Beckmann,* no. 54
1963 Karlsruhe, Badischer Kunstverein, *Max Beckmann – Das Portrait, Gemälde, Aquarelle, Zeichnungen,* no. 40
1968–69 Paris, Musée National d'Art Moderne/Munich, Haus der Kunst/Brussels, Palais des Beaux-Arts, *Max Beckmann,* no. 58 (in Munich no. 56)
1993 Hamburg, Kunsthalle/Munich, Staatsgalerie Moderner Kunst, no. 18
2003 Riehen/Basel, Fondation Beyeler, *Expressive!*

Literature
MB list 1936: Selbstbildnis mit Glaskugel. Simolin Lackner 1938
Bihalji-Merin 1955, fig. XXXII
Busch 1957, vol. 12, p. 10, no. 1 with fig.
Buchheim 1959, no. 61
Busch 1960, pp. 31–32, 66, fig. 12
Jedlicka 1962, pp. 124–25
Max Beckmann Gesellschaft 1962, p. 262, fig. 58
Overy 1965, p. 120
Lackner 1967, pp. 38, 62
Lackner 1969, pp. 41, 59
Zahn 1969/69, fig. p. 54
Schade 1969, vol. 94, pp. 236–37, fig. 4
Kessler 1970, p. 156
Fischer 1972, pp. 52, 119, fig. no. 18
Göpel 1976, vol. I, no. 434, p. 286, vol. II, fig. 148
Zenser 1984, p. 23, fig. no. 33
Erpel 1985, no. 145, fig. p. 151
Selz 1992, p. 65, fig. p. 64
Buck 1993, pp. 35, 94, no. 18
Spieler 1994, fig. p. 123

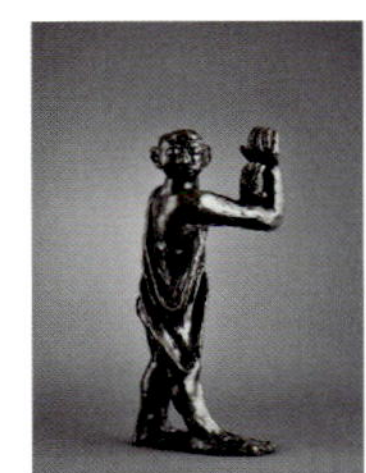

7
Max Beckmann
Mann im Dunkeln
1934

Provenance
Galerie Springer, Berlin
Private collection, Germany

Literature
Fischer 1972, pp. 116–17, fig. no. 34
Lackner 1979, p. 22, fig. 25
Amyx 1981, p. 98
Beckmann 1982, p. 60, fig. p. 57
Dube 1982, p. 70
Beckmann 1983, p. 21
Uthemann 1983–84, p. 40, fig. p. 41
Lackner 1984, pp. 64–65
Franzke 1984, pp. 93ff., fig. no. 1, p. 95
Stabenow 1984–85, pp. 139ff., fig. no. 2, p. 140
Erpel 1985, no. 144/A, fig. no. 152
Rosenthal 1985, no. 90
Wiese 1985, fig. 4
Franzke 1987, pp. 26–29, fig. no. 1
Noll 2002, pp. 26–51, fig. pp. 30–31
Rainbird 2003, pp. 157–64

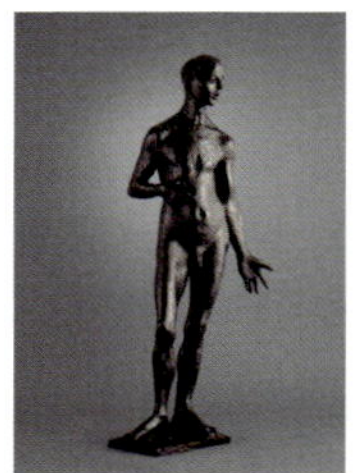

8
Germaine Richier
Juin 40
1940

Provenance
Studio of the artist
Jean Richier, 1950
Private collection

Exhibitions
1942 Winterthur, Kunstmuseum, *René Auberjonois, Gemälde und Zeichnungen – Germaine Richier, Plastiken* (a different cast on view)
1946 Geneva, Galerie Georges Moos, *Germaine Richier,* no. 2 (a different cast on view)
1963 Zurich, Kunsthaus, *Germaine Richier,* no. 63 (a different cast on view)
1996 Saint-Paul-de-Vence, Fondation Maeght, *Germaine Richier, Rétrospective,* no. 6 (a different cast on view)
1997 Berlin, Akademie der Künste, *Germaine Richier,* no. 6 (a different cast on view)
2013–14 Bern, Kunstmuseum/Mannheim, Kunsthalle, *Germaine Richier. Retrospektive,* no. 17, fig. pp. 80–81 (a different cast on view)

Literature
Francastel 1954, pp. 316–20, p. 399

9
Alberto Giacometti
Diego dans un intérieur
1949–50

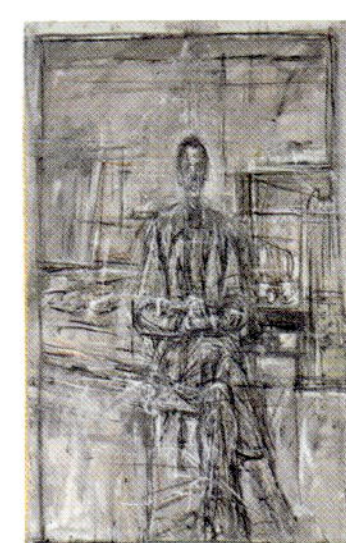

Provenance
Christoph Bernoulli, Basel (acquired from the artist)
Sotheby's, London, 4 December 1984, lot 58
Thomas Ammann Fine Art, Zurich
Private collection, USA
Vivian Horan Fine Art, New York
Private collection, New York

Exhibitions
1960 Paris, Musée d'Art Moderne, et al., Swiss Art from Hodler to Klee, no. 17
2002–03 Zurich, Kunsthaus (loan)
2005 Vaduz, Kunstmuseum Liechtenstein, *Werke aus der Hilti Art Foundation. Von Paul Gauguin bis Imi Knoebel,* p. 72, no. 28
2011 Wolfsburg, Kunstmuseum, et al., *Alberto Giacometti. Der Ursprung des Raumes,* pp. 142, 252

Literature
Wieczorek 2005, p. 72, no. 28

10
Alberto Giacometti
Buste d'homme (Eli Lotar II)
1964–65
(AGD 1620)

Provenance
Annette Giacometti
Thomas Gibson Fine Art London, 1987
Private collection, New York

Exhibitions
1977 Duisburg, Wilhelm-Lehmbruck-Museum, *Alberto Giacometti. Plastiken. Gemälde. Zeichnungen,* no. 54
1992 Riehen/Basel, Galerie Beyeler, *Homage to Francis Bacon,* no. 25

Literature
Salzmann 1977, no. 54, fig. p. 166

11
Willem de Kooning
Cross-Legged Figure
1972

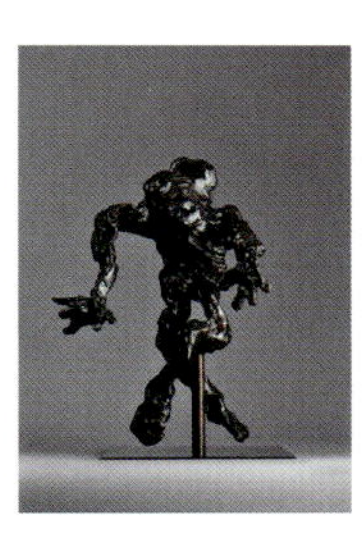

Provenance
Willem de Kooning
Estate of Willem de Kooning
The Pace Gallery, New York
Private collection, New York

Exhibitions
1975 Chicago, *The Art Institute of Chicago, The 34th Annual Society for Contemporary Art Exhibition: The Small Scale in Contemporary Art,* no. 26
2011 New York, The Pace Gallery, *Willem de Kooning, The Figure: Movement and Gesture,* fig. no. 25, p. 44
2011–12 New York, The Museum of Modern Art, *De Kooning, A Retrospective,* fig. no. 162, p. 414

Literature
Gaugh 1983, no. 89, p. 100 (fig.)
Neff 1984, p. 59
Joosten 1984, no. 440
Sollers 1988, no. 76 (fig.)
Washington D.C., 1994
Yard 1997, no. 86, p. 101 (fig.)
Hess 2004, p. 65

12
Georges Seurat
Le tas de pierres
c. 1882–84

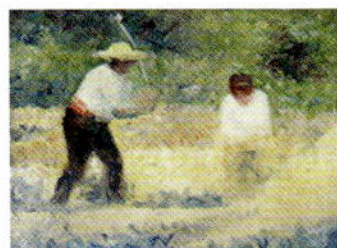

Provenance
Paul Signac, Paris
Berthe Signac, St. Tropez
Léon Salavin, Paris, c. 1957
Wildenstein & Co., Paris
Mr. & Mrs. Sidney R. Barlow, London
Sotheby's, London, 2 April 1979, lot 9
Waddington Galleries, London
Christie's, New York, 12 December 1996, lot 5
Mr. & Mrs. Anton C.R. Dreesman, Niederlande
Christie's, London, 9 April 2002, lot 69
Private collection
Sotheby's, New York, 2 November 2010, lot 52

Exhibitions
1900 Paris, Galerie de la Revue Blanche, *Georges Seurat 1860–1891: Œuvres peintes et dessinées,* no. 9
1908 Paris, Galerie Georges Seligmann
1908–09 Paris, Galerie Bernheim-Jeune, *Georges Seurat,* no. 32
1920 Paris, Galerie Bernheim-Jeune, *Georges Seurat,* no. 15
1952–53 Paris, Musée Carnavalet, *Chefs d'Œuvre des Collections Parisiennes: Ecole française du XIX siècle,* no. 94

1957 Paris, Musée Jaquemart-André, *Seurat,* no. 21
1958 Stockholm, Nationalmuseum, *Fem Sekler Fransk Konst,* no. 163
1963 Hamburg, Kunstverein, *Wegbereiter der modernen Malerei: Cézanne, Gauguin, Van Gogh, Seurat,* no. 97
1969 Phoenix, Museum of Art (on loan)
1974 Los Angeles, County Museum of Art (on loan)
2004 Chicago, The Art Institute of Chicago, *Seurat and the Making of the Grande Jatte,* no. 10

Literature
Coquiot 1924, p. 246
Laprade 1945, fig. no. 17
Rewald 1959, no. 22, fig. p. 21
Herbert 1959, p. 24
Hauke 1961, no. 102, fig. p. 63
Homer 1963, p. 284
Chastel and Minervino 1973, no. 45
Grenier 1990, no. 43
Distel 1991, no. 12, fig. p. 154

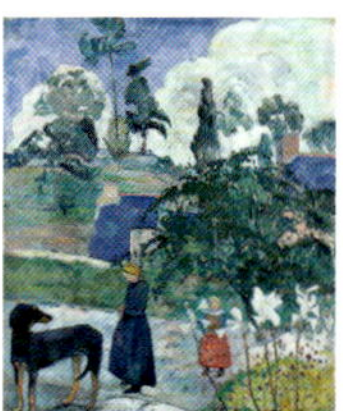

13
Paul Gauguin
Entre les lys
1889

Provenance
Hôtel Drouot, Paris, 23 February 1891, no. 5
M. Matthissen, Paris
Fritz Bendix, Copenhagen
Paul Cassirer, Berlin
Galerie Bernheim-Jeune, Paris
Otto Feldmann
Mario Arbini, Frankfurt am Main
Galerie Thannhauser, Berlin
Rudolf Staechlin, Basel
Sotheby's, New York, 15 November 1989
Private collection, Japan
Private collection, Switzerland

Exhibitions
1893 Copenhagen, Bâtiment des Expositions libres, *Fortegnelse Over Kunstvoerkerne Paa den Frie Udstilling,* no. 151
1928 Basel, Kunsthalle, *Paul Gauguin* 1848–1903, no. 47 and 52 (2nd ed.)
1947–89 Basel, Kunstmuseum (on loan)
1949 Paris, Orangerie des Tuileries, Exposition du Centenaire, *Gauguin,* p. 30, no. 18
1949–50 Basel, Kunstmuseum, *Paul Gauguin zum 100. Geburtstag,* 1949–50, p. 31, no. 27
1956 Basel, Kunstmuseum, *Sammlung Rudolf Staechlin,* no. 33
1964 Paris, Musée National d'Art Moderne, *Fondation Rudolf Staechlin. De Corot à Picasso,* no. 27
1997 Riehen/Basel, Galerie Beyeler, *Joie de vivre,* no. 26
1998–2004 Basel, Kunstmuseum (on loan)
2004–05 Madrid, Museo Thyssen-Bornemisza, *Gauguin and the Origins of Symbolism,* p. 228, no. 104 and p. 324
2005 Vaduz, Kunstmuseum Liechtenstein, *Werke aus der Hilti Art Foundation. Von Paul Gauguin bis Imi Knoebel,* p. 12, no. 1
2007–08 Riehen/Basel, Fondation Beyeler, *Die andere Sammlung. Hommage an Ernst und Hildy Beyeler,* p. 23
2011 Copenhagen, Ny Carlsberg Glyptotek, *Gauguin. Polynesia,* p. 50, no. 27 and p. 363

Literature
Malingue 1948, no. 139
Lewandowski (Lee van Dovski) 1950, p. 345, no. 176
Wildenstein 1964, p. 140, no. 366
Pichon 1986, p. 131
Schneider 2005, p. 12, no. 1

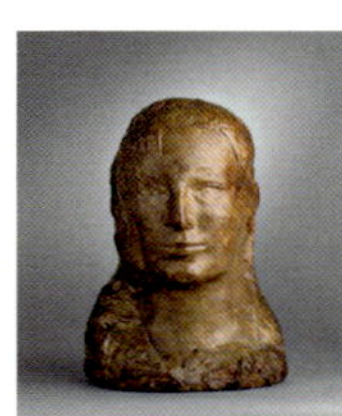

14
Pablo Picasso
Tête de femme (Fernande)
1906

Provenance
Ambroise Vollard, Paris
Jacques Ullman, Paris
Heinz Berggruen, Paris
Pierre Matisse Gallery, New York
Private collection, New York
Stephen Mazoh & Co., Inc., New York
Nathan and Marion Smooke, California, 1986–2001
Phillips de Pury & Luxembourg, New York, 5 November 2001, lot 10

Exhibitions
1983 New York, Stephen Mazoh & Co., Inc., *Twentieth Century Works of Art,* no. 15, fig. p. 32
1987 Los Angeles, Los Angeles County Museum of Art, *Degas to Picasso: Modern Masters from the Smooke Collection,* fig. p. 108
2005 Vaduz, Kunstmuseum Liechtenstein, *Werke aus der Hilti Art Foundation. Von Paul Gauguin bis Imi Knoebel,* p. 20, no. 4

Literature
Zervos 1942, vol. I, no. 323
Merli 1942, p. 292
Boeck and Sabartés 1955, p. 489, no. 68
Penrose 1967, pp. 17, 221, no. 6
Spies 1971, p. 301, no. 6
Johnson 1976, pp. 38–42, 165, no. 5
Palau i Fabre 1981, pp. 436–37, no. 1205
Spies and Piot 1983, pp. 28, 372, no. 61
Wilson 1987, p. 98
Baker 1987, p. 12
Spies 2000, pp. 31–32, 38, 394, no. 6
Schneider 2005, p. 20, no. 4

15

Karl Schmidt-Rottluff

Die Lesende

1911

Provenance

Alfred Hess, Erfurt
Städtisches Museum, Erfurt (now Angermuseum), gift of Alfred Hess, 1919
J. A. Benkert, Berlin
Galerie Ketterer, Munich 1976
Private collection, Munich
Diethelm Hoener Collection, USA
Phillips de Pury & Luxembourg, New York, 5 November 2001, lot 12

Exhibitions

1952 Florence, Museo della Commune di Firenze, *Mostra dell'Espressionismo*
1957 Oldenburg, Kunstverein, *Maler der Brücke in Dangast von 1907 bis 1912,* p. 79, no. 70
1964 London, Tate Gallery, *Painters of the Brücke,* p. 76, no. 253
1966 Paris, et al., Musée National d'Art Moderne, *Le Fauvisme Français et les Débuts de l'expressionnisme Allemand, Paris,* p. 350, no. 273
1989 Bremen, et al., Kunsthalle, *Karl Schmidt-Rottluff, Retrospektive,* p. 233, no. 83
2005 Vaduz, Kunstmuseum Liechtenstein, *Werke aus der Hilti Art Foundation. Von Paul Gauguin bis Imi Knoebel,* p. 30, no. 8

Literature

Niemeyer 1911
Apollonio 1952, p. 27, no. 75
Grohmann 1956, p. 284
Wietek 1955, p. 596, no. 211
Schneider 2005, p. 30, no. 8

16

Ernst Ludwig Kirchner

Paar unter Japanschirm

1913

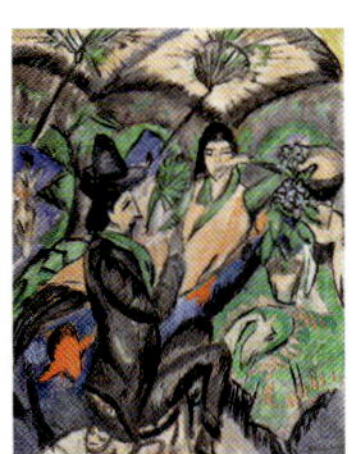

Provenance

Galerie Ludwig Schames, Frankfurt am Main
Ludwig & Rosi Fischer, Frankfurt am Main, c. 1916–18 until after 1945
Ernst Fischer, Richmond, Virginia
The New Gallery, New York
Larry Aldrich, New York
Parke-Bernet Galleries, New York, 1963
Marlborough Fine Art, London
The Yaseen Family Collection
Christie's, New York, 14 November 1990, lot 24
Private collection, Germany

Exhibitions

1958 Raleigh, North Carolina, The Museum of Art, *E. L. Kirchner, German Expressionist,* no. 18, fig. p. 78
1959 Richmond, The Virginia Museum of Fine Arts, *Paintings and Sculpture collected by Mr. and Mrs. Larry Aldrich,* no. 19, pl. 20
1960 Berkeley, University of California, *Art from Ingres to Pollock, Painting and Sculpture since Neoclassicism,* no. 27, with fig.
1963 New York, Marlborough-Gerson Gallery, *A Tribute to Curt Valentine*
1964 London, Tate Gallery, *Painters of the "Brücke",* no. 84
1973 New York, Serge Sabarsky Gallery, *Expressionists: Major Paintings, Watercolors, Drawings and Sculptures by 17 German Expressionists,* no. 25 mit fig.
1983–84 New York, Neuberger Museum, *Selections from the Yaseen Family Collection*
2002–03 Rome, Complesso del Vittoriano, *Gli Espressionisti,* fig. p. 71
2009–10 Salzburg, Museum der Moderne, *Ernst Ludwig Kirchner,* cat. no. 15, fig. p. 103
2010 Frankfurt am Main, Städel Museum, *Ernst Ludwig Kirchner. Retrospektive,* cat. no. 47, fig. p. 126

Literature

Kirchner Archiv, II, no. 31
Gordon 1968, no. 318
Branat, et al. 1987, p. 8
Grisebach 2009–10, pp. 103, 297, no. 15
Brandmüller 2010, p. 100

17

Ernst Ludwig Kirchner

Kniende, nach links gewandter Kopf, rechte Hand auf der linken Brust

1912

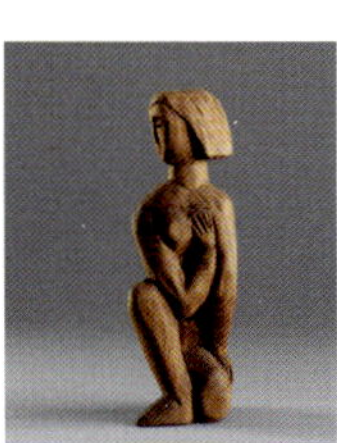

Provenance

Elisabeth Harkort, Hagen, c. 1915–2006/07
Christie's, London, 20 June 2012, lot 44
Private collection

Exhibitions

2002–03 Davos, Kirchner Museum, *Ernst Ludwig Kirchner – Das plastische Werk,* no. 123
2003 Stuttgart, Staatsgalerie, *Ernst Ludwig Kirchner. Der Maler als Bildhauer,* cat. no. 14

Literature

Kirchner Archiv, V, no. 10
Nachbaur 1962, no. 90
Hesse-Frielinghaus 1974, nos. 1–4, p. 19 (fig.)
Gabler 1980, no. 37
Henze 2002, no. 1912–13, p. 330, fig. pp. 139, 140, 330

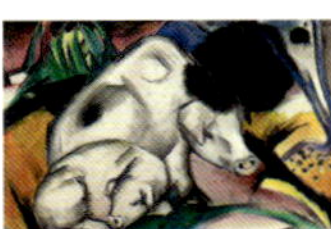

18

Franz Marc

Schweine (Mutterschwein)

1912

Provenance

Galerie Der Sturm, Berlin
Maria Marc, Ried
Fritz Schön, Berlin, 1920
Kronprinzenpalais Berlin (on loan from 1928 to 1933)
Robert C. Schön, 1937
Irene Freund (nee Schön), Toronto, c. 1938
M. Stern, Dominion Gallery Montreal, 1942
Fred S. Mendel, Saskatoon, 1942
Eva Miller (nee Mendel), c. 1970
Karl & Faber, Munich, 1977
Christie's, New York, November 1983, lot 74
Marlborough Fine Art Ltd., London, 1983–87
Private collection, Germany

Selected Exhibitions

1913 Munich, Galerie Thannhauser, *Franz Marc*
1913 Jena, Kunstverein, *Tierbild-Ausstellung, Franz Marc* et al.
1913 Berlin et al., Galerie Der Sturm, 14th exhibition, *Franz Marc*
1928 Berlin, National-Galerie, *Neuere Deutsche Kunst aus Berliner Privatbesitz,* no. 113
1956 Ottawa, National Gallery/Montreal, Museum of Fine Arts 1956, *The Fred Mendel Collection*
1962 Ottawa, National Gallery, *Corot to Picasso*
1971–72 New Orleans, Museum of Fine Art, *German & Austrian Expressionism,* no. 59
1979–80 Berkeley, University Art Museum/Fort Worth, The Fort Worth Art Museum/Minneapolis, Walker Art Center, *Franz Marc: 1880–1916,* published in conjunction with the exhibition *Franz Marc: Pioneer of Spiritual Abstraction,* no. 19, fig. p. 78
1985 London, Royal Academy of Arts and Stuttgart 1986, Staatsgalerie, *German Art in the 20th Century. Painting and Sculpture 1905–1985,* no. 43 (no. 41 in Ger. ed.)
2005–06 Munich, Städtische Galerie im Lenbachhaus und Kunstbau, *Franz Marc – Die Retrospektive,* p. 148, no. 57

Literature

Walden 1919 (fig.)
Weiss 1933, fig. 43
Schardt 1936, 1-1012-10
Lankheit 1970, no. 179
Lankheit 1976, fig. 17
Rosenthal 1989, fig. 29
Hoberg/Jansen 2003, p. 216, no. 191

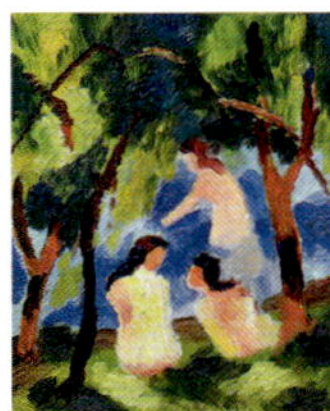

19

August Macke

Badende Mädchen

1913

Provenance

Joseph Haubrich, Cologne, until 1947
Private collection, Germany
Wolfgang Werner, Bremen, 1983
Diethelm Hoener, Germany
Phillips, de Pury & Luxembourg, New York, 5 November 2001, lot 24
Private collection
Sotheby's, New York, 2 November 2010, lot 19

Exhibitions

1914 Berlin, *Erste Ausstellung der freien Sezession,* no. 145
1928 Berlin, Galerie Ferdinand Moeller, *Neuere deutsche Kunst aus Berliner Privatbesitz,* no. 15
1947 Köln, Museen der Stadt Köln in der Alten Universität, *August Macke, Gedächtnisausstellung,* no. 48
1954 Braunschweig, Kunstverein, *August Macke,* no. 63
1957 Münster, Westfälischer Kunstverein, *August Macke, Gedenkausstellung zum 70. Geburtstag,* no. 78
1964 Amsterdam, Stedelijk Museum, *Expressionisme van Gogh tot Picasso,* no. 81

Literature

Cohen 1922, p. 710
Vriesen 1953, no. 436
Vriesen 1957, no. 436, p. 332
Gordon 1974, no. 145, p. 818
Heiderich 2008, no. 515, p. 484 with fig.

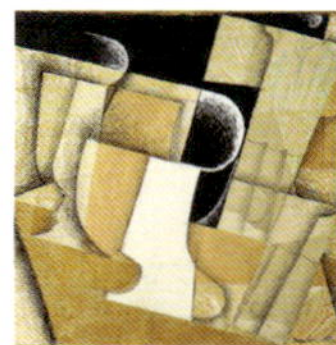

20

Juan Gris

Le verre

1914

Provenance

Daniel-Henry Kahnweiler, Bern
Galerie Simon, Paris
Howard Putzel, San Francisco
Adolfe Mack, San Francisco
Alexander Rabow Galleries, San Francisco
Perls Gallery, New York
Private collection, New York

Exhibitions (selection)

1940 San Francisco, San Francisco Museum of Art, Contemporary Art, no. 119

Literature

Cooper 1977, no. 110, p. 170

21
Fernand Léger
Contraste de formes
1914

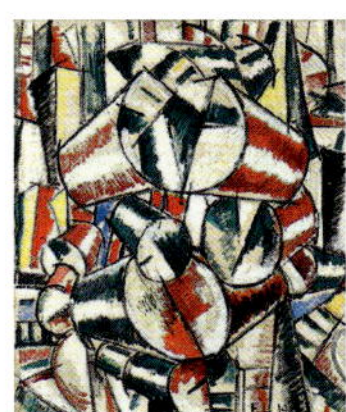

Provenance
Maurice Laffaille, Paris
Ernst Beyeler Collection, Riehen/Basel, since 1961

Exhibitions (selection)
1969 Basel, Galerie Beyeler, *Fernand Léger,* no. 5
1969 Madrid, *Colección Beyeler, Centro de Arte Reine Sofia,* p. 68
1969–70 Düsseldorf, Städtische Kunsthalle Düsseldorf, *Fernand Léger,* no. 15
1993 Berlin, Nationalgalerie, *Wege der Moderne – Die Sammlung Beyeler,* no. 61
1993 Basel, Kunstmuseum, et al., *Fernand Léger 1911–1924. Der Rhythmus des modernen Lebens,* pp. 96, 244, no. 15
1996 Sapporo, Hokkaido Museum of Modern Art, et al., *The Exhibition from Swiss Private Collections,* no. 17, p. 50
1996–97 Sydney, The Art Gallery of South Wales, *Masterpieces of the Twentieth Century, The Beyeler Collection,* no. 35
2005 Vaduz, Kunstmuseum Liechtenstein, *Werke aus der Hilti Art Foundation. Von Paul Gauguin bis Imi Knoebel,* p. 44, no. 14
2007–08 Riehen/Basel, Fondation Beyeler, *Die andere Sammlung. Hommage an Ernst und Hildy Beyeler* (p. 128)
2008 Riehen/Basel, Fondation Beyeler, *Fernand Léger. Paris – New York,* p. 31, no. 10 and p. 202

Literature
Jullian et al., 1969, no. 10
Néret 1990, no. 5
Bauquier 1990, no. 67, fig. p. 125
Los Pintores Cubistas, in: *Saber Ver,* 10 Contemporáneo del Arte, Mexico City 1993, pp. 49ff.
Fondation Beyeler, Sammlungskatalog, Riehen/Basel 1997, no. 85, p. 31
Wieczorek 2005, p. 44, no. 14

22
Piet Mondrian
Tableau No. VIII
with Yellow, Red, Black and Blue
1925

Provenance
Sophie Küppers, Hannover/Dresden, 1925, acquired from the artist
Kunstausstellung Kühl, Dresden, 1926–27
Kaiser Wilhelm Museum, Krefeld, c. 1929–50
Galerie Alex Vömel, Düsseldorf, 1950–55
Karl Anselmino, Wuppertal, c. 1955–77
Private collection, Germany, on loan 1977–88 to Staatsgalerie Moderner Kunst, Munich, inv. no. L 1641
Private collection

Exhibitions
1925 Dresden, Kunsthandlung Kühl und Kühn, *Piet Mondrian – Man Ray*
1926 Munich, Galerie Goltz, *Lissitzky: Moskau, Mondrian: Paris, Man Ray: New York*
1927 Mannheim, Städtische Kunsthalle, *Wege und Richtungen der Abstrakten Malerei in Europa,* no. 261
1929 Frankfurt am Main, Kunstgewerbemuseum, *Der Stuhl*
1958 Wuppertal, Kunsthalle, *Moderne Kunst in Wuppertaler Privatbesitz,* no. 99
1966 Recklinghausen, Städtische Kunsthalle, *Variationen (über ein Thema),* no. 154
1967 Düsseldorf, Städtische Kunsthalle, *Kunst des 20. Jahrhunderts aus rheinisch-westfälischem Privatbesitz,* no. 247
1972 Wuppertal, Von der Heydt-Museum, *Um 1930: Bild, Bau, Gerät,* no. 128
2005 Vaduz, Kunstmuseum Liechtenstein, *Werke aus der Hilti Art Foundation. Von Paul Gauguin bis Imi Knoebel,* p. 62, no. 23

Literature
Piet Mondrian, letter to Til Brugman, 13 Nov. 1924
Piet Mondrian, letter to p.B. Slijper from "Dinsdagavond", c. July 1925
Piet Mondrian, postcard to M. Seuphor, 9 Aug. 1925
Sophie Küppers, Bilderliste, Hannover, 20 Dec. 1926, no. 6, Komposition No. VIII, 25. 51/45. Mark 400
Stuhl-Ausstellung, in: *Das Neue Frankfurt,* p. 64, with photograph of the exhibition, March 1929
Wember 1973, p. 21
Joosten and Welsh 1998, vol. II, p. 316, no. B 160
Wieczorek 2005, p. 62, no. 23

23
Joan Miró
Untitled
1924

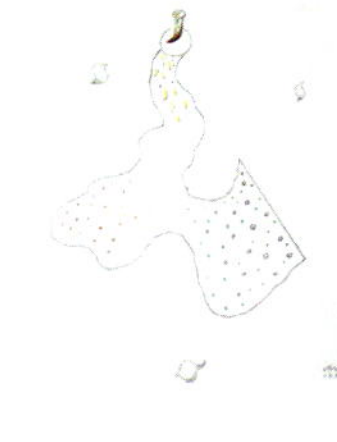

Provenance
The New Gallery, New York
Richard L. Feigen & Co., Chicago
Leo Castelli Gallery, New York
Jane B. Holzer, New York
Private collection, USA

Literature
Dupin/Lelong-Mainaud 2008, no. 201, p. 102

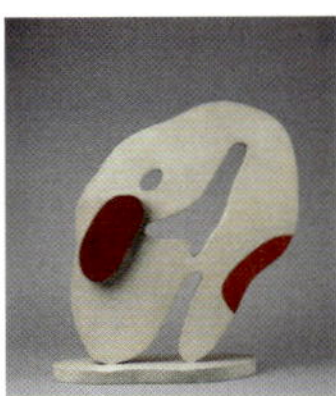

24
Hans Arp
Kopf-Stabile
1926

Provenance
Pierre Janlet Collection, Brussels, 1930
Leo Simon, New York, 1969
Agenzia d'arte moderna, Rome
Johannes Wasmuth Collection, 1982
Stiftung Hans Arp und Sophie Taeuber-Arp e. V., Remagen

Exhibitions
1994 Munich, Haus der Kunst, *Elan vital oder Das Auge des Eros. Kandinsky, Klee, Arp, Miró, Calder,* no. 46, fig. 122
1996 Rolandseck, Stiftung Hans Arp und Sophie Taeuber-Arp e.V., Bahnhof Rolandseck, *Hans Arp. Sophie Taeuber-Arp,* p. 98, no. 26, fig. p. 99 and cover
2004 Basel, Kunstmuseum, *Schwitters. Arp,* no. 29, fig. p. 108
2007 Rolandseck, Arp Museum Bahnhof Rolandseck, *Hans Arp. Die Natur der Dinge,* no. 49, fig. p. 129

Literature
Marchiori 1964, cat. 69, fig. p. 90
Trier 1968, no. V
Andreotti 1989, cat. 9, fig. 21, p. 97
Hartog/Fischer 2012, p. 60, fig. V

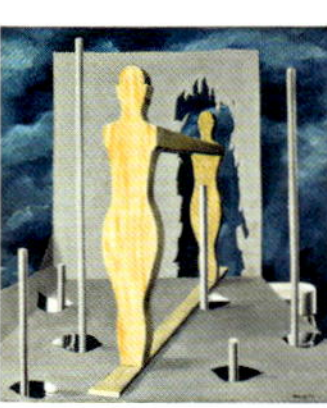

25
René Magritte
La chambre du devin
1926

Provenance
Galerie Le Centaure (P.G. van Hecke), Brussels
E.L.T. Mesens, Brussels, 1931
Grosvenor Gallery, London, 1961
Private collection, Monte Carlo
Studio Bellini, Milan
Private collection, 1996
Christie's, London, 18 June 2013, lot 37

Exhibitions
1927 Brussels, Galerie Le Centaure, *Exposition Magritte,* no. 35
1931 Liège, Palais des Beaux-Arts, *Salon quatriennal de Belgique,* no. 134
1956 Antwerp, Zaal Comité voor Artistieke Werking, *De Vier hoofdpunten van het surrealisme: René Magritte, Max Ernst, Joan Miró, Yves Tanguy,* no. 20
1961 London, Grosvenor Gallery, *Magritte,* no. 12
1979 Venice, Palazzo Grassi, *La pittura metafisica,* no. 118

Literature
Van Hecke 1927, p. 445
Sylvester and Whitfield 1992, no. 88, p. 174
Sylvester 2009, pp. 82, 111 and 424 (illustrated p. 78)

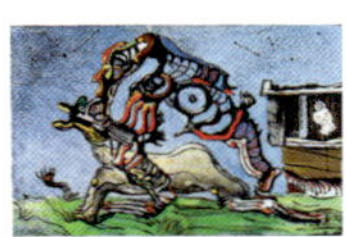

26
Max Ernst
Le paradis
1927

Provenance
Paul Gustave van Hecke, Brussels
Victor Servranckx, Brussels
Private collection, Switzerland

Exhibitions
1927 Brussels, Galerie Le Centaure
1949 Ostende und Den Haag, *Hommage à Ensor,* no. 71
2005 Vaduz, Kunstmuseum Liechtenstein, *Werke aus der Hilti Art Foundation. Von Paul Gauguin bis Imi Knoebel,* p. 56, no. 20
2007–08 Wien, Belvedere, *Wien – Paris. Van Gogh, Cézanne und Österreichs Moderne 1880–1960,* p. 355
2009–10 Münster, Westfälisches Landesmuseum, *"Max Ernst lässt grüssen". Peter Schamoni begegnet Max Ernst,* p. 51
2013 Riehen/Basel, Fondation Beyeler, *Max Ernst – Retrospektive,* p. 215, no. 131

Literature
Spies 1976, p. 147, no. 1076
Malsch 2005, p. 56, no. 20

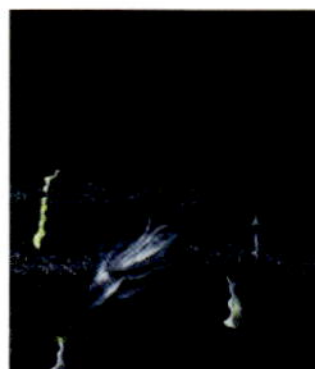

27
Yves Tanguy
Titre inconnu (noyer indifférent)
1929

Provenance
Kunsthaus Zurich (acquired from the artist)
Carl Gustav Jung, Zurich (1929–61)
Private collection, Switzerland
Christie's, London, 6 February 2001, lot 58
Jan Krugier Estate
Sotheby's, New York, 8 May 2014, lot 357

Exhibitions
1929 Zurich, Kunsthaus, *Abstrakte und Surrealistische Malerei und Plastik,* no. 136
1982–83 Baden-Baden, Staatliche Kunsthalle, *Yves Tanguy, Retrospektive 1925–1955,* no. 34
2000 Stuttgart, Staatsgalerie Stuttgart, *Yves Tanguy und der Surrealismus,* no. 31
2007 Munich, Kunsthalle der Hypo-Kulturstiftung, *Das ewige Auge: Von Rembrandt bis Picasso. Meisterwerke der Sammlung Jan Krugier und Marie-Anne Krugier-Poniatowski*

Literature
Matisse 1963, no. 90, fig. p. 68
Waldberg 1977, fig. p. 78
Hohl, 1982, pp. 64–65
Jung 1986, no. 4
Maur, 2000, pp. 58–59
Bihan, Mabin, Sawin 2001, pp. 58–59
Cariou 2007, p. 114
Berk 2009 (cover page)

28

Alexander Calder

Untitled

1935

(A00236)

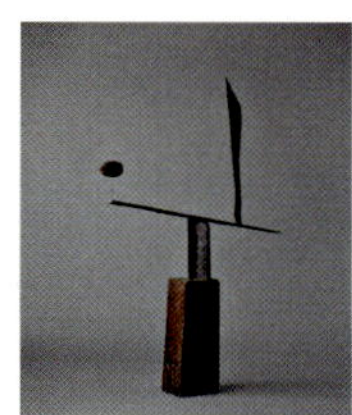

Provenance

Galerie Claude Bernard, Paris
Henry Hecht, New York
Ralph and Helyn Goldenberg, Chicago

Exhibitions

1936 New York, Pierre Matisse Gallery, *Mobiles and Objects by Alexander Calder*
1969 Saint-Paul de Vence, Fondation Maeght, et al., *Calder*
1974 Chicago, Museum of Contemporary Art, *Alexander Calder: A Retrospective Exhibition (Works from 1925-1974)*
1977 New York, Whitney Museum of American Art, *Calder's Universe,* fig. p. 226
1987–88 New York, Whitney Museum of American Art, *Alexander Calder: Sculpture of the Nineteen Thirties*
1998 Washington D.C., National Gallery of Art, et al., *Alexander Calder: 1898–1976,* no. 79
2005 Houston, The Menil Collection, *The Surreal Calder,* fig. 50, fig. p. 130

Literature

Arnason 1971, fig. 20
Fondation Maeght 1971, fig. p. 51
San Lazzaro 1972, fig. p. 226

29

Paul Klee

Clown

1929

133 (D3)

Provenance

Ida Bienert, Dresden/Munich, until 1952
Curt Valentin, Buchholz Gallery/Valentin Gallery, Berlin/New York, 1952–54
Gertrude Lenart Bernoudy, St. Louis, 1954–94
The Gertrude Bernoudy Trust, 1994
Private collection, Switzerland

Exhibitions

1929 Berlin, Galerie Alfred Flechtheim, *Paul Klee,* no. 116
1950 Munich, Haus der Kunst, *Die Maler am Bauhaus,* no. 140
1953 New York, Curt Valentin Gallery, *Paul Klee,* no. 19
1967 New York, The Solomon R. Guggenheim Museum, *Paul Klee 1879–1940. A Retrospective Exhibition,* no. 104
1987–88 New York, Museum of Modern Art, et al., *Paul Klee,* no. 22
1995 Riehen/Basel, Galerie Beyeler, *Joie de vivre,* no. 37
2000–01 Turin, Galleria Civica d'Arte Moderna e Contemporanea, *Paul Klee*
2005 Vaduz, Kunstmuseum Liechtenstein, *Werke aus der Hilti Art Foundation. Von Paul Gauguin bis Imi Knoebel,* p. 48, no. 16
2006–07 Dresden, Staatliche Kunstsammlungen, Galerie Neue Meister, *Von Monet bis Mondrian. Meisterwerke der Moderne aus Dresdner Privatsammlungen der ersten Hälfte des 20. Jahrhunderts,* pp. 76–77, 198, no. 75
2007 Bern, Zentrum Paul Klee, *Überall Theater,* pp. 156, 171, 269
2007–08 Riehen/Basel, Fondation Beyeler, *Die andere Sammlung. Hommage an Ernst und Hildy Beyeler,* p. 195
2009 Ulm, Ulmer Museum, *Paul Klee und die Romantik,* p. 79, no. 50 and p. 143 and front cover
2010 Bern, Zentrum Paul Klee, *Klee trifft Picasso,* pp. 160, 171, 269
2012–13 Bern, Kunstmuseum, et al., *Itten – Klee. Kosmos Farbe,* p. 264, no. 106 and p. 366

Literature

Documents, 1st vol., no. 5, October 1929, pp. 286–87
Grohmann 1929, fig.
Hirsch 1929, fig. p. 210
Crevel 1930, fig. p. 61
Einstein 1931, fig. p. 548
Volné sm ry, vol. 29, nos. 7–8, November 1932, pp. 187, 195, fig.
Grohmann 1933, pp. 14, 21, fig.
Giedion-Welcker 1952, fig.
Grohmann 1954, p. 246, fig.
San Lazzaro 1957, fig. 78
Plant 1978, pp. 43, 76, 97–98, 118, fig.
Müller 1979, p. 112, note 1
Kagan 1983, p. 102, fig.
Löffler 1986, p. 45
Bischoff 1992, fig.
Roskill 1992, fig.
Paul-Klee-Stiftung 2001, p. 336, no. 4889
Malsch 2005, p. 48, no. 16

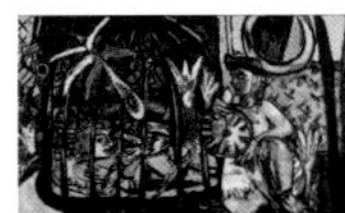

30
Max Beckmann
Traum des Soldaten
1942/43

Provenance
Max Beckmann studio
Buchholz Gallery, Curt Valentin, New York
Elise V.H. Ferber, Washington D.C., 1946
Private collection

Exhibitions
1948–49 St. Louis, Saint Louis City Art Museum, et al., *Max Beckmann 1948. Retrospective Exhibition*
1950 Northampton, Smith College, *Works of Art Belonging to Alumnae,* no. 37
1957 Boston, Museum of Fine Arts, *European Masters of our Time,* no. 6, fig. 106
1959 Northampton, Smith College, *Works of Art Belonging to Alumnae,* no. 33
1961 Kansas City, William Rockhill Nelson Gallery of Art and Mary Atkins, Museum of Fine Art, *The Logic of Modern Art,* no. 10 with fig.
1984 Munich, Haus der Kunst, et al., *Max Beckmann – Retrospektive*
2007 Munich, Pinakothek der Moderne, *Max Beckmann. Exil in Amsterdam,* no. 21
2012 Munich, Pinakothek der Moderne, *Frauen. Picasso, Beckmann, de Kooning,* no. 84
2013–14 Mannheim, Kunsthalle, *Dix/Beckmann: Mythos Welt,* no. 62, fig. p. 181

Literature
MB-Liste Amsterdam 1942
Reifenberg (checklist) 519
Swarzenski 1948, p. 8
Göpel 1976, vol. 1, p. 372, no. 616, vol. 2, pl. 222, no. 616
Schulz-Hoffmann 2007, p. 192, no. 21
Schulz-Hoffmann 2012, p. 288, no. 84
Von Bormann 2013, p. 159

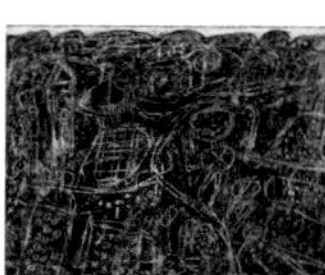

31
Jean Dubuffet
Paysage noir avec Joueur de fifre
1949

Provenance
Studio of the artist
Pierre Matisse, New York

Exhibitions
1994 Avignon, Palais des Papes, *Dubuffet. Haute Lieux, Paysages 1944–1984,* fig. p. 37
2001 Paris, Centre Georges Pompidou, *Dubuffet,* fig. p. 113
2010 Berlin, Wolfgang Werner, *Dubuffet,* exh. cat. no. 2

Literature
Loreau 1965, WV no. 58, fig. p. 40

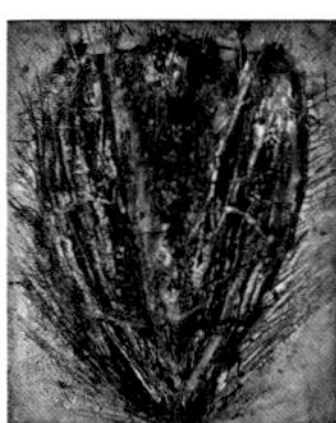

32
Wols
La flamme
1946–47

Provenance
Galerie René Drouin, Paris
Private collection (Bernard Collin), Paris, 1948
Sotheby's, Paris, 31 May 2011, lot 5

Exhibitions
1947 Paris, Galerie René Drouin, *Wols*
1949 Milan, Galleria del Milione, *Wols*
1957 Paris, Studio Paul Facchetti, *Jean Dubuffet, Henri Michaux, Wols,* fig.
1958 Venice, XXIX Esposizione Biennale Internazionale d'Arte, p. 152, no. 3
1973 Berlin, Nationalgalerie SMPK, *Wols 1913–1951. Gemälde, Aquarelle, Zeichnungen*, no. 20, fig. p. 52
1973–74 Paris, Musée d'art moderne de la ville de Paris, *Wols 1913–1951,* no. 16
1974 Ginals, Abbaye de Beaulieu en Rouergue, Centre d'art contemporaine, *Matière e Mémoire. L'informel, l'expressionisme abstrait, cobra...*
1989–90 Zurich, Kunsthaus/Düsseldorf, Kunstsammlung NRW, *Wols. Bilder, Aquarelle, Zeichnungen, Photographien, Druckgraphik,* no. 220, fig. p. 274
1990 Edinburgh, Scottish National Gallery of Modern Art, *Wols. Paintings, Watercolours, Photographs and Prints,* no. 3
1995–96 Paris, Musée d'art moderne de la ville de Paris, *Passions privées. Collections particulières d'art moderne et contemporain en France,* p. 297, no. 18, fig.
2013 Bremen, Kunsthalle, *Wols: Die Retrospektive,* p. 227, no. 189 and p. 270

Literature
Anonymous 1955, fig. p. 19, upper right
Roh 1958, fig. p. 258
Hofmann 1959, p. 183
Platschek 1959, 3rd fig. after p. 40
Restany 1962, fig. p. 56
Celebonovic 1965, fig. p. 11
Chiba 1974, p. 107
LeCris-Bergmann, 1976, no. 163
Glozer 1978, p. 8, fig. 2
Damme 1985, no. 428, p. 270
Bonnefoi 1988, fig. cover
Lévêque 2001, fig. cover

33

Alberto Giacometti

Petit buste d'homme

1950–51

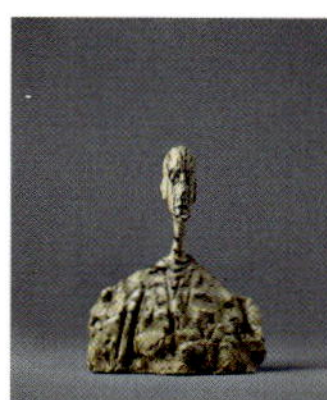

Provenance

Herbert Matter
Harold Diamond, New York
Galerie Beyeler, Basel, 1971
Private collection, Germany, 1974
Sotheby's, New York, 3 May 2005, Impressionist & Modern Art, Part One, lot 60

Exhibitions

1977 Duisburg, Wilhelm Lehmbruck Museum, *Alberto Giacometti,* p. 223, no. 32
1987–88 Berlin, Nationalgalerie SMPK, et al., *Alberto Giacometti,* p. 248, no. 143
1991–92 Paris, Musée d'Art Moderne de la Ville de Paris, *Alberto Giacometti,* p. 217, no. 121

Literature

Hohl/Honisch/Beye 1987–88, p. 248, no. 143
Page 1991–92, p. 121, fig. p. 217

34

Norbert Kricke

Raumplastik Gelb – Weiss – Schwarz

1952

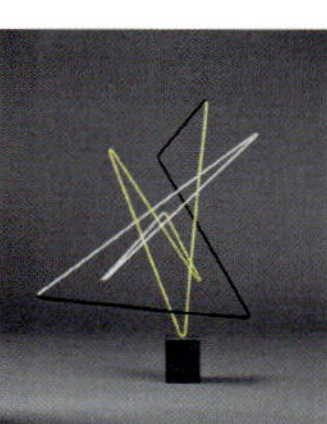

Provenance

Estate of Norbert Kricke
Edith Wahlandt Galerie, Stuttgart

35

Josef Albers

Homage to the Square

1959

(JAF 0916)

Provenance

André Emmerich, New York, Zurich
Karsten Greve, Cologne
Private collection, Switzerland

36

Gianni Colombo

Spazio elastico

1968

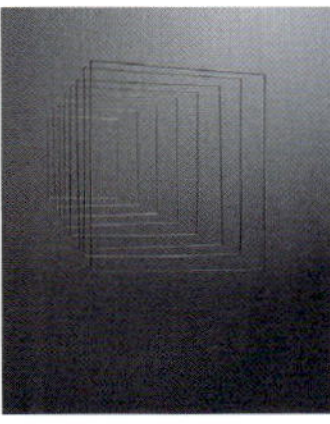

Provenance

Private collection, Germany

Exhibitions

1970 Kempfenhausen/Starnberg, Thomas Keller Galerie, *Gianni Colombo*
2009–10 Rivoli-Turin, Castello di Rivoli, Museo d'Arte Contemporanea, *Gianni Colombo,* p. 163 with fig. and p. 196

Literature

Gomringer 1970

37

Lucio Fontana

Concetto spaziale – Attese

1966

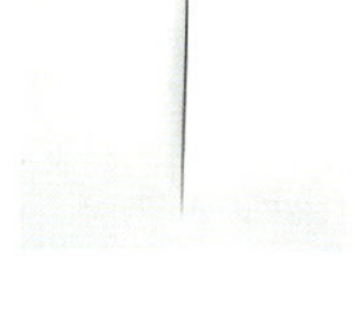

Provenance

Galerie H.J. Müller, Cologne
Op Art Galerie, Esslingen
Galerie Denise René – Hans Mayer, Krefeld
K. Schröer Collection, Krefeld
Private collection, Germany

Exhibitions

1967 Cologne, Kunstmarkt
1981 Cologne, Galerie Reckermann. *Nice-Milano-Paris-Düsseldorf,* fig.

Literature

Crispolti 1986, vol. II, p. 651, no. 66 T 116

38

Yves Klein

Monochrome (IKB 180)

1958

Provenance

Mme. R. Gaspérini, Nizza

Exhibitions

1994 London, Gimpel Fils, Yves Klein
2005 Vaduz, Kunstmuseum Liechtenstein, *Werke aus der Hilti Art Foundation. Von Paul Gauguin bis Imi Knoebel,* p. 88, no. 36

Literature

Wember 1969, p. 75
Schneider 2005, p. 88, no. 36

39

Piero Manzoni

Achrome

1959–60

(1132/A/95)

Provenance

Private collection, Viareggio

Exhibitions

2005 Vaduz, Kunstmuseum Liechtenstein, *Werke aus der Hilti Art Foundation. Von Paul Gauguin bis Imi Knoebel,* p. 92, no. 38
2008 Vienna, BA-CA Kunstforum, *Monet Kandinsky Rothko und die Folgen. Wege der abstrakten Malerei,* p. 132
2013 Wolfsburg, Kunstmuseum, Art & Textiles. Fabric as Material and Concept in Modern Art from Klimt to the Present, p. 190

Literature

Malsch 2005, p. 92, no. 38

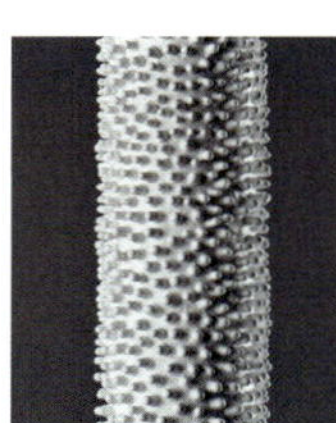

40

Gerhard von Graevenitz
weisse struktur, rundstab mit homogener verteilung
1959

Provenance
Estate of the artist

Exhibitions
2014 Berlin, Kunsthandel Wolfgang Werner, *Gerhard von Graevenitz,* no. 3, with fig.

Literature
Bremer 1985, no. 28
Berswordt-Wallrabe, 1994–95, no. 314

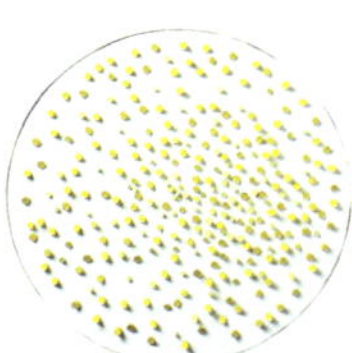

41

Klaus Staudt
Kreisformation II
1965
(FA-RE 5)

Provenance
Studio of the artist, Galerie am Lindenplatz, Vaduz

Literature
Enzweiler/Rompza 1999, no. 1/77, p. 226

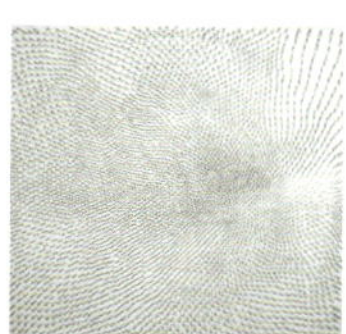

42

Günther Uecker
Grosses Feld
1967

Provenance
Galerie Schmela, Düsseldorf
Marianne and Viktor Langen Collection, Düsseldorf
TRW Collection, Düsseldorf

43

Gotthard Graubner
Lichter Körper
1968

Provenance
Fritz and Ilona Busse Collection, Germany

Exhibitions
1969 Hannover, Kestner-Gesellschaft, *Gotthard Graubner,* no. 68
1969 Düsseldorf, Kunstverein für die Rheinlande und Westfalen, *Gotthard Graubner,* no. 81
1985 Bremen, Kunsthalle Bremen, *Kunst des 20. Jahrhunderts aus privaten Sammlungen,* no. 281

44

Imi Knoebel
Untitled
(119 Linien / 11 mm Abstand)
1968

Provenance
Studio of the artist
Private collection

Exhibitions
1999 St. Gallen, Kunstverein, Kunstmuseum, *IMI KNOEBEL, Linienbilder 1966 bis 1968,* no. 29
2002–03 Braunschweig, Kunstverein, *IMI KNOEBEL, IMI GEGEN GROBEN SCHMUTZ,* p. 36

Literature
Stüttgen 1999, pp. 7ff.
Bitterli 1999, pp. 31ff.

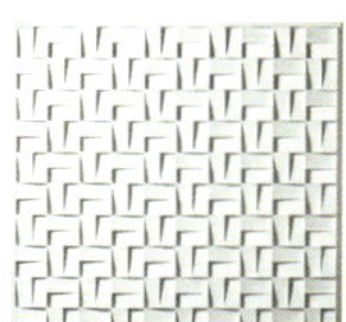

45

Jan Schoonhoven
R 72–25
1972

Provenance
Private collection, Essen

Exhibitions
1995–96 Essen, Museum Folkwang/Maastricht, Bonnefantenmuseum/Aarau,
Aargauer Kunsthaus, *Jan J. Schoonhoven retrospektiv,* pp. 142, 176

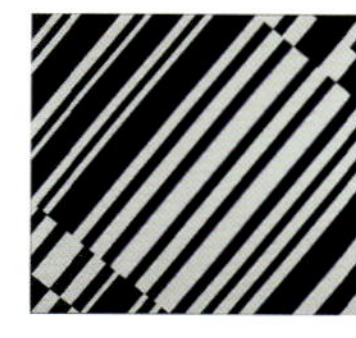

46

Günter Fruhtrunk
Diagonale Progression Schwarz-Weiss
(Studie II)
c. 1970

Provenance
Günter Fruhtrunk Estate

Exhibitions
2012 Vaduz, Kunstmuseum Liechtenstein, *Günter Fruhtrunk, Farbe Rhythmus Existenz,* pp. 87, 160

Literature
Franz 2012, p. 9

47

Gottfried Honegger
Tableau-Relief
1979
(Z.825.1)

Provenance
Studio of the artist
Private collection, Switzerland

48

Verena Loewensberg
Untitled
1984–85

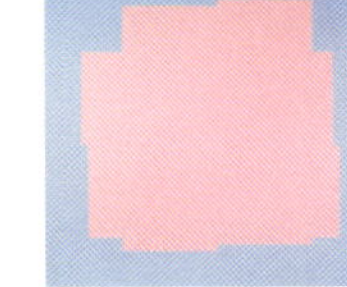

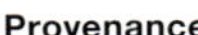

Provenance
Studio of the artist
Private collection, Switzerland

Exhibitions
1986 Zurich, Galerie Jamileh Weber, *verena loewensberg bei jamileh weber*
1993–94 Zurich, Haus für konstruktive und konkrete Kunst, *Thematische Veränderungen: Bill – Graeser – Loewensberg – Lohse*

Literature
Coray Loewensberg 2012, p. 240, no. 612
Grossmann 2012, pp. 124ff.

49

Verena Loewensberg
Untitled
1985

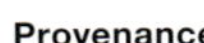

Provenance
Studio of the artist
Private collection, Switzerland

Literature
Coray Loewensberg 2012, p. 243, no. 632 and fig. 160, p. 132
Grossmann 2012, pp. 124ff.

50

Imi Knoebel
Untitled
(Schwarzes Bild Nr. 9 [von 24], Schlachtenbild)
1990

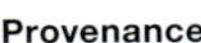

Provenance
Studio of the artist
Kewenig Galerie, Cologne

Bibliography

Affentranger-Kirchrath, Angelika: Die Frage nach dem Menschen. Portraitmalerei um 1900 am Beispiel Ferdinand Hodlers und Edvard Munchs, in: Zeitschrift für Schweizerische Archäologie und Kunstgeschichte, vol. 4, 1994

Alley, Ronald: Catalogue of The Tate Gallery's Collection of Modern Art, other than works by British Artists, London 1981, pp. 60–61 (with additional listings)

Amyx, Clifford: Max Beckmann: Die Ikonographie der Triptychen, in: Max Beckmann. Die Triptychen im Städel, exh. cat., Frankfurt am Main 1981

Arnason, H. Harvard: Calder, New York 1971

Andreotti, Margherita: The Early Sculpture of Jean Arp, London 1989

Anonym: **Wols**, in: I 4 soli. Rassegna d'arte attuale, 2/5, 1955

Apollonio, Umbro: Die Brücke e la Cultura dell'Espressionismo, Venice 1952

Badt, Kurt: Die Plastik Wilhelm Lehmbrucks, in: Zeitschrift für Bildende Kunst, vol. 55, Leipzig 1920

Bätschmann, Oskar / Brunner, Monika / Walter, Bernadette: Ferdinand Hodler, Catalogue raisonné der Gemälde, vol. 2, Die Bildnisse, Zurich 2012

Baker, Kenneth: The Modern and the Ancient, San Francisco Chronicle, May 31, 1987

Bauquier, Georges: Fernand Léger, Catalogue raisonné de l'œuvre peint, vol. 1, 1903–1919, Paris 1990

Beckmann, Peter: Max Beckmann, Leben und Werk, Stuttgart / Zurich 1982

Beckmann, M. Q.: Mein Leben mit Max Beckmann, Munich 1983

Berk, Tjeu van den: Eigenzinnig kunstzinnig, De visie van Carl Gustav Jung op kunst, Zoetermeer/Kapellen, 2009

Berswordt-Wallrabe, Kornelia von: Gerhard von Graevenitz, Werkverzeichnis, in: Gerhard von Graevenitz, exh. cat. Staatliches Museum Schwerin 1994, Von der Heydt-Museum Wuppertal 1995

Bihalji-Merin, Oto: Savremena Nema ka Umetnost (German Contemporary Art), Belgrade 1955

Bihan, René le / Mabin, Renée / Sawin, Martica: Yves Tanguy, Quimper, 2001

Bischoff, Ulrich: Paul Klee, Munich 1992

Bitterli, Konrad: Raster und Strukturen. Imi Knoebels Linienbilder und die Erweiterung des Bildbegriffs, in: IMI KNOEBEL, Linienbilder 1966 bis 1968, St. Gallen 1999

Bonnefoi, Geneviève: Les années fertiles 1940–1960, Paris 1988

Bloesch, Hans: Zur internationalen Kunstausstellung in Interlaken, in: Die Alpen. Monatsschrift für schweizerische und allgemeine Kultur, 5, 1910, vol. 1, pp. 25–32

Boeck, Wilhelm / Sabartés, Jaime: Picasso, New York 1955

Bormann, Beatrice von: Triebträume – Von Bordell und Lustmord, in: Dix / Beckmann. Mythos Welt, Mannheim 2013

Branat, F. / Hight E. / Kistler A. / Schultz S.: German Expressionist Art, The Ludwig and Rosi Fischer Collection, Virginia Museum of Fine Arts, 1987

Brandmüller, Nicole: Der Expressionist in Berlin, in: Ernst Ludwig Kirchner. Retrospektive, exh. cat. Städel Museum, Frankfurt am Main 2010

Bremer, Jaap: Gerhard von Graevenitz, Werkverzeichnis, in: Gerhard von Graevenitz, exh. cat. Rijksmuseum Kröller-Müller, Otterlo 1985

Buchheim, Lothar-Günther: Max Beckmann, Feldafing 1959

Busch, Günter: Max Beckmann, in: Mededelingen Gemeentemuseum, Den Haag, vol. 12, 1957

Busch, Günter: Max Beckmann, Eine Einführung, Munich 1960

Calvesi, Maurizio / Coen, Ester: Boccioni, Milan 1983

Cariou, André: Yves Tanguy. L'Univers surréaliste, exh. cat. Musée des Beaux-Arts, Quimper & Museu Nacional d'Art de Catalunya, Barcelona 2007

Celebonovic, Aleska: Novi oblici u posleratnom slikarstvu, in: Umetnost, April – June 1965

Chastel, A. / Minervino, F.: Tout L'Œuvre peinte de Seurat, Paris 1973

Chiba, Shigeo: L'œuvre de Wols (diss.), Paris 1974

Coen, Ester: Umberto Boccioni, New York 1988

Cohen, Walter: August Macke, in: Der Cicerone, Leipzig 1922

Cooper, Douglas: Juan Gris, Catalogue raisonné de l'œuvre peint, vol. 1, Paris 1977

Coquiot, Gustave: Seurat, Paris 1924

Coray Loewensberg, Henriette (ed.): Verena Loewensberg 1912–1986, Katalog der Gemälde (unter Mitarbeit von Renate Holliger), Zurich 2012

Crevel, René: Paul Klee, Peintres nouveaux, Paris 1930

Crispolti, Enrico: Fontana, Catalogo generale, Milan 1986

Damme, Claire van: Kunst als catharsis en psychogenese. Het extreem subjectivistisch kunstscheppen van de Duitse surrealistische en informele kunstnaar Wols 1913–1951, Ghent 1985

Distel, Anne: Seurat, Chêne 1991

Dube, Wolf-Dieter: Auferstehung im Werke Max Beckmanns, in: Kunst und Kirche 2, 1982

Dupin, Jacques / Lelong-Mainaud, Ariane: Miró: Catalogue raisonné of Drawings, vol. 1 (1909–1937), Paris 2008

Einstein, Carl: Die Kunst des 20. Jahrhunderts, 3rd ed., Berlin 1931

Enzweiler, Jo / Rompza, Sigurd: Klaus Staudt. Werkverzeichnis 1960–1999, Saarbrücken 1999

Erpel, Fritz: Max Beckmann, Leben im Werk. Die Selbstbildnisse, Berlin 1985

Fischer, Friedhelm Wilhelm: Max Beckmann, Symbol und Weltbild, Munich 1972

Fischer, Marcel: Sammlung Arthur Stoll. Skulpturen und Gemälde des 19. und 20. Jahrhunderts, SIK, Zurich / Stuttgart 1961

Fondation Maeght: Calder: L'Artiste et l'Œuvre, Archives no. 1, Paris 1971

Francastel, Pierre: La nouvelle sculpture, Richier Germaine, Les sculpteurs célèbres, Paris 1954

Franz, Erich: Günter Fruhtrunk – Rhythmus des Sehens, in: Günter Fruhtrunk, Farbe Rhythmus Existenz, exh. cat. Kunstmuseum Liechtenstein, Vaduz 2012

Franzke, Andreas: Max Beckmanns Skulpturen, in: Max Beckmann, exh. cat. Josef-Haubrich-Kunsthalle, Cologne 1984

Franzke, Andreas: Max Beckmann, Skulpturen, Munich 1987

Gabler, Karlheinz: E. L. Kirchner. Dokumente, Fotos, Schriften, Briefe, Aschaffenburg 1980

Gaugh, Harry F.: Willem de Kooning, New York 1983

Giedion-Welcker, Carola: Paul Klee, London 1952

Glozer, Laszlo: Wols. Photograph, Munich 1978

Göpel, Erhard and **Barbara**: Max Beckmann, Katalog der Gemälde, vol. I und II, Bern 1976

Gomringer, Eugen: Gianni Colombo, in: exh. cat. Galerie Thomas Keller, Starnberg 1970

Gordon, Donald E.: Ernst Ludwig Kirchner, Munich 1968

Gordon, Donald E.: Modern Art Exhibitions 1900–1916, Munich 1974

Grenier, Catherine: Seurat, Catalogo Completo, Milan 1990

Grisebach, Lucius: Ernst Ludwig Kirchner, in: exh. cat. Museum der Moderne, Salzburg 2009–10

Grohmann, Will: Paul Klee, with contributions by René Crevel, Paul Eluard, Roger Vitrac, Tristan Tzara, Louis Aragon, Philippe Soupault and Jean Lurçat, Paris 1929

Grohmann, Will (ed.): Privatsammlungen neuer Kunst. Die Sammlung Ida Bienert Dresden, vol. 1, Potsdam 1933

Grohmann, Will: Paul Klee, Geneva/Stuttgart 1954

Grohmann, Will: Schmidt-Rottluff, Stuttgart 1956

Grossmann, Elisabeth: Verena Loewensberg, Werkmonografie, in: Verena Loewensberg 1912–1986, ed. by Henriette Coray Loewensberg, Zurich 2012

Hartog, Arie / Fischer, Kai: Hans Arp, Skulpturen – Eine Bestandsaufnahme, Ostfildern 2012

Hauke, Cesar M. de: Seurat et son Œuvre, vol. 1, Paris 1961

Hecke, P. G. van: René Magritte, peintre de la pensée abstraite, in: Sélection, Antwerp 1927

Heiderich, Ursula: August Macke, Gemälde, Werkverzeichnis, Ostfildern 2008

Henze, Wolfgang: Die Plastik Ernst Ludwig Kirchners. Monografie mit Werkverzeichnis, Wichtrach-Bern 2002

Herbert, Robert L.: Seurat and Puvis de Chavannes, in: Yale University Art Literature Gallery Bulletin, October 1959

Hess, Barbara: Willem de Kooning, Inhalt als flüchtiger Eindruck, Cologne 2004

Hesse-Frielinghaus, Herta: Ernst Ludwig Kirchner und das Museum Folkwang Hagen. Briefe von ihm, an und über ihn, in: Westfalen 52, 1974, vols. 1–4

Hirsch, Karl Jakob: Maler Paul Klee, in: Musaion, vol. 9, December 1929

Hoberg, Annegret/ Jansen, Isabelle: Franz Marc. Werkverzeichnis, vol. 1, Gemälde, Munich 2004

Hofmann, Werner: Der Maler Wols, in: Werk. Schweizer Monatsschrift für Architektur, Kunst und künstlerisches Gewerbe 46, 1959

Hohl, Reinhold: Tanguy und die surrealistische Figuration, in: Yves Tanguy, exh. cat. Staatliche Kunsthalle Baden-Baden, 1982–83

Hohl, Reinhold / Honisch, Dieter / Beye, Peter: Alberto Giacometti, in: Alberto Giacometti, exh. cat. Nationalgalerie Berlin, Staatsgalerie Stuttgart 1987–88

Homer, W. I.: Seurat's Paintings and Drawings, in: Burlington Magazine, June 1963

Jedlicka, Gotthard: Max Beckmann in seinen Selbstbildnissen, in: Blick auf Beckmann, Dokumente und Vorträge, Munich 1962

Johnson, Ron: The Early Sculpture of Picasso, 1901–1914, New York 1976

Joosten, Joop M.: Twenty Years of Collecting, Stedelijk Museum Amsterdam, 1984

Joosten, Joop M. / Welsh, Robert P.: Piet Mondrian, Catalogue Raisonné of the Work of 1911–1944, Antwerp 1998

Jullian, René et al.: Fernand Léger, Edition Beyeler, Basel 1969

Jung, Carl Gustav: Ein moderner Mythus. Von Dingen die am Himmel gesehen werden (Zurich and Stuttgart 1958), in: Zivilisation im Übergang, Freiberg 1986

Kagan, Andrew: Paul Klee. Art & Music, Ithaca / London 1983

Kessler, Charles S.: Max Beckmann's Triptychs, Cambridge 1970

Kraft, Hartmut: Objektverlust und Kreativität – eine Darstellung anhand Ferdinand Hodlers Werkzyklus über Valentine Godé-Darel, in: Psychoanalyse, Kunst und Kreativität heute. Die Entwickling der Kunstpsychologie seit Freud, Cologne 1984

Lackner, Stephan: Das Welttheater des Malers Max Beckmann, 1938, in: Benno Reifenberg und Wilhelm Hausenstein, Max Beckmann, Munich 1949

Lackner, Stephan: Ich erinnere mich gut an Max Beckmann, Mainz 1967

Lackner, Stephan: Max Beckmann, Memories of a Friendship, Coral Gables 1969

Lackner, Stephan: Max Beckmann, Cologne 1979

Lackner, Stephan: Max Beckmann, in: Skulptur des Expressionismus, exh. cat. Josef-Haubrich-Kunsthalle, Cologne 1984

Lankheit, Klaus: Franz Marc. Katalog der Werke, Cologne 1970

Lankheit, Klaus: Franz Marc. Sein Leben und seine Kunst, Cologne 1976

Laprade, J. de: Georges Seurat, Monaco 1945

LeCris-Bergmann, Françoise: Composantes plastiques et pôles référentiels dans l'œuvre de Wols (diss.), Paris 1976

Lévêque, Jean-Jacques: Wols, Neuchâtel 2001

Lewandowski, Herbert (Lee van Dovski): Gauguin oder die Flucht vor der Zivilisation, Olten-Bern 1950

Löffler, Fritz: Theodor Däubler sowie Ida Bienert und Klee, in: Akten, Dresden 1986

Loosli, Carl Albert: Ferdinand Hodler, Zurich 1919–20

Loosli, Carl Albert: Ferdinand Hodler, Leben, Werk und Nachlass, 4 vols., Bern 1921–1924

Loreau, Max: Catalogue des travaux de Jean Dubuffet, vol. V, Paysages grotesques, Lausanne 1965

Malingue, Maurice: Gauguin, Le peintre et son œuvre, Paris 1948

Malsch, Friedemann: in: Werke aus der Hilti Art Foundation. Von Paul Gauguin bis Imi Knoebel, exh. cat. Kunstmuseum Liechtenstein, Vaduz 2005

Marchiori, Giuseppe: Arp. Cinquante ans d'activité, exh. cat., Bruno Alfieri, Milan 1964

Matisse, Pierre: Yves Tanguy, Un Recueil de ses œuvres, Paris 1963

Maur, Karin von: Yves Tanguy oder „Die Gewissheit des Niegesehenen", in: Yves Tanguy und der Surrealismus, exh. cat. Staatsgalerie Stuttgart, 2000

Max Beckmann Gesellschaft: Blick auf Beckmann, Munich 1962

Merli, Juan: Picasso, el artista y la obra de nuestro tiempo, Buenos Aires 1942

Mühlestein, Hans / Schmidt, Georg: Ferdinand Hodler 1853–1918. Sein Leben und sein Werk, Zurich 1942

Müller, Carola: Das Zeichen in Bild und Theorie bei Paul Klee (diss.), TU Munich, 1979

Nachbaur, Wenzel: Verzeichnis der Plastiken Ernst Ludwig Kirchners, 1962

Neff, Terry Ann R.: The Museum of Contemporary Art, Selections from the Permanent Collection, vol. I, exh. cat., Chicago 1984

Néret, Gilles: Fernand Léger, Paris 1990

Niemeyer, Wilhelm: Malerische Impressionen und koloristischer Rhythmus. Denkschrift des Sonderbundes, Düsseldorf 1911

Noll, T.: Max Beckmann – Mann im Dunkeln, in: Christian Lenz, Max Beckmann, Aufsätze, Max Beckmann Archiv, Munich 2002

Overy, Paul: Three German Self-Portraits, in: Apollo, vol. 81, London 1965

Page, Suzanne: Alberto Giacometti. Sculptures. Peintures. Dessins, in: exh. cat. Musée d'Art Moderne de la Ville de Paris, Paris 1991–92

Palau i Fabre, Josep: Picasso – The Early Years 1881–1907, New York 1981

Paul-Klee-Stiftung, Kunstmuseum Bern (ed.): Paul Klee, Catalogue Raisonné, vol. 5, 1927–1930, Bern 2001

Penrose, Roland: The Sculpture of Picasso, exh. cat. The Museum of Modern Art, New York 1967

Pichon, Yann le: Sur les traces de Gauguin, Paris 1986

Plant, Margaret: Paul Klee. Figures and Faces, London 1978

Platschek, Hans: Neue Figuration. Aus der Werkstatt der heutigen Malerei. Munich 1959

Pradel De Grandy, Marie N. de: Duchamp-Villon, in: exh. cat. Centre Georges Pompidou, Paris 1998

Prather, Marla: Willem de Kooning, exh. cat. National Gallery of Art, Washington DC 1994

Rainbird, Sean: A Gathering Storm: Beckmann and Cultural Politics 1925–1938, in: Max Beckmann, exh. cat. The Tate Gallery, London 2003

Restany, Pierre: Une peinture existentielle. Wols, in : XXe siècle, 24/19, Paris 1962

Rewald, H. Dorra and John: Seurat, Paris 1959

Roh, Franz: Geschichte der deutschen Kunst von 1900 bis zur Gegenwart. Deutsche Kunstgeschichte, vol. VI, Munich 1958

Rosenthal, Mark: Franz Marc, Munich 1989

Rosenthal, Norman et al.: German Art in the 20th Century, exh. cat. Royal Academy, London 1985

Roskill, Mark: Klee, Kandinsky, and the Thought of Their Time. A Critical Perspective, Urbana/Chicago 1992

Salzmann, Siegfried: Alberto Giacometti. Plastiken. Gemälde. Zeichnungen, exh. cat. Wilhelm-Lehmbruck-Museum, Duisburg 1977

San Lazzaro, Gualtieri di: Klee. La vie et l'œuvre, Paris 1957

San Lazzaro, Gualtieri di: Xxe Siecle: Hommage à Calder, Paris 1972

Schade, Herbert: Max Beckmann, Gestaltung ist Erlösung, in: Stimmen der Zeit, Freiberg 1969

Schardt, Alois J.: Franz Marc. Mit hundertfünfzehn Abbildungen, Berlin 1936

Schneede, Uwe M.: Umberto Boccioni, Stuttgart 1994

Schneider, Angela: in: Werke aus der Hilti Art Foundation. Von Paul Gauguin bis Imi Knoebel, exh. cat. Kunstmuseum Liechtenstein, Vaduz 2005

Schubert, Dietrich: In ihrer wunderbaren Gusshaut, in: Frankfurter Allgemeine Zeitung, No. 137, 16 June 2001

Schubert, Dietrich: Anmerkungen zur ersten Ausstellung der "Freien Secession" in Berlin, April 1914, in: Jahrbuch der Berliner Museen, vol. 52, 2012

Schulz-Hoffmann, Carla: in: Max Beckmann. Exil in Amsterdam, exh. cat. Pinakothek der Moderne, Munich 2007

Schulz-Hoffmann, Carla: Frauen. Picasso, Beckmann, de Kooning, exh. cat. Pinakothek der Moderne, Munich 2012

Selz, Peter: Max Beckmann, The Self-Portraits, New York 1992

Sollers, Philippe: De Kooning, Vite, Paris 1988

Spieler, Reinhard: Max Beckmann – Der Weg zum Mythos, Cologne 1994

Spies, Werner: Pablo Picasso. Das plastische Werk, Stuttgart 1971

Spies, Werner: Max Ernst, Œuvre-Katalog, Werke 1925–1929, Cologne 1976

Spies, Werner / Piot, Christine: Picasso. Das plastische Werk, Bonn 1983

Spies, Werner: Picasso, The Sculptures: Catalogue Raisonné of the Sculptures, Ostfildern/Stuttgart 2000

Stabenow, Cornelia: Metaphern der Ohnmacht. Zu den Plastiken Max Beckmanns, in: Max Beckmann Retrospektive, exh. cat., Munich et al., 1984–85

Stüttgen, Johannes: Bevor sich überhaupt etwas zeigt. Über die Linienbilder und die ersten Etappen der Arbeit von IMI Knoebel, in: IMI KNOEBEL, Linienbilder 1966 bis 1968, St. Gallen 1999

Swarzenski, Hanns: Max Beckmann 1948. Retrospective Exhibition, exh. cat. Saint Louis City Art Museum, St. Louis 1948–49

Sylvester, David / Whitfield, Sarah: René Magritte, Catalogue Raisoneé, vol. 1, Oil Paintings, 1916–1930, Antwerpen 1992

Sylvester, David: Magritte, Brussels 2009

Thévoz, Michel: Louis Soutter, Catalogue de l'œuvre, Lausanne/Zurich 1976

Trier, Eduard: Hans Arp. Skulpturen 1957–1966, Stuttgart 1968

Uthemann, Ernest W.: Mann im Dunkeln, in: Max Beckmann, Werke aus der Sammlung des Kunstmuseums Hannover mit Sammlung Sprengel, Hannover 1983–84

Vignau-Wilberg, Peter: Gemälde und Skulpturen. Museum der Stadt Solothurn, Zurich 1973

Vriesen, Gustav: August Macke, Stuttgart 1953

Vriesen, Gustav: August Macke, Suttgart 1957

Waldberg, Patrick: Yves Tanguy, Brussels, 1977

Walden, Herwarth: Die neue Malerei, Berlin 1919

Weiss, Elisabeth: Franz Marc. Ein Versuch zur Deutung expressionistischer Stilphänomene und ihrer Voraussetzungen (diss.), Frankfurt am Main 1933

Wember, Paul: Yves Klein, Cologne 1969

Wember, Paul: Kunst in Krefeld. Öffentliche und private Kunstsammlungen, Cologne 1973

Wieczorek, Uwe: Werke aus der Hilti Art Foundation. Von Paul Gauguin bis Imi Knoebel, exh. cat. Kunstmuseum Liechtenstein, Vaduz 2005

Wiese, Stephan von: Max Beckmann, in: Sprengel Museum Hannover. Malerei und Plastik des 20. Jahrhunderts. Bearb. v. M. M. Moeller, Hanover 1985

Wietek, Gerhard: Schmidt-Rottluffs Oldenburger Jahre 1907–1912, Mainz 1955

Wildenstein, Georges: Gauguin, Paris 1964

Wilson, William: A Heartfelt Compendium of Modernism, Los Angeles Times, April 26, 1987

Yard, Sally: Willem de Kooning, New York 1997

Zahn, Leopold: Das Kunstwerk, vol. 22, 1968–69

Zenser, Hildegard: Max Beckmann, Selbstbildnisse, Munich 1984

Zervos, Christian: Pablo Picasso, Catalogue raisonné, Paris 1932–1978

This book is published in conjunction with the exhibition
Painting and Sculpture – From Classical Modernism to the Present Day
23 May 2015 – 9 October 2016

Hilti Art Foundation / Kunstmuseum Liechtenstein, Vaduz
Städtle 32, FL 9490 Vaduz

www.hiltiartfoundation.li

Editor
Uwe Wieczorek / Hilti Art Foundation
Vaduz / LI

Texts
Angela Schneider
Berlin / DE
Uwe Wieczorek
Vaduz / LI

Translation
Catherine Schelbert
Weggis, Hertenstein / CH

Proofreading
Vajra Spook
Berlin / DE

Project management
Karin Osbahr, Hatje Cantz
Ostfildern / DE

Reproductions
Heinz Preute
Vaduz / LI

Visuals
Thomas Pircher, MRS
Wolfurt / A

Graphic design and typesetting
Kurt Dornig
Dornbirn / A

Corporate Identity Hilti Art Foundation
Brigitte Lampert
Zurich / CH

Typefaces
Helvetica by Max Miedinger
Didot Elder by François Rappo

Printing
Thurnher Druckerei GmbH
Rankweil / A

Book jacket
Mader Werbetechnik
Lauterach / A

Paper
PhoeniXmotion Xenon 150 g/m²

Binding
GG Buchbinderei
Hollabrunn / A

ISBN 978-3-7757-3947-4

Printed in Austria

Published by
Hatje Cantz Verlag
Zeppelinstrasse 32
73760 Ostfildern
Tel. +49 711 4405-200
Fax +49 711 4405-220
www.hatjecantz.de
A Ganske Publishing Group Company

You can find information on this exhibition and many others at www.kq-daily.de.

Cover illustration
Max Beckmann
Selbstbildnis mit Glaskugel, 1936
(Cat. 6)